W9-BBE-438

THE HUMAN SHAPE
OF GOD

THE HUMAN SHAPE OF GOD

Religion in Hegel's *Phenomenology of Spirit*

By Daniel P. Jamros, S. J.

Paragon House
New York

First Edition, 1994

Published in the United States by

Paragon House
370 Lexington Avenue
New York, NY 10017

Copyright 1994 by Paragon House

Library of Congress Cataloging-in-Publication Data

Jamros, Daniel Peter.
  The human shape of God : religion in Hegel's Phenomenology of spirit / by Daniel P. Jamros. — 1st ed.
      p.   cm.
  Includes bibliographical references and index.
  ISBN 1-55778-703-4
      1. Hegel, Georg Wilhelm Friedrich, 1770–1831. Phänomenologie des Geistes.   2. Hegel, Georg Wilhelm Friedrich, 1770–1831—Views on religion.   I. Title.
B2929.J35   1994
193—dc20   94-15657
                                                                                      CIP

Manufactured in the United States of America

CONTENTS

FOREWORD

THERE HAS BEEN much disagreement over Hegel's interpretation of religion in *The Phenomenology of Spirit*, largely because of his obscure style and difficult subject matter. Was he a humanistic atheist, or a serious Christian thinker? Both positions have been maintained in recent years. In my view neither one corresponds to the philosophical theist who wrote the *Phenomenology*. For Hegel divine essence is universal essence; the development of this essence into human existence describes God. Since divine essence determines this whole movement, God must be affirmed, and so the left-wing interpretation of Hegel is rejected. But since on the other hand God is the essence of earthly human existence, Hegel's version of Christianity excludes divine personality and eschatology, and so the right-wing interpretation also must be rejected. The metaphysical interpretation I accept is not unknown in Hegelian philosophical circles, but it has received little support in religious journals and in English commentaries on the *Phenomenology*. It does correspond however to the view of Kierkegaard, whose *Philosophical Fragments* consider Hegel a non-Christian yet philosophical theist.

I expound this philosophical theism through a careful study of the texts dealing with religion, amounting to about a third of the whole *Phenomenology*. Since the texts are the fundamental evidence for any interpretation, I examine them closely; I often explicate important passages in detail. My method looks to Alexandre Kojève's lectures on the *Phenomenology* as a model of clear and detailed exposition, even if their Marxist interpretation does not do justice to Hegel's metaphysical depth.

In general I have used secondary literature only insofar as it examines the text of *Phenomenology* in some detail. Thus, my fifth chapter uses *La Christologie de Hegel* by Emilio Brito but not *The Christology of Hegel* by James Yerkes, who does not deal with the *Phenomenology* at all. The same principle applies to many other works on Hegel's philosophy of religion. They may be excellent in themselves, but they still provide little assistance for a detailed examination of the *Phenomenology*.

Acknowledgment must be given to the many fine Hegelian scholars whose works have helped me produce this one. Our points of agreement have consoled me, and our disagreements have stimulated me to a clearer formulation of my own position. A special acknowledgment goes to Peter C. Hodgson, who directed long ago the dissertation that the present work revises and who continues to be a helpful resource. Special thanks have also been merited by Stephen Crites, W. ver Eecke, and Oliva Blanchette, all of whom offered much encouragement along with challenging criticism and specific suggestions for improving the manuscript.

Translations from Hegel's *Phenomenology* are my own, based on the German critical edition in the *Gesammelete Werke* published by Felix Meiner Verlag. An appendix following my final chapter correlates the paragraphs of this German edition with section numbers used by Miller's English translation.

CHAPTER I

ORIENTATION

WHEN HEGEL GRADUATED from the theological seminary at Tübingen in 1793, at the age of twenty-three, he did not pursue a career in the church. Philosophy had been one of his major subjects at the seminary, and perhaps he already sensed a call to philosophize. After some years as a private tutor in Bern and Frankfurt, he finally became a lecturer in philosophy at the University of Jena in 1801.[1] And so, at the age of thirty-one, Hegel began an academic career that continued to the end of his life.[2] When he died in 1831, Hegel was a professor of philosophy and rector at the University of Berlin. By then he was famous as the creator of a systematic philosophy he had begun to develop at Jena. His first major work, *Die Phänomenologie des Geistes*,[3] completed in 1806 and published in 1807 around the time he left Jena,[4] was an introduction to a system already present in his mind. That system remained basically the same throughout Hegel's career; since he had several opportunities to test it intellectually, both in his university lectures and in his published works, it must have been a solid one. Hegel did not miss his calling when he gave his life to philosophy rather than to theology or religious ministry.

In Hegel's decision to pursue philosophy instead of religion, one finds a symbol of his thinking about these two disciplines. Philosophy ranks higher than religion, claims Hegel, because it comprehends what religion merely believes. Such a position, however, is not a simple rejection of one in favor of the other. Hegelian dialectical thinking preserves what it surpasses. His philosophy therefore preserves his early interest in religion: there are lectures on the philosophy of religion, and religious

1

themes are discussed in many of his other works. Even more fundamental is the apparently religious aim of his philosophy: it shares religion's desire to approach God, and in fact claims to provide a better knowledge of God than religion does. This point appears in many of his analyses of religion, which are never purely descriptive, since they attempt to comprehend the reality that religion reveals.[5]

RELIGION IN THE HEGELIAN CORPUS

For one to gain a thorough understanding of how Hegel understood religion, several of his works would have to be consulted[6] and digested. Each of them contributes something different. *Hegels Theologische Jugendschriften*[7] contain youthful essays written in the 1790s while Hegel was still in his twenties.[8] While these essays do not contain his mature thinking about religion, they nevertheless reveal his tendency to comprehend religion in rational categories. Within a few years this tendency will lead Hegel to place philosophy above religion. In *Glauben und Wissen* (1802)[9] the need to surpass religion is suggested if not actually made explicit: "believing" falls short of "knowing" because it fails to possess its object. Religion however is not directly treated in this work. "Believing" refers not to religion but to the philosophies of Kant, Jacobi, and Fichte, all of whom Hegel criticizes for the limitations they place on human knowing. Their thought appeals to belief because they claim that human beings cannot comprehend what is ultimately true.

But the goal of surpassing belief affects not only the philosophy of belief but also religion itself. The "knowing" that Hegel had in view as superior to "believing" finally came to light in his own system, which he was mulling over during the early 1800s. His *Phänomenologie des Geistes* (1807) announced itself as the "first part of the system of science"[10] and therefore the years preceding it must also have been devoted to planning an entire system of knowledge. *PhG* does not present the system Hegel had in mind, but it does show that a scientific philosophy is called for by the contemporary intellectual situation.[11] In other words, human spirit has reached a point in its history where true systematic knowing is possible; it does not have to be content any longer with merely "believing."[12] In *PhG*, this point is made by showing that religion is a limited knowing about God.

Hegel never published his complete system in detail. His *En-*

zyklopädie is only an outline of it made for the use of his students.[13] Nevertheless, this outline does prove that the system did exist in Hegel's own thinking and that it could be set down on paper. The system itself, apart from its introduction by *PhG*, was to consist of a logic, a philosophy of nature, and a philosophy of spirit.[14] After *PhG* Hegel published his *Wissenschaft der Logik*,[15] but no other fully developed part of the system; perhaps the thinking through of that first part was such a strenuous intellectual undertaking that it could not be duplicated for the two remaining domains of nature and spirit. At any rate the *Logik* alone (published in three parts: 1812, 1813, 1816) is a great achievement of speculative thought. It deals not with religion but with pure concepts and their progressive enrichment by the dialectical movement of pure thinking. This set of pure concepts is not an encyclopedic assembly of different ideas but rather a systematic integration of a single developing concept that represents, as Hegel describes it in the language of religion, "God . . . in his eternal essence before the creation of nature and of a finite spirit."[16] Thus, the *Logik* is of fundamental importance for Hegel's theory of deity as an eternal essence.

However, the truth that the *Logik* portrays is incomplete, inasmuch as the world of nature and spirit is missing; the logical scheme is not yet nature and spirit but only their logical prelude. Hegel's *Enzyklopädie* (in three editions: 1817, 1827, 1830)[17] does present all three parts (logic, nature, and spirit) of the system, but only in outline. The logical part is far less detailed than the earlier and longer *Logik*. And since corresponding works on nature and spirit were never published by Hegel, he apparently never fulfilled his ambition of producing a philosophy of nature and of spirit comparable to the great *Logik*. Part three of the *Enzyklopädie* does, however, contribute to the religious component of the Hegelian corpus: "die geoffenbarte Religion" (§564–71, 1830 ed.) occupies the middle position between art (§556–63) and philosophy (§572–77) in the development of absolute spirit (§553–77).

In Berlin Hegel lectured on the philosophy of religion four different times (1821, 1824, 1827, 1831) without ever publishing a text himself on this important topic. Two volumes (XI and XII) of the *Werke* (1832–1845) published after his death (1831) reproduce these lectures mainly on the basis of notes from students, although for the 1821 cycle Hegel's own manuscript was available to the editors. As a result, there exists in print a work called *Vorlesungen über die Philosophie der Religion*.[18]

This work offers Hegel's most detailed discussion of religion. Even though a large part of it consists of students' notes published after their teacher's death, it does seem to bring one reasonably close to what Hegel actually said in the classroom. Furthermore, these lectures contain far more material on religion than *PhG*, partly because more religions are included, partly because the discussion tends to be more leisurely and more thorough, and partly because the printed text of the lectures contains material from all four cycles (1821, 1824, 1827, 1831).

There exists another set of lectures called *Vorlesungen über die Beweise vom Dasein Gottes*, given by Hegel in 1829, and first printed after his death in the *Werke* on the basis of his own manuscript, now lost.[19] The printed text is not a polished one, so reading it requires some labor. In spite of this difficulty, however, it offers a sustained discussion about human thinking's attempt to grasp the being of God. Such a topic is evidently relevant to the study of religion.

TEXTS ON RELIGION IN *PhG*

Within this group of writings on religion itself and on topics connected with religion, *PhG* has an importance all its own. From a historical point of view, it provides a fairly lengthy discussion completed fifteen years before Hegel first lectured on religion in Berlin, and in this respect contains material that students of the Berlin lectures would be interested in. From a philosophical point of view, *PhG* offers a perspective on religion that is duplicated in no other work of Hegel's. In *PhG* his reflections on religion are part of a broader analysis of the human spirit as it has developed throughout its history, especially in the Western world. Religion is thus interpreted in relation to other forms of thinking, and all these forms are analyzed with a rigor that is rarely found in writings on religion. Because of his ambition to examine many varieties of human thinking and to put them into a systematic order, Hegel is forced to relate religion to other areas of human life, as well as to understand it as part of a larger historical development.

Even though there are many fewer pages on religion in *PhG* than in the printed version of the lectures, the former work still offers a great deal of material on religion. At the beginning (pp. 363–64) of chapter VII, itself entirely devoted to "Die Religion," Hegel reminds his reader that religion has also been discussed in earlier chapters of the book. He identifies six such occurrences, each of them occupying several pages of text in those earlier chapters.

First is the consciousness of the supersensible or inner side of being (363.9–13), which appears in a chapter devoted to physical science and its laws (chapter III, "Kraft und Verstand"). Second is the famous unhappy consciousness (363.13–17), which is actually a type of self-consciousness that feels itself separated from the divine goal of its yearning. Third is the religion of the underworld as practiced in ancient Greece (363.21–33), where the self begins to be aware of its personal individuality. Fourth is what Hegel calls faith in heaven (364.1–6), the Christian faith of Europe before the Enlightenment. Gradually this faith loses its credibility for the educated world and is replaced by the Enlightenment's own religion. There are thus two forms of religion in this section: Christian faith in heaven and the religion of the Enlightenment. I treat them together as one occurrence of religion because Hegel analyzes them together as opposing sides of one basic kind of consciousness. The fifth occurrence is Kantian morality (364.10–16), one of the varieties of religion after the Enlightenment, and presumably the most convincing one too, since it carries forward the development of spirit after faith in heaven has been undermined. Sixth is conscience (364.21–32), a post-Kantian development of morality.[20]

The seventh occurrence of religion is found in *PhG* VII, which is divided into five religions, so that chapter VII contains the seventh through eleventh occurrences of religion in *PhG*, according to the counting I have been following. *PhG* VII–A, "Natural Religion," is subdivided into Persian, Indian, and Egyptian religion; VII–B, "The Religion of Art," is a long treatment of Greek religion; and VII–C, "Manifest Religion," is Christianity itself. There are thus three generic and five specific types of religion in chapter VII.

Greek religion appears both in *PhG* VII and in VI–A, but from different points of view. In chapter VII, Hegel considers it as living human individuality expressing itself in art; in chapter VI–A, Hegel analyzes its cult of the dead as a first instance for the valuing of personal individuality. In the number of appearances, however, Greek religion is outranked by Christianity.

Christianity first came into view as the unhappy consciousness of Roman Catholicism; this identification is hardly to be doubted, even though it has been contested. It then appears as the (probably Protestant) faith in heaven discredited by the Enlightenment in Europe. Finally its original idea is examined in *PhG* VII–C as the highest form of religion. This exalted role is due to its revelation of divine-human unity, first as the incarnation of God in Jesus and then as the Christian church. Such a unity is what Hegel means by "spirit"; the Christian religion is a revelation of "spirit" and thus it leads to the "Absolute Knowing" (*PhG* VIII) of Hegelian philosophy.

Given all these occurrences of religion—six before *PhG* VII and five more in *PhG* VII, with some historical overlapping but no confusion from an analytical point of view—some principle of ordering them needs to be established. There is no better way to perform this task than to follow Hegel's own indications. According to him, *PhG* VII differs from earlier chapters as self-consciousness differs from consciousness: before chapter VII religion occurs as "consciousness of absolute essence," but in VII it occurs as "absolute essence in and for itself"[21] or as the "self-consciousness of spirit" (363.3–8). Before chapter VII the human mind is conscious of an absolute essence distinct from itself, but in VII this absolute essence incarnates itself as human being and so acquires human self-consciousness. What exactly is meant by this is of course the crucial point in interpreting Hegel, whose thinking on this topic is revealed throughout this study as various texts are examined in detail. But one can immediately obtain a preliminary grasp of his meaning from the idea of the incarnation of God in human being, the idea that makes Christianity the final religion for Hegel and the point to which all other religions lead.

The incarnation establishes a unity of divine and human being, so that the absolute essence expresses itself as human. Consequently in Christianity, human consciousness also achieves a breakthrough: it is no longer separate from God but knows itself as the very expression of God's absolute essence. The other religions treated in *PhG* lead up to this revelation. Before chapter VII, religions are portrayed as keeping God and human being separate, while in chapter VII their gradual unification is examined.[22] Therefore, the distinction between consciousness and self-consciousness and the merging of the two in *PhG* VII in general and in Christianity in particular are crucial to the sense of Hegel's argument: religion reaches its highest development when divine essence exists as the human self; God is no longer an object separate from consciousness but an object that *includes* human consciousness. As a result human self-consciousness belongs to divine essence.[23] Such a unification is what Hegel means by "spirit."

Before *PhG* VII, this unification is not yet reached. In the earlier chapters human consciousness has a divine object from which it is separated. This feature is shared by all the religions Hegel analyzes before chapter VII. In them divine essence is considered separate from human consciousness of it. But in *PhG* VII this essence is viewed as an incarnation, and so it gradually absorbs human being. From the point of view of the *Logik*, one would say that divine essence is inseparable from human being because the latter belongs to the essence itself; the concept of absolute essence is expanded to include human consciousness. And that is the goal to which spirit is moving through the religions studied in *PhG*. Thus the main organizing principle of religion in *PhG* is this distinction between the religions of consciousness, treated before *PhG* VII, and the religions of self-consciousness analyzed in chapter VII.

Still another term that helps classify the different stages of religion's development is "faith," which Hegel uses for faith in heaven but which seems applicable to other religions, too. "Faith" is defined as referring to "essence in the element of pure consciousness, beyond what is actual" (287.31, 33–35); such "believing" is necessarily the "opposite of actuality as *this* [actual world of individual things] in general and of self-consciousness in particular" (287.39–288.1), because faith looks to something beyond this world and beyond the human self. As faith, religion is not yet "*in and for itself*" (287.27–29), an expression that corresponds to the "absolute essence *in and for itself*" (363.7) mentioned at the beginning of *PhG* VII; faith is not yet "the self-consciousness of spirit" (363.7–8) because the object of belief does not include the believer's consciousness. Instead this object is always beyond the self. What Hegel says about faith is similar to what he writes about religion from the standpoint of consciousness (363.3–7). In both, the object of which the self is conscious appears to exist beyond the conscious self.

Thus, religion as it appears before *PhG* VII may be considered as faith, and more precisely as faith in a divine other beyond the self. This type of religion is distinguished from that of *PhG* VII, where this divine other is not beyond the self but is present to it and even unified with it, so that otherness is minimized. The term "faith," then, is a good equivalent for the religions of consciousness portrayed before *PhG* VII.[24]

However, I use the term "faith" for only the first four of these religions, namely those of the supersensible inner, the unhappy consciousness, faith in the underworld (see 287.31–32 for the term "faith" in connection with the underworld), and faith in heaven. For the next two forms of religion—morality and conscience—"faith" would also be an accurate term, especially for morality, which is Kant's practical reason; but for convenience of presentation, morality and conscience are treated in a separate chapter. My chapters thus adopt the distinctions Hegel uses, but stretch them a bit further for ease of organization. My chapter II ("Faith") examines the first four religions of consciousness: the supersensible inner, the unhappy consciousness, the Greek religion of the underworld, and Christian faith in heaven. My chapter III ("Morality") examines both morality and conscience. This chapter ends the religions of consciousness.

Two other chapters then study the religions of self-consciousness analyzed in *PhG* VII. Natural religion and the Greek religion of art are examined in my chapter IV ("Religion"), while Christianity as "Manifest Religion" supplies the subject of my chapter V. Finally, my chapter VI, called "Conclusion: Hegel and Christianity," examines the result of Hegel's analysis.

INTERPRETING HEGEL'S ARGUMENT

The preceding pages have explained what sections of *PhG* I discuss and how I organize them. More significant is my argument—the interpretation of Hegel it expounds. In my view, religion for Hegel is grounded in human thinking and not in revelation, if by revelation is meant an extraordinary intervention of God into the ordinary course of human life. As a form of thinking, however, religion is a legitimate revelation of God, for God is the logical ground of all that can be thought. Furthermore, humanity's religious thinking leads to a more specific concept that is peculiarly Hegelian. This is the concept that Hegel deals with in *PhG* VII and that Christianity decisively reveals, namely the concept of spirit as divine-human unity, which thinking itself discovers.[25]

Nevertheless, there are different ways in which this unity can be understood. One can understand it simply as the mental unity between thought and thinker: God and human thinking are united whenever someone thinks of God. Such a unity is however contingent, because it does not show why human thinking must exist; it does not develop the object of thought (or God) into one that *must* be thought. For even when thinking reaches an unknown first cause that *must* be thought of as the ultimate explanation of things, this "must" is only from the point of view of the thinker. By itself the object does not entail the thinker, whose existence is contingent. There is nothing in the concept of God that links it necessarily to the human thinker. Consequently, such a concept seems to go no further than the religions of consciousness. A deeper unity is needed: one grounded in the concept of God "in itself,"[26] which must be reconstructed so that divine essence will include the actual existence of human thinking. Failing such a concept, human being is not linked to God in a necessary way.

A second way of defining divine-human unity tries to remedy this defect. This approach understands God as the totality of all things, including human being. Human thinking necessarily falls into such a totality because everything is ascribed to the all-inclusive divine totality. But this concept also has a major problem: although human thinking is contained in the concept of totality, it does not follow rigorously from this initial concept.[27] "Totality" is too amorphous and undifferentiated an idea; it contains anything and everything, or even nothing at all. Such a concept does not necessitate human existence. If there were no human beings on earth, there would still be a totality composed of other beings. And if there were no other beings, there would still be a totality of emptiness.

Consequently, a third way of comprehending divine-human unity is desirable. This method derives human existence from the concept of God in such a way that this concept necessitates human being and its thinking. This approach seems to be that of Hegel's *Logik*, in which a series of abstract thoughts leads to the idea of a being that thinks and that acts according to its thought. How Hegel proves this conclusion cannot be explained in my study of *PhG*. But his general plan seems clear enough: starting from the abstract concept of being, he proceeds to enrich it by means of negation and synthesis, step-by-step, until the concept of being reaches its highest differentiation in the concept of a thinking that includes all that can be thought. This thinking contains the whole preceding series. As the logical development of the simple thought of being, it is both the final member of the series and its summation.

Now if God is considered to be this entire chain of logical ideas, then human being falls within the concept of God, and it does so necessarily. God is seen to engender human existence in a necessary way, by strict conceptual necessity. Here there is a rigorous unity of divine and human being. Divine being contains human being and has this being as its internal goal. Divine purposiveness culminates in the positing of human being, which is able to return to God by thinking the whole series of abstractions that make up divine essence. In this way God can be called a thinking that thinks itself.[28] Spirit then exists necessarily; it is the result of the abstract idea of being. The divine-human unity that is thereby implied is the highest thought of speculative philosophy. One might even say that human thinking that grasps its divine origin expresses the whole idea of God. This expression comes about as the inevitable result of a dialectical development of the idea of being. In other words, the concept of being can be developed rigorously enough to posit its being thought. And since the final part of this development contains all that precedes it, the thinking of the whole is said to contain the entire idea of God.

This third way of understanding divine-human unity is Hegelian, for it is accomplished in his *Logik*. And since *PhG* was intended as an introduction to his system,[29] Hegel probably had such a derivation in mind when he wrote *PhG*. In this way the *Logik* does help illuminate the concept of spirit found in *PhG*, and one can see why *PhG* attributes this concept to both Christianity and to speculative thinking (407.1–7): the concept of spirit that *PhG* finds in Christianity resembles the one developed by Hegel's own system.

Of course, *PhG* arrives at this concept by a different route, namely by a phenomenology of human consciousness. Whereas the *Logik* envisions divine essence as the pure objectivity of being that develops itself into subjective human being (the absolute idea), *PhG* assumes the empirical existence of both simple objective being and subjective human being. In *PhG* this objective empirical being becomes universalized into objective divine essence, kept separate from human subjectivity throughout the first six chapters. When *PhG* VII unifies them by making human being the expression or existence of divine essence, it arrives at a concept of spirit similar in content to the *Logik*'s absolute idea.

However, the existence of certain manuscripts drafted before *PhG* complicates matters. Some interpreters[30] claim that *PhG* in fact relics not so much on the later published versions of the system as on those earlier manuscripts Hegel wrote at Jena between 1803 and 1806. These manuscripts (which Hegel himself never published) have appeared in recent years as *Jenaer Systementwürfe I–III*.[31] Of these three volumes, the most systematic is the second, which deals with logic, metaphysics, and nature. In this volume's table of contents there is no separate heading for spirit; human subjectivity is treated as part of metaphysics (*GW* 7: v–vi). Therefore, the outline of his mature system does not appear here.

But *GW* 8, the last of these three volumes, does contain a concept of spirit similar to that of *PhG*, in which divine substance finally becomes human subjectivity. In this "Vorlesungsmanuskript zur Realphilosophie (1805/06)," Hegel describes the Trinity (*GW* 8: 282.15–283.16; 286.9–15) in language resembling that of *PhG*. This concept of the Trinity also corresponds to the three parts of the *Enzyklopädie*. Likewise, his description of "Naturphilosophie" as the "expressing of the idea in the shapes of immediate being" and its "becoming spirit" (*GW* 8: 286.9–11) clearly anticipates the three parts of his mature system and their interconnection. Therefore, this final Jena manuscript already contains the outline of the system, but not in systematic form.

The outline is finally worked out in rigorous and explicit form as the *Logik* and *Enzyklopädie*; the concept of spirit found in *GW* 8 requires the later system (at least in its main outlines) rather than the earlier one of *GW* 7. And between the last Jena manuscript (*GW* 8) and Hegel's *Logik*, one has *PhG*, where one can expect to find the same concept of spirit along with corresponding hints of the later system. That *PhG* does contain such a concept of spirit (as divine essence differentiating itself into human existence) is demonstrated in my fourth and fifth chapters. This concept helps to link *PhG* with Hegel's later system and also with his thinking before *PhG*.

In *PhG*, Christianity is the final religion because it reveals what spirit is, namely God existing as human being. The content of this revelation is also found in the *Logik*, in which divine essence differentiates itself into a thinking being. Thus, thinking in general is the revelation of God. But in order for thinking to reveal the specific character of God, it must somehow discover the inner logic of divine essence. There must then be a connection between the history of human thought and the structure of divine essence, so that the historical movement of thinking can grasp itself as the intrinsic goal of divine self-differentiation. Such a grasp appears at the very end of *PhG* as "Absolute Knowing," or Hegelian philosophy.[32] In general Hegel's *PhG* intends to show how thinking discovers itself to be absolute. This "Absolute Knowing" is reached only after a long history of human thinking, to which religion makes a significant contribution.

As a type of thinking, however, religion is not the highest kind. Religion approaches the right conclusion without reaching it in a definitive way. Religion grasps the unity of divine essence and human existence, but cannot really capture it because it lacks the proper logical tools. Its use of "Vorstellungen" or mental "images"[33] afflict its thinking with a sensory character that has a serious consequence for its way of understanding divine-human unity. The consequence is that imagination treats its thought like a sensory object, separate and distinct from other things. Even philosophy can have mental images and when it has them it is deficient; Kant's postulates of practical reason are a good example in Hegel's view.[34] But religion has mental images in a more obvious way, notably in its thought of a God beyond the world. The essential point in this type of image is the separateness entailed by sensory thinking.[35] In contrast to this kind of thinking is Hegel's version of conceptual thought. Defining ideas abstractly and precisely, the philosopher is able to grasp the necessary relations between ideas and thereby is able to derive one from another by dialectical thinking. Hegel's *Logik* even aims to derive human existence from divine essence and to grasp the necessity of such a derivation.

Religion, however, cannot accomplish this step because for religion God is imagined in the form of a pure idea separate from the world, and as having the sensory attribute of separate existence. As a result, God always remains a holy other for religion, no matter how deeply the Spirit of God may be said to dwell in the human soul. In religion the object of knowledge—divine presence—remains a gift or a grace. Consequently, the religious spirit is never quite able to think of God as necessarily related to itself. That is why religion has to be given up for a higher kind of knowing, which will know itself in God. But religion does lead the human spirit to this goal, not only because the inwardness of Christian spirituality points to the purity of thought (420.16–19), but also because Christianity provides (in unconceptual form) the concept of spirit, according to which individual human existence is the real existence of divine essence.

As the internal goal of *PhG*, this concept explains the history of consciousness as a necessary movement of self-discovery. Implicit in the concept is the whole structure of Hegelian metaphysics, in which everything is derived from divine essence; human existence with its philosophical thinking is the complete unfolding of that essence. A lesser type of thinking like religion would then be an incomplete realization of divine essence. But this metaphysical outlook is only implicit in *PhG*, which merely aims to show that Hegelian metaphysics is the next necessary step for human spirit to take. That divine essence realizes itself in human existence is a truth to be discovered by consciousness at the end of *PhG*, though Hegel has been aware of it all along; describing the journey of consciousness toward that truth, Hegel's book surpasses the types of consciousness that are not yet aware of it. This truth is, therefore, a phenomenological explanation for the structure and history of human consciousness rather than its metaphysical explanation. These two kinds of explanation are different. Hegel's phenomenology of spirit analyzes types of consciousness in order to display their origin in God, whereas a Hegelian metaphysics of spirit would analyze divine essence to discover its existent realization as human spirit.

For example, religion in *PhG* is not portrayed as an incomplete development of divine essence (as it would be in a metaphysical work by Hegel) but rather as part of the "appearance" ("Schein," 61.1)[36] of consciousness that must proceed to its "true existence" (61.37) of "absolute knowing" (62.5) where "it grasps its essence" (62.5) of being the existence of divine substance. In contrast to this absolute and true knowing, religion belongs to the appearance of consciousness "afflicted with an alien [divine essence] that is only [an object] for it and . . . an other [than it]" (62.1–2). Hegel's focus, then, is not on religion as an incomplete existence of God but as an incomplete form of human consciousness. To understand *PhG*, therefore, one needs to recognize not only Hegel's concept of spirit but also his intention to write a phenomenology rather than a metaphysics of spirit.

Hegel's use of the term "phenomenology" seems to have been an afterthought because the term appears only[37] in the Preface (24.2; 30.5), which Hegel wrote after completing the body of the work.[38] His original designation when he began the book with the Introduction was the "Science of the *Experience of Consciousness*" (*GW* 9: 61.29–30). Substituting "spirit" for "consciousness" made no great difference, since the former brings the latter to its fullest form; the two terms are used equivalently in the "Introduction" (61.31–33). But using "phenomenology" in place of a "science of experience" calls for some explanation. A few passages in the Introduction help explain the substitution.

The "Science of the *Experience of Consciousness*" (61.29–30) is also described as "the portrayal of knowing [as it] appears" (55.30); such knowing contains a great deal of "untruth" (56.11). Thus, "knowing [as it] appears" (55.30, 32; 56.11; 58.13) can also be characterized as "apparent knowing," in order to emphasize its lack of complete truth. Since Hegel plans to describe this "apparent knowing" from the viewpoint of one who has overcome it, his analysis of consciousness reflects "an *attitude* [*Verhalten*] of *science* towards *apparent* [erscheinenden] knowing" (58.12–13). He can say this because he (the all-knowing author) already knows the outcome of his analysis, the point at which consciousness "lays aside its appearance" (62.1) and "grasps its essence" (62.5). When this point is reached, consciousness becomes "absolute knowing" (62.5). Before arriving there consciousness contains the "untruth" (56.11) that makes its knowing incomplete.

The instances of incomplete knowing Hegel analyzes often refer to real instances of knowing that he was familiar with from his wide reading. There would be little point in conjuring up imaginary cases of errors that had no factual existence. Hegel's reference to "the *experience of consciousness*" (61.29–30) therefore should be interpreted as a reference to actual cases of real knowing. He may have discovered some of them (such as "Absolute Knowing") for himself, but usually he is referring to something already known from the cultural history of the West. Furthermore, he does not normally identify the instances of knowing he has in mind at various points in *PhG*. For example, Hegel uses Sophocles's *Antigone* at great length in his analysis of the Greek religion of the underworld (*PhG* 241–64), without ever naming any of the characters. Another example comes from Christianity: although the name of Jesus never occurs in Hegel's text, there can hardly be any doubt that by "the individual man" in whom "absolute essence is manifest" (407.33) Hegel means Jesus Christ. Such allusive language throughout *PhG* contributes to the difficulty of interpreting it. Nevertheless, scholars often have succeeded in providing plausible identifications for the types of consciousness Hegel has in mind.

Taken from the patrimony of Western culture, these types constitute a phenomenology of knowing as it has appeared in history. Consequently, Hegel affirms at the end of *PhG* that absolute knowing has been produced by "*actual history*" (430.6); in Hegel's own time, spirit has come to a "*true knowing of itself*" (430.4). Previous forms of spirit have all been incomplete, but they nevertheless contribute something to the emergence of "absolute knowing" (433.38), which depends upon its "recollection" (433.39) of past actual spirits. *PhG* itself— "the *science* of *knowing [as it] appears*" (434.4)—is nothing other than the "comprehended organization" (434.3–4) of the actual spirits that have appeared in "history" (434.3). As a result, the types of consciousness that make up *PhG* correspond to real historical cases[39] in the evolution[40] of spirit toward absolute knowing.

Such then is the interpretation of Hegel maintained by my pages, which examine the gradual emergence of spirit in the texts about religion in *PhG*. Since these texts are difficult to decipher, a careful exegesis of them is necessary. Through such exegesis I hope to show that *PhG*'s analyses of religion use a concept of spirit that appears in the Jena lecture manuscript of 1805/06 and is then developed by Hegel's later system. I understand Hegel to view spirit as the human existence of divine essence rather than as an existing divine Holy Spirit that relates itself to human spirit.

In the field of Hegelian scholarship such an interpretation of *PhG* seems to be lacking. Jean Hyppolite's commentary is generally accurate about Hegel, yet is not lucid enough in explaining fundamental terms and concepts. The clearest and most thorough commentary for exegesis of selected points is that of Alexandre Kojève.[41] But Kojève's interpretation has a number of serious flaws. It assumes that the only possible God is a transcendent one beyond the world. Thus, in Kojève's view Hegel's analysis of the incarnation of God in Jesus amounts to atheism[42] because the transcendent God then disappears in a human being. According to Kojève's Marxist view, this transcendent God is really the ideal state[43] that as an unrealized ideal is separated from real human individuality, and so "the moment the ideal is *realized*, the dualism disappears, and with it [also disappears] religion and theism."[44] For Kojève God is nothing more than a human idea[45] and more precisely an ideal goal to be realized[46] in real life by the French Revolution and the Emperor Napoleon, who is the true God-man.[47] Kojève's interpretation ignores the metaphysical side of Hegel, who considers God as the underlying substance of all reality—a substance that reaches its logical goal by differentiating itself into human being. For Hegel human being is "absolute spirit" only as the real existence of a divine logical substance.

Kojève's view is also the one held in a recent and lively work by Robert C. Solomon,[48] who maintains that Hegel is at heart an atheist[49] because he does not believe "in a God other than ourselves."[50] Like his predecessor Kojève, Solomon does not entertain the possibility of God as the absolute idea that differentiates itself into nature and human spirit. Since this is precisely Hegel's idea of God, it follows that Solomon (like Kojève) cannot recognize God in *PhG*. For him, Hegel is an "anti-metaphysical . . . anthropologist rather than an ontologist."[51] Consequently, Solomon admits that when "Hegel seems to find a certain 'levity' in the proposition 'The Self is absolute Being' (748), I must confess that I miss the joke."[52] This joke would, of course, be unappreciated by anyone who does not consider divine essence as the underlying logical substance of the universe. But the brief text that Solomon quotes is itself enough to show that his humanistic interpretation[53] of Hegel is too one-sided.

My interpretation also differs from that of Quentin Lauer, who has written a stimulating commentary on *PhG*.[54] For Lauer, Hegel's God is a divine Spirit[55] speaking to human spirit.[56] In other words, there are two different spirits, instead of a single spirit seen from two different points of view, namely the purely divine or logical and the human or existing side of the divine idea. Lauer's idea of two different spirits (divine and human) enables him to align Hegel with the classical Christian view of a Holy Spirit revealing itself to human spirit, but it also seems to retain something of the separate God of religious imagination. Lauer's interpretation is encouraged by parts of Fackenheim's excellent book,[57] which describes religion as it *precedes* philosophy,[58] even while acknowledging that Hegel describes it from the point of view of his own philosophical comprehension.[59] Thus, Hegel's interpretation of religion is not really described by Fackenheim, whose intention is actually to examine Christianity rather than Hegel's understanding of it. The result is a clear portrayal of Christianity from the point of view of its own mental images.

Kainz's careful commentary[60] provides excellent background information along with an intricate analysis of *PhG*. Like Lauer, Kainz offers a Christian interpretation of the text: Hegel's absolute spirit is understood as a divine self that relates itself to human selves. Although Kainz never discusses this point formally, a few passages in his work indicate such a position. For example, Hegel adapts a verse from Schiller[61] to illustrate the relation between absolute spirit and history: " 'from the chalice[62] of this realm of [historical] spirits foams . . . its [own] infinity' " (434.8–9). In Kainz's translation "its" becomes "his,"[63] because he understands "absolute spirit" (434.4–5) as a person rather than as an essence.[64] Elsewhere, Kainz describes the Christian God as "the universal Essence which has evolved to a stage of ultimate *abstraction*, where this Essence makes a clean break with all its embodiments in Nature and appears as it is in itself, i.e., as an individual *Self*."[65] In this passage divine essence is understood as a transcendent God with a divine personality before its incarnation. Given this understanding of a transcendent divine self, Kainz's reference to a "divine Spirit expressing itself in and through finite consciousnesses"[66] has to be taken as a divine self related to human beings but also conscious of itself prior to any such relation.[67] This point may not be central to Kainz's interpretation, which emphasizes religion as intersubjectivity[68]; but his understanding of God as a divine (rather than human) consciousness must also affect his treatment of intersubjectivity, which Hegel uses for the appearance of deity.[69] The question of divine personality is so fundamental to Hegel that one's answer to it influences the interpretation of many other themes in *PhG*. Kainz's answer reflects Christian tradition, and in this respect he resembles Lauer.

Of the commentators mentioned, I think that Hyppolite comes closest to Hegel's meaning when he claims that Hegel does not reduce God to human being by suppressing divine transcendence.[70] But how this balanced position is possible is not explained very clearly by his commentary. In my view the answer lies in the Hegelian system, which treats God as an essence that posits its own existence as the world. Evidence for this interpretation must, however, come from *PhG* itself, whose texts on religion are examined in the following four chapters.

NOTES

1. For detailed information on Hegel's lectures at Jena, see Heinz Kimmerle, "Dokumente zu Hegels Jenaer Dozententätigkeit (1801–1807)," *Hegel-Studien* 4 (Bonn: H. Bouvier, 1967): 53–56, 78–87. According to this documentation, during those years Hegel lectured on logic and metaphysics, as well as the philosophy of nature and of mind.
2. Hegel's university career was interrupted from 1807 when he left Jena, until 1816 when he went to Heidelberg. From spring 1807 until fall 1808 he was an editor of a newspaper in Bamberg. From the fall of 1808 until 1816 he was rector of the Gymnasium at Nürnberg. Hegel's great *Logik* appeared in his years at Nürnberg. See the chronology of his life in Walter Kaufmann, *Hegel: Reinterpretation, Texts, and Commentary* (Garden City, NY: Doubleday, 1965), pp. 24–25.
3. Georg Wilhelm Friedrich Hegel, *Gesammelte Werke*, vol. 9: *Phänomenologie des Geistes*, ed. Wolfgang Bonsiepen and Reinhard Heede (Hamburg: Felix Meiner, 1980). This edition is used as the primary source for my study, which cites it by page and line numbers without further identification. The title will usually be abbreviated as *PhG*, but sometimes as *GW* 9, with page and line numbers following. For example, a reference to 420.16–19 means page 420, lines 16–19 of this edition. Other volumes from the *Gesammelte Werke* are also referred to in the same way. The *Gesammelte Werke* are also known as the Akademie-Ausgabe, from the sponsoring Rheinisch-Westfälische Akademie der Wissenschaften.
4. Hegel left Jena around March 1807. See *Hegel: The Letters*, trans. Clark Butler and Christiane Seiler, with commentary by Clark Butler (Bloomington, IN: Indiana University Press, 1984), pp. 125–28.
5. This fact has been noted by many commentators and students of Hegel. See, for example, Emil L. Fackenheim, *The Religious Dimension in Hegel's Thought* (Bloomington, IN: Indiana University Press, 1967), p. 23; and Jean Hyppolite, *Genèse et Structure de la Phénoménologie de l'Esprit de Hegel* (1946; reprint ed., Paris: Aubier, Editions Montaigne,

1974), p. 543. Hyppolite's remark refers to a particular topic, namely the Christian church's speculative knowing (pp. 541–42).

6. A very helpful bibliographic description of Hegel's writings may be found in Kaufmann, pp. 470–78 (with different pagination in the paperback edition). Kaufmann's bibliography was compiled before the Akademie-Ausgabe of Hegel's *Gesammelte Werke* began to appear.

7. G. W. F. Hegel, *Hegels Theologische Jugendschriften*, ed. Herman Nohl (Tübingen, 1907; reprint ed., Frankfurt/Main: Minerva GmbH, 1966). The English version called *Early Theological Writings*, trans. T. M. Knox, with an introduction and fragments trans. Richard Kroner (Chicago: University of Chicago, 1948; reprint ed., Philadelphia: University of Pennsylvania Press, 1977), does not include all the essays found in Nohl. The others are now available in G. W. F. Hegel, *Three Essays, 1793–1795*, ed. and trans. with an introduction and notes by Peter Fuss and John Dobbins (Notre Dame, IN: University of Notre Dame Press, 1984).

8. See the chronology in Kaufmann, pp. 22–23.

9. Hegel, *Gesammelte Werke*, vol. 4: *Jenaer Kritische Schriften*, ed. Hartmut Buchner and Otto Pöggeler (Hamburg: Felix Meiner, 1968), pp. 315–414.

10. *PhG* was published in 1807 with the following title: "*System der Wissenschaft [:] Erster Theil, die Phänomenologie des Geistes.*" See *GW* 9, pp. V, 1, 3.

11. See the brief article in *Encyclopedia Judaica* (New York: Macmillan, 1971), s.v. "Hegel," by Emil L. Fackenheim.

12. Near the beginning of his Introduction (Einleitung) to *PhG*, Hegel attributes a "fear of the truth" (54.20) to those thinkers who separate human knowing from the absolute (54.16–19). In printed versions this Introduction is preceded by the Preface (Vorrede), which in fact was written after the rest of the book (see Kaufmann, p. 91, and his chronology, p. xxiv; *GW* 9, "Editorischer Bericht," pp. 462–63). Hegel actually began writing *PhG* with his Introduction, which itself begins with the problem he describes in *Glauben und Wissen*. The Introduction to *PhG* ends by expecting a solution (61.37–62.5) that is presumably found in the body of the book.

13. See the title page of G. W. F. Hegel, *Enzyklopädie der Philosophischen Wissenschaften im Grundrisse (1830)*, ed. Friedhelm Nicolin and Otto Pöggeler, Philosophische Bibliothek 33 (Hamburg: Felix Meiner, 1959), p. 1.

14. Hegel, *GW* 11: *Wissenschaft der Logik*, Erster Band, ed. Friedrich Hogemann and Walter Jaeschke (Hamburg: Felix Meiner, 1978), 8.21–26.

15. To the previous reference must be added the second volume: *GW* 12:

Wissenschaft der Logik, Zweiter Band, ed. Friedrich Hogemann and Walter Jaeschke (Hamburg: Felix Meiner, 1981). Together, the volumes constitute the whole of this work, which is hereafter referred to as *Logik*. *GW* 11 corresponds to the parts published in 1812 and 1813; *GW* 12 to the part published in 1816.

16. *GW* 11: 21.19–21.
17. Although the 1830 version of the *Enzyklopädie* is commonly available, the 1817 version is found only in the *Werke* and in the Jubiläumsausgabe reprinting. The 1827 version seems to have never been reprinted (see Kaufmann, pp. 474–75) until recently, when it appeared as *GW* 19: *Enzyklopädie der philosophischen Wissenschaften im Grundrisse (1827)*, ed. Wolfgang Bonsiepen and Hans-Christian Lucas (Hamburg: Felix Meiner, 1989).
18. G. W. F. Hegel, *Vorlesungen über die Philosophie der Religion*, ed. Georg Lasson, 4 vols. in 2, Philosophische Bibliothek 59–60, 61, 63 (1925; reprint ed., Hamburg: Felix Meiner, 1966). Long the standard text, Lasson's edition has now been superseded by Jaeschke's edition. See Hegel, *Vorlesungen*, Band 3 (1983), Band 5 (1984), Band 4 (1985), ed. Walter Jaeschke (Hamburg: Felix Meiner, 1983–1985). These volumes have been translated into English and edited by Peter C. Hodgson under the title *Lectures on the Philosophy of Religion* (Berkeley and Los Angeles: University of California Press, 1984–1987). Among the many virtues of this new edition (both in German and in English) is the separation of the lectures into chronological order. The German title is referred to as *VPR*; the English title as *LPR*. An electronic version of Hodgson's English edition is available from Georgetown University; see my bibliography.
19. G. W. F. Hegel, *Vorlesungen über die Beweise vom Dasein Gottes*, ed. G. Lasson, Philosophische Bibliothek 64 (1920; reprint ed., Hamburg: Felix Meiner, 1973). For textual information, see pp. 178–82.
20. Occurrences three through six are all found in *PhG* VI, "Der Geist," which in Hegel's introduction to *PhG* VII is called "immediate spirit" and is distinguished from "the self-consciousness of spirit" (365.22–24) that is developed in *PhG* VII, "Die Religion." The difference between these two forms of spirit seems to be that in the "immediate" kind human being does not yet know itself as the existence of divine essence. I develop this point in my chapters IV and V.
21. The expression "in and for itself" can be understood as a combination of "in itself" as an objective self-identity and "for itself" as subjective knowing. The term "absolute essence in and for itself" would then mean that the concept of God as an essence "in itself" posits its knowing in human subjectivity that is "for itself." In other words, divine essence

becomes subjectivity in human knowing. But then "for itself" would refer to the human self rather than to a divine subjectivity, and so would not be "absolute essence . . . for itself." Therefore, one must understand a deeper meaning: in human subjectivity absolute essence returns to itself and so is for its *own* self in human being. The end of *PhG* VI–C and all of *PhG* VII amply demonstrate how universal essence is present as universal human thinking. However, this precise meaning of "in and for itself" does not seem to be present in all contexts. Often the phrase simply means "absolute" or "complete," a meaning that could be derived from the more precise one that has just been given.

22. The Greek and Christian religions occur more than once (both before *PhG* VII and then within it) because in some respects they emphasize the separation and in other respects the unification.

23. Hegel's position therefore implies that the divine object knows itself through human knowing of God—a point first impressed upon me by Professor Peter Hodgson. In *PhG* this point is clearly made in Hegel's analysis of the Christian Trinity. The pretemporal Trinity is God's own self-knowing (410.18–23), but only as the logical prototype of the real divine self-knowing that occurs in human being.

24. Even the supersensible inner of human understanding (studied in my chapter II) seems to qualify as a faith according to the definition of faith in 287.31, 33–35 (quoted in my text). This inner side of actuality is not present to empirical consciousness; thus it is beyond it.

25. In his Einleitung to *PhG*, Hegel claims that the object of consciousness develops "through a *conversion of consciousness* itself" (61.4–5). In *PhG* VII Christianity requires a "conversion *for* and *through self-consciousness* itself" (400.26), whereby an unhappy Roman consciousness turns into Christian faith. Belief thus produces a new object of consciousness, namely God incarnate. Produced by subjectivity, this new object is also objective; it results from a necessary logic dictated by divine substance. See my chapter V for a fuller discussion.

26. The phrase "in itself" seems to refer to any object considered apart from its relation to a knowing subject. See above, n. 21. But Hegel does not share Kant's view that the object "in itself" is beyond one's thinking. This point holds for all kinds of objects. For Hegel, even divine essence comes to be known by human thinking. See the treatment of Kant in *PhG* VI–C (studied in my chapter III), which criticizes him for placing God beyond our knowing.

27. Such would seem to be Hegel's complaint against Spinoza in his lectures on the history of philosophy. See Hegel's *Werke*, Theorie-Werkausgabe, ed. Eva Moldenhauer and Karl Markus Michel (Frankfurt am Main:

Suhrkamp Verlag, 1969–1971), 20: 157–97, especially 173 and 175. The Theorie-Werkausgabe is hereafter cited as TWA.

28. See Hegel's remarks on Aristotle in *Werke*, TWA, 19 (1971): 165, where he praises Aristotle for unifying subject and object in his theory of thinking. According to Hegel, Aristotle placed himself "on the highest standpoint"; there can be "nothing deeper" than Aristotle's position on thinking. These remarks of Hegel's are, of course, a good clue to his own view as well.

29. See above, n. 10 , as well as the passage from the *Logik* (*GW* 11: 8.21–26) cited in n. 14. In the latter passage, Hegel writes that *PhG* was the first part of a system that was to include as its second part the three sciences of logic, nature, and spirit. He furthermore indicates (in lines 28–29) that his *Logik* of 1812–1813 "constitutes . . . the first sequel to the Phenomenology of Spirit." Therefore, the system promised by *PhG* must be the one offered by Hegel's *Logik* and *Enzyklopädie*.

30. Howard Kainz in his *Hegel's Phenomenology, Part II: The Evolution of Ethical and Religious Consciousness to the Dialectical Standpoint* (London and Athens, OH: Ohio University Press, 1983), pp. 183–85 nn. 19–20, points out some correspondences between *PhG* and the 1805/06 Realphilosophie. In this he follows Otto Pöggeler, "Selbstbewußtsein und Identität," *Hegel-Studien* 16: 189–217. Emilio Brito's *La christologie de Hegel* (Paris: Beauchesne, 1983) makes frequent reference to Hegel's *Jenenser Logik, Metaphysik und Naturphilosophie* of 1804/05, ed. Georg Lasson, Philosophische Bibliothek 58 (Hamburg: Felix Meiner, 1923; reprint ed., 1967). Brito relies on the study by Johannes Heinrichs, *Die Logik der «Phänomenologie des Geistes»* (Bonn: Bouvier Verlag Herbert Grundmann, 1974).

31. *Jenaer Systementwürfe I*, "Fragmente aus Vorlesungsmanuskripten zur Philosophie der Natur und des Geistes (1803/04)," ed. Klaus Düsing and Heinz Kimmerle, *GW* 6 (Hamburg: Felix Meiner, 1975); *Jenaer Systementwürfe II*, "Fragment einer Reinschrift (1804/05): Logik, Metaphysik, Naturphilosophie," ed. Rolf-Peter Horstmann, and Johann Heinrich Trede, *GW* 7 (Hamburg: Felix Meiner, 1971); *Jenaer Systementwürfe III*, "Vorlesungsmanuskript zur Realphilosophie (1805/06): Naturphilosophie und Philosophie des Geistes," ed. Rolf-Peter Horstmann, assisted by Johann Heinrich Trede, *GW* 8 (Hamburg: Felix Meiner, 1976). Two of these documents were published earlier in Felix Meiner's "Philosophische Bibliothek" series. *GW* 7 replaces *Jenenser Logik, Metaphysik und Naturphilosophie*, Philosophische Bibliothek 58, ed. Georg Lasson (Hamburg: Felix Meiner, 1923). *GW* 8 replaces *Jenaer Realphilosophie*, Philosophische Bibliothek 67, ed. Johannes Hoffmeister (Hamburg: Felix Meiner, 1931).

32. In the 1830 *Enzyklopädie*, philosophy (§572–77) is the highest activity of "Absolute Spirit" (§553–77).
33. Following Copleston's translation of "Vorstellung" in his discussion of Fichte, *A History of Philosophy*, vol. 7: *Fichte to Nietzsche* (Westminster, MD: The Newman Press, 1963), p. 51, one could translate "vorstellen" and its derivatives as "to present," "presentation," and "presented." Others translate by "represent," etc., and this translation is the usual one because it expresses a nuance not contained in "present": what is "represented" is not an immediate or present experience but is rather a reshaping of immediate experience by thought (although in a way that falls short of the concept's necessary connections). But mental "image" offers a more idiomatic equivalent to "Vorstellung." I therefore translate "vorstellen" and its derivatives as "imagine," "imagined," "imagination," and "image" whenever possible. Hegel does not usually mean that "Vorstellungen" are "imaginary." They contain a good amount of truth even though they do not express it as accurately as the concept.
34. Hegel often refers to Kant's "Vorstellungen" (e.g., 331.7–10; 340.13–16), which I examine in my chapter III. With reference to Kant, one is tempted to translate "Vorstellung" by "idea" rather than "image." But even here the term "image" seems appropriate since Kant postulates a world beyond this one.
35. For a clear description of "Vorstellung" (as imagination), see 407.27–32; 408.11–25.
36. Cf. "Erscheinung" (62.2).
37. As determined by searching an electronic version of Baillie's translation. See G. W. F. Hegel, *The Phenomenology of Mind*, trans. J. F. Baillie (Washington, DC: The Center for Text & Technology, Academic Computer Center, Georgetown University, 1990).
38. See Hoffmeister's editorial introduction to Hegel's *Phänomenologie des Geistes*, ed. Johannes Hoffmeister, Philosophische Bibliothek 114 (Hamburg: Felix Meiner, 1952), p. xxxvii.
39. A similar point appears in the *Realphilosophie* of 1805/06: in world history, spirit discovers for itself the essence of nature and spirit (*GW* 8: 287.22–24).
40. A term inspired by Kainz, *Hegel's Phenomenology, Part II*, p. x: "I use the word 'evolution' instead of 'phenomenology' in order to emphasize the difference of Hegel's *Phenomenology*, which is concerned primarily with *movement* . . . from contemporary phenomenologies, which seem to be concerned primarily with the eidetic and/or linguistic *structures* of subjective, intersubjective and/or objective experience." Also in his first volume, *Hegel's Phenomenology, Part I: Analysis and Commentary*,

Studies in the Humanities 12 (Tuscaloosa, AL: University of Alabama Press, 1976), p. 47, Kainz distinguishes between Hegelian and Husserlian phenomenology: "Husserl, like Kant, concentrates more on the structures in the knowledge of being than on the dynamisms. . . ." Kainz makes no special reference to historical dynamisms in these passages, but his commentary (especially in the second volume) is a fine example of identifying the actual historical examples Hegel had in mind. These two volumes are referred to hereafter as Kainz 1 and 2.

41. Alexandre Kojève, *Introduction à la lecture de Hegel*, Leçons sur la *Phénoménologie de l'Esprit* professées de 1933 à 1939 à l'Ecole des Hautes Etudes, réunies et publiées par Raymond Queneau (1947; reprint ed., Paris: Editions Gallimard, 1979).

42. Ibid., p. 257.

43. Ibid., pp. 200–02, 211, 230–31, 235.

44. Ibid., p. 213.

45. Ibid., p. 228.

46. Ibid., p. 257.

47. Ibid., p. 266.

48. Robert C. Solomon, *In the Spirit of Hegel [:] A Study of G. W. F. Hegel's Phenomenology of Spirit* (New York: Oxford University Press, 1983). On p. 7, Solomon allies himself with Kojève and others.

49. Ibid., p. 582 and elsewhere.

50. Ibid., p. 630.

51. Ibid., p. 27. In the same passage, Solomon also calls Hegel "anti-religious." I agree with this, if by religion one means the conventional form of it. Hegel is not a conventional Christian. But he *is* a metaphysician whose metaphysics is a theism without any supernatural beyond. For Hegel, God is the underlying substance or essence of the empirical world.

52. Ibid., p. 612. The reference "748" is to Hegel's *Phenomenology of Spirit*, trans. A. V. Miller (Oxford University Press, 1977), § 748. In the *GW* edition used in my study, it is 400.13.

53. His pp. 5–7 offer a convenient summary of his position.

54. Quentin Lauer, S. J., *A Reading of Hegel's Phenomenology of Spirit* (New York: Fordham University Press, 1976; reprint ed., 1982).

55. Ibid., p. 231.

56. Ibid., p. 234.

57. See above, n. 5.

58. Fackenheim, pp. 117–18.

59. Ibid., pp. 23, 117–18.

60. See above, n. 40.

61. *GW* 9: 523–24 (note to 434.8–9). Hegel ends *PhG* by this quotation from Schiller.
62. Because Hegel has already mentioned "the recollection and the Golgotha of absolute spirit" (434.5–6), the chalice in his text probably alludes to the Eucharist.
63. Kainz, 2: 186: " 'out of the chalice of this kingdom of spirits does his own infinity foam up to [the Absolute].' "
64. Without history, according to Hegel (following Schiller—see above, note 61) "absolute spirit . . . would be the lifeless [and] solitary [One]" (434.5–7). Hegel's use of the neuter "das leblose Einsame" suggests to me that he is thinking of "absolute spirit" as an essence rather than as a person; he could have written "der" instead of "das."
65. Kainz, 2: 159.
66. Kainz, 2: 180.
67. As in 1 Cor. 12 4, 11.
68. See the subheadings on his pp. 131, 138, 154.
69. Notably in "Evil and Its Pardon," at the end of *PhG* VI–C. Kainz describes the divine appearance in these terms: "Absolute Spirit is explicitly present in the world, appearing necessarily in the midst of the mutually reconciled consciousnesses" (2: 123). Although such wording does not require the meaning of a conscious divine self, this meaning is implied by Kainz's interpretation of other passages noted above.
70. Hyppolite, *Structure*, p. 524; p. 525 n. 1.

CHAPTER II

FAITH

SOME JUSTIFICATION NEEDS to be provided for the title of this chapter, which includes many different kinds of material. This chapter deals with all the sections on religion found in *PhG* before its analysis (in VI–C) of Kant and German idealism. As noted earlier, these sections are identified by Hegel himself in the early paragraphs (363.9–364.9) of his chapter VII, "Die Religion."

According to that summary review, religion first appears as the understanding of the supersensible inner in *PhG* III, then as the unhappy consciousness in *PhG* IV, next as religion of the underworld in *PhG* VI–A, and finally as faith in heaven that turns into the Enlightenment, all in *PhG* VI–B.

The last-named section furnishes the term "faith" (286.26), which I somewhat arbitrarily extend to the earlier sections on religion. This extension is justified inasmuch as "faith" is described in terms that apply to the other sections. Faith is "essence posited in the element of pure consciousness beyond actual [consciousness]" (287.33–34). But the same can be said of the underworld, which is evidently a world beyond the empirical one; in this respect it is a "faith" (287.31–32; 363.22), although in another respect it has an actual reference in the family (287.32–35) that honors a dead relative. Likewise, the unhappy consciousness must be a faith because the reason for its unhappiness lies in its inability to join itself with the object of its yearning, which lies forever beyond it. Thus, one can easily consider the second, third, and fourth occurrences of religion in *PhG* as forms of faith in something beyond empirical knowledge.

But is the first occurrence of religion—the supersensible inner—also a form of faith? The answer to this question depends on whether the "inner" is understood as beyond the actuality of the sensible world. Yet as supersensible, the inner must lie beyond what is perceived, even if it is "in" this perceived actuality. Consequently, Hegel more than once (89.8, 26) calls the supersensible inner a "beyond." If that does not entitle it to be called an object of faith, the inner is nevertheless a stage in the development of spirit that soon leads to the faith of the unhappy consciousness. The very attempt to think of a supersensible essence is what brings spirit to believe in a transcendent beyond. Even when the essence is the essence of what lies before one in the world of experience, it is already beyond experience, simply in virtue of its being essence. Therefore, the acknowledgment of a supersensible inner is, if not yet faith in a transcendent other, a strong step toward it.

The four occurrences of religion studied in this chapter as instances of "faith" are also among the six religions of consciousness (363.3–8), a term Hegel uses for a religion whose object does not contain the knowing subject. In such a religion the object of knowing is separate from the knower and detachable from its being known; the object belongs to a transcendent world that would exist even if the knower did not. Curiously, the object of such knowing exists in "the element of pure consciousness" (287.33) and yet consciousness does not recognize itself in it, probably because the object is understood as being beyond the actual world in which consciousness lives; as such, it is beyond consciousness itself. Were human thinking conscious of itself in its object, it would no longer be mere consciousness, but self-consciousness. And its object then would not be a transcendent other, beyond consciousness, but something like the incarnate God of Christianity in *PhG* VII. At present, in the religions that precede that seventh chapter of *PhG*, human being does not yet think itself within its object. It is conscious of itself as a separate being and so has not yet become absolute spirit.

Hegel also includes in his list of six religions of consciousness two more instances—morality and conscience (364.10–32)—that I discuss in my third chapter, "Morality." I separate "faith" and "morality" partly for convenience, and partly for reasons intrinsic to Hegel's text.

With "morality" the interest of spirit shifts away from an otherworldly object and toward human behavior in this world; the difference between faith and morality, then, is the difference between looking away from oneself and looking at oneself. Thus, the distinction between faith and morality is justified; it goes back to the sequence of Hegel's text.

However, one caution is necessary. Although "faith" and "morality" have been distinguished, they should not be understood as mutually exclusive because the religions treated under "faith" may have moral concerns, and those treated under "morality" are not without faith. The unhappy consciousness, for example, is an instance of faith and yet its faith leads it to sacrifice immediate enjoyment in this life; it is a consciousness that acts in conformity with what it thinks. Likewise, "morality" itself is not without faith: by "morality" Hegel means Kant's practical reason that looks beyond this world to a holy lawgiver and to a future where virtue and happiness coincide. In fact, it is the faith of Kant's morality that receives special criticism from Hegel, rather than the morality itself. And so faith and morality do not represent tendencies that mutually exclude one another.

But over the course of time, spirit's interest does move away from an otherworldly God and toward its life in this world. This development, historically linked to the Enlightenment, can be symbolized as a shift from faith to morality, provided that the development is understood as a change in direction rather than as an abandonment of faith. In fact, the change can be more precisely understood as the attempt to ground faith in human morality. Furthermore, since Kant's attempt to derive faith from morality was really a derivation of religion from reason, Kantian morality ultimately leads to Hegel's "absolute knowing," where human reason does without faith. However, that development lies outside the scope of my study. In Kantian morality, faith does remain, and that is just what Hegel finds wrong with Kant's "moral world-view."

A closer look at the broad sweep of the development just discussed reveals another significant detail. In between the two extremes of an otherworldly God and human morality in this world are two religions that I call "faith" but that also begin to move away from the transcendent beyond toward actual human being. These are belief in the underworld and in heaven, both of which are populated by human shapes. To be sure, they are human beings in another world, but human beings nevertheless. Their presence in the movement of *PhG*'s religious interest gives them a transitional role between God and this world's human beings. Spirit's movement from the former to the latter passes by way of otherworldly human forms that are an appropriate middle factor between a transcendent God and actual human being.[1]

Finally, the shift in spirit away from its thought of a transcendent God and toward its own actual existence is intelligible as a movement from the object of thought to the being that thinks. God is not merely an object of thought for human being, but also the thinking existence of human being, whose true nature is to think of itself as the final goal of divine self-differentiation. These insights occur in the movement from faith to morality. They indicate a shift from objectivity to subjectivity; more precisely, they suggest a shift from thinking about a transcendent object to thinking about one's own existence within that object, which thereby loses its transcendence.

THE SUPERSENSIBLE INNER (82–102)

Before spirit discovers itself in its thinking, it shapes for itself a system of universal thought that is the first appearance of religion in *PhG*. Hegel's analysis of the supersensible inner[2] is evidently based on works about natural science and philosophy from the eighteenth and early nineteenth centuries.[3] Although the supersensible inner is thus a relatively recent form of religion, it is nevertheless the first one analyzed in *PhG*, because it "still is far distant from being spirit knowing itself as spirit" (363.12–13).[4] As a type of consciousness (even apart from its religious character), the supersensible inner is inferior to other shapes that preceded it in history.

Thus, religion first appears in *PhG* in an imperfect type of thinking called "understanding" ("Verstand"). Religion occurs here because understanding has for its object the universal inner side of being (363.9–13). This type of consciousness is treated in great detail in *PhG* III, a long and complicated chapter[5] that I do not examine in comparable detail since most of it does not appear to concern religion.[6] However, the general idea of the chapter is quite relevant to my topic. Human understanding that grasps a supersensible side of being already has a resemblance to religion because both are the mind's attempts to go beyond the sensible world into an intelligible one.

This remark holds true for many different understandings of the supersensible. An unchanging realm of ideal forms (of the sort commonly attributed to Plato) is a transcendent world that represents one kind of supersensible. But even when these forms are acknowledged as existing only in the actual beings of our empirical world (a thesis typical of Aristotelian thinking), a supersensible entity of some sort is posited; because the form is grasped by thinking rather than by sensation, it is beyond sense or "supersensible." So too is the Newtonian[7] attempt to frame universal laws of the movement of forces in the world; these laws are known to thinking but not to sensation. They too are "supersensible."

Understanding therefore points to a world beyond sensation because it discovers universal forms and laws that only thinking can grasp. Consequently, scientific understanding and religion have something in common. And so it is not surprising to find Hegel calling the understanding of the supersensible a form of religion, even when understanding has no interest in religion, or even when it considers religion as "pre-scientific." Hegel's position here is correct for it points out that scientific understanding and religion resemble one another: both claim to reach ideas that lie beyond what one perceives.

Furthermore, the link between religion and understanding of the supersensible has more to it than mere resemblance. If thinking of the supersensible is in Hegel's view religious, then religion must be for him a similar type of thinking. One may then infer that for Hegel, religion is thinking; its object, divine being, is accessible only to thought. Specifically, it is from thinking's ability to grasp universal objects that religion derives its knowledge of God. From this point of view, God is the most universal concept[8] of all, as well as the law that rules the world. That is why God is thought to be omnipresent and all-powerful. Through its ability to grasp an omnipresent essence, thinking produces the idea of God in one's mind. In scientific thinking this universal essence is given determinate and specific forms or laws. In religion it is grasped as an all-inclusive generality and often put into imaginative shapes. In Hegelian thought it is the absolute essence that includes and explains everything, even thinking itself.

These general considerations must now be developed by a closer look at Hegel's analysis of the supersensible inner side of empirical being. His treatment of this supersensible inner offers some parallels to his later chapter on religion.[9] This fact is not surprising because the supersensible inner is, after all, an instance of religion. A closer look at is worth the effort (even if the look is not as detailed as it could be) because the way Hegel examines this supersensible inner and its relation to both sensible things and self-consciousness resembles the way he thinks of God's relation to the world and to human being.

It would be too extreme a hypothesis to consider that this chapter (*PhG* III) contains the genesis of the idea of God since that idea begins to be shaped in the very first pages of *PhG* I, where the truth of the "here and now" is seen to be the universal thought rather than the sensory immediate. Consciousness's movement toward the universal is already its ascent to God. But in the chapter called "Force and Understanding" (*PhG* III), this universal becomes more definite and all-embracing; its comprehensive character makes it the basis for the thought of God that religion draws upon.

Inner Laws and Supersensible Worlds

The inner arises in thought first of all as the result of reflection on the nature of a thing: the thing is one, yet with many properties that express the thing's oneness; therefore, the thing is a force or movement toward self-expression (84.6–8). Force however is not a thing, but a thought; with the thought of force, the thing is de objectified; its inner nature is grasped as a universal that is no longer a thing ("unbedingt") (85.7).

Furthermore, the play of inner and outer is the play of two aspects of the thing, each of which seems to act upon the other; thus, two forces are at work in the thing (85.31–86.11), or two correlative forces that are the same insofar as both are instances of force (86.12–28). This correlation of forces means that forces do not exist independently of each other, by themselves, but only in correlation; forces therefore have a higher unity, which is the concept or thought of force, an essence or a universal (87.22–37). The inner nature of things appears as the concept, essence, or universal of force (88.1–9). Concrete material things thereby show themselves to have an inner truth which only thought can grasp.

But then the outer or perceived movements of things are only an appearance; the play of forces is said to belong to a world of appearances (88.24–89.3) that is not their ultimate truth. This kind of understanding starts out as a scientific meditation and soon becomes "Platonic" by its attempt to find unchanging truth. The inner side of appearance, then, is different from the external appearance; it is a supersensible truth (89.7; 90.8) which the mind is led to by its need to unify diversity in the world. This supersensible is indeed a "beyond" (89.7–8, 16–17) for it is unlike the initial appearance that consciousness perceived. It is "a *realm of laws at rest* . . . beyond the perceived world, for this [latter] portrays the law only through continual change, but also *present* in it and its immediate [though] tranquil copy" (91.27–30). From the empirical world comes its content: the simple law of force is that everything is different yet related (91.12–16) and consequently subject to the law of universal attraction—a law that lacks determinacy, according to Hegel, because it simply asserts that everything is different and is subject to law (92.17). Thus its content is fairly indeterminate.

This kind of supersensible resembles the God of theism. It is universal and all-powerful, subjecting everything to itself. As supersensible, it is beyond the world of material bodies and forces, which are therefore only an appearance of what is hidden. It is also transcendent insofar as any supersensible beyond is transcendent. But in this transcendence there is a definite relation to the world; God is conceived as the idea of the world, not as a mind whose thinking contains the idea of the world along with all other kinds of ideas, which would be possibilities not yet realized by our world or even possibilities of wholly different kinds of worlds.

Although the supersensible inner of *PhG* III is never called God, it resembles in many ways the God of Hegel's *Logik*. There are also notable differences. The supersensible inner of *PhG* III has not yet been conceived as positing real existence, nor as positing the highest part of real existence, human spirit, in which its supersensible quality at last appears. These limitations in the supersensible inner are only to be expected. This kind of entity does not represent Hegel's own concept of God in final form, but only God from the point of view of understanding. "Verstand" or understanding is not even self-consciousness, and still less spirit. Its view of God is therefore limited.

Understanding comes closer to Hegel's own view when it modifies the supersensible inner into a second supersensible known as the "inverted world." This variation is an attempt to account for the determinate differences in a given law, such as the difference between space and time in gravitational attraction (94.20–25). Since every law unifies a set of such differences (93.1–6), understanding now places dynamic difference in the supersensible world (96.30–34) so that the different factors of a law can evoke their opposites. A "force . . . repels itself from itself, and thus essentially attracts to itself this repelled [force], since it is *the same* [as the original force]" (96.18, 21–22). Here, difference is explained by repulsion of like from like, which then become opposites; these opposites attract one another because they are really alike. This law constitutes the second supersensible world, where internal repulsion inverts the relationships of the first (96.36–37; 97.27–28). Also inverted in the second supersensible is the empirical[10] world (97.28–29), of which the first supersensible world is a copy (91.29–30; 96.27–28). These reversals give the second supersensible its name: it is the so-called "inverted . . . supersensible world" (99.4), where black becomes white, or sweet becomes sour (97.8–9). As the hidden inner substance holding the empirical world's potential for difference, the second supersensible world contains the opposite of what appears empirically at any given time.

By dealing with opposition and unity, this odd inverted world resembles Hegel's own dialectic.[11] Nevertheless he considers it an unsatisfactory "image of inversion" (98.27), another "*sensory world . . .* [existing only] in *imagination*" (98.7–8). By imagining this world, understanding places differences "in two worlds or in two substantial elements" (101.21), one empirical and the other supersensible.

The true unity of opposites is to be found instead in the Hegelian concept: one must "*think* pure change or *opposition within itself, contradiction*" (98.32–33). Without its being explicitly named, one meets here the famous Hegelian dialectic, in which "*the opposite in and for itself*" (99.2) emerges. Through this dialectic, the first supersensible world would become "the inverted [version] of itself; it is itself and [also] its opposite in one unity" (99.5–6). In Hegel's version of the supersensible inner, the two supersensible worlds would form a single unity of "difference as *inner*, or difference *in itself*" (99.7) because every difference contains its other.[12]

Infinity

Their unity is the occasion for Hegel to introduce the term "infinity" (99.7–8), by which he means something unbounded inasmuch as it logically passes over into its opposite. Opposites are correlative, each one calling for the other so that each one has the other in itself; together they constitute a higher unity (99.23–29). With each opposite the other is expressed (99.39–100.2). Every determinacy is also its contrary; their correlation is what is meant by "infinity" (100.29).

From this discussion, one can infer what Hegel would mean by an infinite God. In Christian imagery, divine essence would be infinite (according to Hegel) only if it passed beyond itself and constituted an other, that is, a world different from itself. A second way of being infinite would be to pass into human being; the Incarnation would then be an example of divine infinity applied to a single human person. A third way would be the presence of the Holy Spirit in the faithful; this, too, would be an example of divine self-communication or deity's moving outward into something other than itself. But such examples[13] become truly Hegelian only if they are shown to be necessary movements because Hegelian dialectic posits itself with logical necessity. Without such logic the movement would have no conceptual necessity. And if the movement is not intrinsic to its concept,[14] the concept is not really infinite.[15]

Self-Consciousness

Although understanding fails to grasp its object as infinite (101.24–30), it has nevertheless attempted to explain movement and difference within its object: it posits an inverted world, where force repels and unifies differences (96.18–23). But instead of grasping this object "in its essential form as pure concept . . . *infinity* as such" (101.24–26), understanding prefers to see itself as the unification of differences: it is "consciousness of difference as a [difference that is] also *immediately* surmounted; it is *for itself* . . . or *self-consciousness*" (101.31–33).[16] For understanding, the surmounting of differences is not objective but subjective (100.35–101.2; 101.30–33); its explaining of difference and unity in its object now leads it inward into itself (101.13–16; 102.16–20).

Perhaps Hegel is alluding to Kant or someone like him. For Kant, synthesis derives from the mind, not from the object as given; the unified object is a synthesis made by the understanding. But whether Hegel had in mind Kant or someone else, the main result is clear:

consciousness is now self-consciousness. By trying to explain the logical movement of its supersensible object, consciousness discovers itself as distinct from this object. For this consciousness, the inner that differentiates itself and then unifies the differences is consciousness itself; thus, understanding "experiences *itself*" (102.11) in "the inner [side] of appearance" (102.8). The ascent of consciousness to a supersensible world now turns back into consciousness itself, thereby constituting the transition from consciousness to self consciousness. The supersensible inner vanishes from view as *PhG* begins a new chapter (IV) centered around self-consciousness.

By itself, however, human self-consciousness is not yet spirit, for which an objective divine essence is also necessary. In the development of *PhG*, "self-consciousness has come to be only *for itself*, [but] not yet *as unity* with consciousness [of objectivity] in general" (102.6–7). When the supersensible inner reappears as the transcendent God of the unhappy consciousness, it remains an objectivity separate from that consciousness and so continues the separation of human subjectivity from divine objectivity.

Later on, Hegel calls the supersensible inner object a "selfless universal" (363.9–13). He means that God pictured in the form of this supersensible inner is not yet spirit, not yet a self. In my interpretation of Hegel, "self" refers here not to the selfhood of the universal considered by itself (as though a divine selfhood were meant), but to the self it has when human subjectivity is seen to be a necessary development of it. It is true that religion has another view: it imagines God as an independent self who thinks and acts like a person. But the only self Hegel mentions in his long analysis of the supersensible inner is the human subjectivity that discovers itself as a self-consciousness at the end of the analysis. Consequently, the later description of a "selfless universal" refers to an object without such a self, namely a universal object without a human self. And Hegel's God has a human self at the end of *PhG*, where human thinking is not externally related to God but is contained in the concept of its supersensible object. In other words, God is spirit only when human being is a necessary development within the concept of God.

This conclusion cannot yet be proven fully since a human self has not yet emerged within divine essence. The true meaning of divine selfhood appears only in *PhG* VII, "Die Religion." But Hegel's next analysis of religion also points toward the same conclusion. Since human thinking about the supersensible is reflected back into itself, divine essence now has to be examined in its relation to human being. *PhG* thus advances to another type of consciousness and another kind of object.

UNHAPPY CONSCIOUSNESS (121–31)

If the supersensible inner is said to be without a self, this deficiency is filled to some extent by the "unhappy consciousness," the next occurrence of religion in *PhG*.[17] Here, the object of consciousness is again a universal thought, like the supersensible inner. But in addition to being an unchangeable universal, the object also takes on an individual shape (125.7–21); this is undoubtedly a reference to the incarnation of God in Jesus. This kind of individuality puts a human self into God, who is no longer the "selfless universal" of the supersensible inner, but now a universal with a self. In fact, the discussion of the unhappy consciousness (121.23–131.31) is for the most part a discussion of its relation to that unchangeable universal in human shape (123.38–131.31). But when only Jesus is the incarnation of God, every other human being remains as before, namely separated from God. Thus, despite its individual shape the divine universal remains separated from human consciousness (127.36–128.2), which is consequently unhappy.

Obviously, this religion is Christianity, which in *PhG* VII is presented as the highest one of all. Yet here in *PhG* IV, it is portrayed as the cause of great unhappiness. Why this difference of treatment for the same religion? One reason can be found in the historical situation of the unhappy consciousness, which is not the same as that of Christianity in *PhG* VII. In *PhG* IV, the unhappy consciousness succeeds Stoicism and Skepticism and is a development of those philosophies; it is the religion of Greco-Roman Christianity, which prolonged itself into the Middle Ages.[18]

But this historical period, like any other one in Hegel, is to be understood according to its particular determinacy or character. Why is the period marked by an unhappy consciousness? Hegel explains it in the following way. Most generally, "the *unhappy consciousness* is the consciousness of self as a double essence only contradicting [itself]"

(121.38–39). It is a double consciousness, aware of itself on the one hand as a "simple immutable" (122.14) consciousness of universals, and on the other hand as a "multiple mutable" (122.14–15) consciousness of individual beings. Knowing these two different kinds of objects, the unhappy consciousness is *"split within itself"* (122.1) into "opposed" (122.13) sides.[19]

Moreover, this consciousness keeps the universal separate from the singular.[20] Such a difference is maintained because it considers its "simple immutable [consciousness] as *essence"* (122.14) and its "multiple mutable [consciousness] as the *non-essential"* (122.14–15). And it ranks itself with this non-essential side (122.16–17), thereby keeping itself separate from essence and effecting a distinction between its own actuality and the realm of essence: "for itself [or subjectively] *itself* . . . is not this essence" (122.22–23).[21] In this way the mental picture of a divine essence beyond the actual world arises. Therefore, its religion is an instance of "consciousness of *absolute essence* . . . from the *standpoint of consciousness"* (363.4–5), having its object separate and transcendent. Later on (in *PhG* VII) Hegel considers Christianity from the point of view of "absolute essence *in and for itself"* (363.7) or of divine essence whose becoming other and human is a logical necessity.[22] For unhappy consciousness, however, divine essence is an immutability opposed to mutable human consciousness; it is "only the immutability [that is an object] . . . of consciousness, which consequently is not the true [one] but is still afflicted with an opposite, [and so is] not the immutable *in and for itself"* (123.32–34). In other words, unhappy consciousness believes in a transcendent, immutable God beyond the mutable world. According to Hegel, though, the true God is the essence that includes its opposite or its other; this essence is "the immutable *in and for itself"* (123.34). *PhG* VII considers God from this higher point of view, but the unhappy consciousness of *PhG* IV does not.

Faced with the opposition between its universal thinking and its individual consciousness, the unhappy consciousness attempts to surmount its individuality (122.27) by elevating itself to immutable thought (122.36).[23] However, this attempt is not entirely successful. When "the immutable which enters consciousness is . . . touched by individuality" (123.1–2),[24] there is indeed produced a relation[25] between God and individual human being, the *"emerging of individuality*

IN the immutable and *of the immutable IN the individual"* (123.5–7). But this relation does not remove the individual consciousness's unhappiness. Despite the unity of human individuality and divine immutability (123.7–9), the unhappy consciousness remains divided between its own individuality and its immutable thought (123.5–9), and *"the difference* of both is the dominant" (123.10–11) feature. This difference prevents consciousness from finding happiness.

Linking Human Being with Its Immutable God

In particular there arises a "threefold way" in which "individuality is linked with the immutable" (123.11, 12). This threefold linking is obviously modeled after the Christian Trinity. In the first way, empirical individual consciousness is "opposed to the immutable essence" (123.13), which thus appears as "the *alien* essence condemning [human] individuality" (123.19); undoubtedly Hegel has in mind Judaism, which gives Christianity its transcendent Father. A second way occurs when the immutable essence assumes a singular shape (123.15–16), like that of empirical human being (123.20), so that God incarnate now resembles everything that exists as individual (123.7, 16–17). In the third way, human being "finds . . . *itself* as this individual in the immutable" (123.17–18), presumably because it identifies itself with the incarnate Son, who "is a *shape* of *individuality* like itself" (123.20). This identification is possible because the unhappy consciousness understands the incarnation of God as "individuality *in general in* the immutable essence" (123.7) and therefore as "also *its own"* (123.8), that is, as every individual's. Human being then becomes "spirit" (123.20) because it "has the joy of finding itself in [divine essence] and becomes conscious [that] its individuality is reconciled with the universal" (123.21–22); human being is spirit when its actual, empirical side is reconciled with divine essence.[26]

And yet this joy eludes the unhappy consciousness because *"the difference"* between it and its essence remains "the dominant" (123.10, 11) feature or "the element" (123.14) and milieu of its whole history. Therefore, even when the unhappy consciousness relates itself to a God incarnate in human shape (123.23–25), it still relates itself to a being other than itself, higher and different; the transcendence of Judaism's

God is preserved in medieval Christianity. But the goal of consciousness is to surmount its limited individuality by union with divine
essence. By devotion and self-sacrifice, therefore, the unhappy consciousness "strives to attain this being one" (124.31–32) with Christ,
but does not succeed. If one interprets these works of the individual
consciousness as its futile attempt to become spirit,[27] one can understand most of this section is a description of the third way by which the
unhappy consciousness relates itself to its immutable, incarnate God.

The first two ways (namely Judaism and the individual incarnation
of God in Jesus) are more negative than positive, and they are only
briefly described. When God is known as "the *alien* essence condemning individuality" (123.19), reconciliation between divine essence and
individual human being is obviously impossible. And even when the
divine "*immutable . . .* has *in itself individuality*" (123.15–16) as God
incarnate, it remains separate from other human beings because every
empirical being is "an untransparent sensory *one*" (124.11–12) standing over against other empirical beings. And then like all individual
creatures, it vanishes from the earth (124.16–19) so that its separateness
from others appears even more clearly. Consequently, the third way,
that of "spirit" (123.20), is adopted; it follows from the second way,
inasmuch as empirical consciousness knows from the incarnation of
God that "its individuality is reconciled with the universal" (123.21–
22). Hegel must mean that Christians try to make themselves more like
Christ so that their "initially external relation" to him "becomes
absolute oneness" (124.29–30). As a result, their own individuality
becomes effectually reconciled with universal deity.

Space forbids a detailed examination of how the unhappy consciousness attempts to come closer to its incarnate God. Nevertheless, a brief
summary of its movement as spirit may be given. Spiritual Christian
behavior, the third way of relating to an immutable God, is itself
subdivided into a threefold movement: inner devotion (124.38–
126.23); outward activity (126.24–128.34); and the inner renunciation
of selfish activity (128.35–131.31). All three subdivisions (named in
124.31–36) illustrate how consciousness remains unhappy despite its
various attempts to unite itself with God incarnate.

First, it is "*pure consciousness*" (124.33) or "*inner feeling*"
(128.38–39), a "*devotion*" (125.26) and "infinite *yearning*" (125.33)

that cannot attain its object (125.36–126.6), which by definition is beyond actuality. The Crusades do not obtain it either, because the holy places are not God incarnate (126.7–18).

Second, consciousness is a living self active in the world; it is an "external doing and enjoying" (129.1), an "*individual actuality*" (126.25) expressing itself in "desire and labor" (124.34) and so is no longer the pure consciousness of devotion but a corporeal being marked by conscious individuality. In its devotion, "it has felt the object of its pure feeling, and this [object] is itself" (126.28–29). Consequently, it feels itself as individual. But since this consciousness always views itself and its God as two separate entities, its individual activity merely confirms its distance from God. Thus, "the [self-] confirmation [Bewährung] which it would obtain through work and enjoyment is . . . *broken*; . . . it . . . finds only confirmation of what it [subjectively] is for itself, namely [confirmation] of its disunity" (127.1–4). As a result, the unhappy consciousness acts not by its own power but by "capacities and forces . . . which the immutable [God] . . . gives over to consciousness for it to use" (127.25–27).[28] Every human deed, then, illustrates the "pure universal . . . absolute power" (128.5) of God; since for the unhappy consciousness God is "beyond itself" (128.2), its own activity (based on divine gifts) is viewed as "an alien gift" (127.26). This outlook merely preserves the initial division between God and the unhappy consciousness.

A similar division occurs in the actual world (127.5–8) in which the unhappy consciousness lives, works, and finds enjoyment. This world seems to be centered in the Eucharist, whose elements are divine "essence . . . in the form of independent things" (126.35); by partaking of them, consciousness obtains "*unity* with the immutable" (128.13) for which it *gives thanks* [*dankt*]" (128.9).[29] Such unity is deceptive, however. When "the immutable [deity] itself *hands over* its shape and *leaves* [it] to [consciousness] for enjoyment" (127.18–19; 127.35–36), its gift is a divine act calling for a corresponding human one (128.20–21). Since each party's action is distinct and separate, their "unity is afflicted with separation" (128.13–14). Consciousness has acted as individual (128.15–29) and so it remains individual (128.27–29) and separated from God (128.29–34). Not even the Eucharist can overcome that initial division between human being and its incarnate God.[30]

Third, thanksgiving effects "a return of consciousness into itself"

(129.9). This inner actuality is again "the *relation* of itself as nothingness to the universal essence" (129.12), which is considered the source
of everything else and in comparison to which the human self feels
"defiled" (129.27) by its "animal functions" (129.20–21). And so by
self-mortification, it gives up its own individual will,[31] its enjoyment,
its possessions,[32] and even its thought (130.9–24).[33] By giving up its
individual side, which is oriented to external things, it becomes conscious of its own freedom (130.25–28) from them and so discovers its
universal intellectual side. Then it is able to make its individual will
conform to the universal will of God (131.6–9).

Other Shapes of Consciousness

A new content then arises for consciousness. Even though it is distinct
from its universal object (131.16–17, 28), it nevertheless knows that its
individual activity conforms to universal essence "*in itself*" (131.29).
In this way, there arises "the picture [Vorstellung] of *reason* . . . consciousness's certainty of being in its individuality absolutely *in itself*, or
all reality" (131.30–31). Historically, this new content marks the transition from the Middle Ages to the Renaissance. Conceptually, it seems
to mean that individual consciousness knows itself as unlimited intellect. However, it will take some time for this inner certainty to fill itself
with a more determinate content.

One can understand Hegel's next example of religion as providing
some of this determinate content, even though the religion itself belongs to pre-Christian times. In the Greek religion of the underworld, a
valuing of human individuality that is missing from the unhappy Christian consciousness develops; the latter is displeased with its individual
existence. But before passing on to this early stage of Greek religion,
I wish to examine two particular questions arising from Hegel's analysis of the unhappy consciousness: divine reality and the incarnation
of God.

Divine Reality and Its Incarnation

Hegel's analysis of the unhappy consciousness raises the question of
divine reality. For this unhappy consciousness, God is an immutable
essence beyond the world. In Hegel's view, however, this conscious-

ness deceives itself because all its knowledge of a transcendent God is really its own self-knowing. For example, in devotion "its feeling of essence is [really] this self-feeling" (126.36; 126.26–29); therefore, it should not attribute its own activity to God but should rather "arrive at a feeling of its own independence" (127.14). Furthermore, Hegel writes of the unhappy consciousness that "although *for itself* it may only be mutable, and the immutable alien to it, [in fact] *it itself is* simple and thereby immutable consciousness, which it is thereby conscious of as *its* essence, yet in such a way that *itself* is again for itself not this essence" (122.20–23). In this sentence Hegel appears to mean that the divine essence honored by consciousness is really the human intellect. This raises the question of whether such a God is real or not. To help resolve this question, one must consider the way in which Hegel relates divine essence and human thinking.

For Hegel, the thought of God does arise from the human intellect.[34] But this thinking is not merely subjective. The supersensible inner that arises for understanding consists of the laws of the physical world. Such an idea must be objective and real. Yet as a separate realm, it does seem to be abstract; its reality has to be the physical world itself. As this idea tries to incorporate this mutable reality into itself, it becomes inverted as though it were straining toward a dialectical content in which its concept would be related to its reality. But the immutable God of the unhappy consciousness remains immutable; it does not lead back to the actual world, which is that of nature and spirit. This defect is not remedied when the immutable God becomes incarnate in one human being and inspires other human beings to become spirit. Such acts of God are not conceptually comprehended; they are a contingent "*happening*" (123.2) for the unhappy consciousness and so lack the necessity (306.21; 404.19) and universality of the concept.

But in Hegel's system, God is an idea developing itself by logical necessity into existing nature and spirit. For Hegel, then, human thinking is the culmination of divine essence, which develops itself into human thinking. In this way, human selfhood is independent of God because it is not simply essence, but exists in nature as a free intellect. On the other hand, as the highest development of divine essence one can also understand it as the existence of that essence. Human thinking, then, is God's thinking since divine essence posits itself as human being.

However, the unhappy consciousness does not think of God in this way. It regards divine essence simply as immutable. And because it does not identify its thinking with divine essence, object and subject are separated. For the same reason, this essence is also considered to lie beyond nature, the realm of individual existence. Therefore, consciousness becomes divided into a thinking of immutable essence and a knowing of mutable existence. And then its immutable thought cannot refer to itself because by definition the immutable belongs to God alone.[35]

But when Hegel identifies "immutable consciousness"[36] with the "essence" (122.21, 22) it is conscious of, he does not mean that God is only a thought with no reality. On the contrary, according to his system, God's reality is at its fullest in human thinking. Thus, the unhappy consciousness correctly grasps (through its universal thinking) an immutable essence, but it incorrectly knows this essence *only* as God and not also as itself. Such a God is abstracted from real existence and objectified into a separate entity by unhappy consciousness. In Hegel's own system, however, this immutable God has real existence as human being, as the phrase "*its* essence" (122.22) indicates. Therefore, the separation between God and human being disappears in Hegelian thought.

But the unhappy consciousness is unhappy because it does not yet comprehend itself as a differentiation of divine essence. Hegel's text implies that such a comprehension is legitimate: "for itself [i.e. subjectively] *itself* . . . is not this [divine] essence" (122.22–23); in reality, however, it is the existence of this essence. But the existence of this essence includes the mutable side of human being, and because of its mutability it considers itself alienated from divine essence. The problem is solved later on in *PhG* through the concept of spirit, according to which human being will think itself to be the real existence of divine essence.

Hegel's analysis of the unhappy consciousness also raises a question about the reality of God's incarnation in Jesus. If divine immutability is known by a thinking of immutability, it would be an easy matter for human intelligence to think of God as incarnate by joining its immutable thought to an individual human being. Although Hegel is not very explicit about this point, his discussion supports such an interpretation. When the unhappy consciousness touches its immutable thought with its own individuality (123.1–3), the result is the presence of individuality in the immutable God (123.5–6). This must be the incarnation of God in a single human being, who is first of all contrasted with others (129.29–30) but then is viewed as individuality in general, so that all other individuals can be contained in it (123.7, 15–17), including the unhappy consciousness itself (123.8, 17–18, 20–22). The whole movement seems to occur because the unhappy consciousness attributes a singularity like itself (123.20) to God.

It is hard to escape the suspicion that the unhappy consciousness, "the unity of pure thinking and individuality" (125.16–17), makes itself into an object of thought and in this way obtains God's incarnation of God in Jesus, "the immutable itself essentially as individuality" (125.18). But because it thinks of this divine incarnation as a distinctive individual being rather than as a universal (126.23), it does not see its incarnate God as its own dual nature: "it is not *for it* that this its object, the immutable which for it essentially has the shape of individuality, is *itself*" (125.19–20). In other words, not seeing God as the universal whose individuality is every human being, the unhappy consciousness can never completely identify itself with God incarnate.

Knowing it as a singular event rather than as a universal (and necessary) truth, the unhappy consciousness does not *comprehend* the incarnation of God. This consciousness knows "not the immutable in and for itself" (123.34) but only "immutability as [object] ... of consciousness" (123.32) and distinct from consciousness. If the immutable were known "in and for itself," it would not have human consciousness as its opposite (123.33–34; 125.5–6) but would include it so that human being in general would be comprehended as the real existence of the divine concept (125.28–29). However, the unhappy consciousness does not arrive at this concept, which would eliminate its separation from God (125.30–31). For it, God is a beyond, present only through the behavior[37] of consciousness, not through the divine concept itself (125.1–6). For this reason, most of Hegel's analysis is devoted to the behavior of the unhappy consciousness, which unsuccessfully tries to unite itself to its incarnate God.

THE RELIGION OF THE UNDERWORLD (241–64)

Unhappy consciousness concluded its development by becoming reason or the individual's certainty of being all reality (131.30–31). This conviction, which is the basis of idealism (133.6–7), identifies thinking with the actual world (132.27–29). No doubt it is Hegel's position too, for his *Logik* argues that the actual world is thinkable through pure universals. But to pursue this point would go far beyond the scope of this study. Also outside my investigation is the development of reason in *PhG* V, which has "no religion, because the self-consciousness [of reason] . . . knows or seeks *itself* in the *immediate* present" (363.19–20) rather than in thinking.

Such a limited view of reason is surmounted when reason becomes spirit in *PhG* VI: "reason is spirit, inasmuch as the certainty of being all reality[38] is raised to truth and is conscious of itself as its world, and of the world as itself" (238.3–5). In spirit the inward certainty of reason finds its outward truth or empirical verification. But what exactly is "spirit"? In *PhG* VI, it seems to refer to social and political life, in which universal thought and individual actuality interpenetrate.[39] Hegel's chapter on spirit thus begins with an analysis of ancient Greece, whose "*religion* of the *underworld*" (363.21–22) has a social character that was left out of the treatment of the unhappy consciousness in *PhG* IV.

Hegel examines Greek society in a section called "Die Sittlichkeit," a term that refers to a way of life practiced by a group of individuals (194.1–16). Its "Sitte" is its "ethos."[40] "Sittlichkeit" could, therefore, be translated literally as "ethicality"; Baillie and Miller render it as "ethical order."[41]

Overview of Ethical Life in Greece and Rome

An overview of topics contained in Hegel's section on "Sittlichkeit" (*PhG* VI–A) may help one's understanding of the religion it contains.[42] Subsection "a" (241.21–251.4) is entitled "The Ethical World: Human and Divine Law; Man and Woman." It describes Greek society as formed by the harmonious cooperation of two institutions, civil government and family, each having its own sphere of interest. Human law is the self-conscious law of the state and its ruler (242.18–25); this law is the work of men, who thereby maintain a universal public order against their own individuality (242.29–30). Divine law is the unconscious law of the family (243.2–5). This law is maintained by women (248.17–19), and its sole content (245.18) consists of burying a family member whose individuality (243.24–25; 257.33) is recognized after death (245.25). Obviously Hegel is retelling the story of Antigone, interpreting it for his own purposes. One easily sees that the difference between the two laws, as well as between their corresponding institutions and sexes, is fundamentally a difference between universal thinking and individual actuality: just as the unhappy consciousness excludes its individual existence from its immutable thought, ancient Greek society separates individual personality from universal civic interests. The former is recognized only by women; the latter, only by men.

Subsection "b" (251.5–260.23) bears the title "Ethical Action: Human and Divine Knowing; Guilt and Fate." Ethical action, or action according to either human or divine law, disrupts the harmony between the two laws. The reason is simple: the two laws are opposed, so an individual must follow one or the other (252.15–20). And a given individual has no choice between them. A man will promote human law; a woman will maintain divine law (252.7–14). By nature, the genders have different outlooks. There is some advantage to this limitation: whether male or female, "the ethical consciousness . . . [already] knows what it has to do" (252.7). But its human knowing is limited to the law of its own sex. As a result, human knowing ignores the opposite law that is hidden from its view (255.10–12), but that is presumably known to the gods and hinted at by seers and diviners. This hidden knowledge is the "divine knowing" mentioned in Hegel's title. Only the gods know all; human knowing is either male or female and, as such, is limited. Action according to this knowing therefore leads to tragedy. A deed according to one law "renounces and wounds" the other law and is thereby "guilt" and "crime" (254.7, 9, 10). The law that has been violated then takes its revenge (255.1–8). Thus, the ethical individual necessarily perishes (256.9–14); "ethical substance" or law turns out to be a "negative power" or "fate" (256.32–33) destroying the individual who acts. This ending is necessary because action according to one law violates the other. Greek society therefore consumes itself.

Subsection "c" (260.24–264.6) describes the Roman empire, in which the value of individual personality is at last given legal recognition by human law (260.30–32; 261.11–12; 261.24, 26). This empire is a new synthesis of spirit's two elements, individual actuality and universal thinking, which are opposed to one another in Greece. In Roman law, human individuality is recognized by the state or by universal thought.[43] The Roman synthesis, however, is not perfect. Individuals are recognized only "as the pure *empty one*[ness] of the person" (262.5–6) that, taken by itself, is "without proper content" (262.12). This emptiness is not eradicated by the economic corollary to independent personhood, namely "possession" (262.13) or "*property*" (262.14),[44] because "the actual content or the *determinacy* of [what is] mine—be it an external possession or the inner richness of poverty of spirit and character [—] is not contained in this empty form" (262.20–22) of personhood. Specific norms for property and character do not belong to the abstract idea of "person."

One figure, however, is exempt from the customary Roman understanding of personhood. All the reality missing from this definition of "person" is attributed to the emperor, "the absolute power and absolute actuality . . . lord of the world . . , [and] the   person comprising all existence within himself" (262.34–36). It is not surprising that "this lord of the world is the monstrous [human] self-consciousness that knows itself as the actual God" (263.9–10). When a legally recognized person has no content beyond personhood, all real content belongs to the emperor. But the legal recognition of individual persons is at least an improvement over their submergence into community life, as is the case in ancient Greece.

This rapid overview of ethical life in ancient Greece (and Rome) provides a context for understanding particular points in the Greek religion of the underworld.

Fate

When Hegel summarizes this religion at the beginning of *PhG* VII, he characterizes it as "faith in the frightful unknown night of *fate* and in the Fury of the *departed spirit*" (363.22–23). These two objects of faith derive from the opposition between universal thinking and individual actuality: fate is a version of the immutable God as thought by the unhappy consciousness, while the departed spirit is actual human personality in another world.

Fate is "pure negativity in the form of universality" (363.24), or the universal power of destruction. Hegel also calls it "the nothing[ness] of necessity" (364.1), alluding to the ethical characters of Greek trag-edy who necessarily perish because they violate one law by obeying another. Thus fate appears to be the logic of the universe, or divine substance, in its aspect of negating and destroying; it is "the eternal necessity . . . which devours in the abyss of its *simplicity* the divine as well as the human law, along with the two self-consciousnesses in which these powers have their existence" (251.19–22). When the two antagonists of a tragic conflict perish, as Creon and Antigone do, both they and the laws they embody are shown to be subject to a higher power, "and ethical substance emerges as the negative power which devours both sides, or [as] the all-powerful and just *fate*" (256.32–34). Consequently, fate is not a blind or irrational force but rather an image of dialectical metaphysics. The tragic chorus that believes in fate thereby also "feels . . . the seriousness of the concept" (393.8–9) governing human affairs.

However, this concept is not yet grasped as spirit, or as divine substance that necessarily becomes human; instead it is viewed as an "*alien*" (393.12–13) force, hostile to human being. But if fate is on the one hand mysterious and frightening, on the other hand it is the universal substance that eventually differentiates itself into human knowing. Hegel alludes to this positive development when he de-scribes the limitation of fate: "fate without the self . . . remains the unconscious night, which does not come to differentiation within itself nor to the clarity of self-knowing" (363.31–33). In other words, Greek fate is the forerunner of the God of Christianity: the universal divine substance that comes to know itself in human thinking.

Another meaning that Hegel gives to the word "fate" is related to this future development. When he writes that in Greek "*comedy* . . . actual self-consciousness portrays itself as the fate of the gods" (397.28–29), "fate" refers not to a purely negative force, but to a positive result: human selfhood now is the object of thinking, instead of the gods. This is also true of the Roman empire, where "the necessity of empty fate is nothing other than the *I* of self-consciousness" (261.10–11); Greek culture ends not with an empty fate, but with the human person given legal recognition in Roman law. In this sense, "the ethical world showed . . . *the individual self* as its fate and its truth" (323.25–26). But with this more positive meaning of "fate," the human spirit is beyond the ethical world and its religion because thinking no longer contemplates human life as simply subject to fate, its all-powerful destroyer.

In ancient Greece, human being already contributes to the working of fate, though unwittingly. The Greek world perishes because "ethical consciousness essentially is *immediately* directed to the law . . . [thus] nature in general comes into ethical action" (260.8–10). By nature, Hegel probably means the gender a person is born with. In the ethical world, individual consciousness supports either divine law or human law because the individual has a naturally given gender: a woman is on the side of divine law, while a man is on the side of human law (252.7–14). Nature then limits the ethical decisions of individuals, directing them to one law or the other. Women support human individuality by appealing to divine law, while men promote the universal (political) good by appealing to human law. Greek culture is therefore a house divided against itself, and so it perishes. Its destruction comes about through the agency of human beings who attribute their destiny to fate because they do not understand why their conflicts occur. Limited by nature to knowing only one law, these ethical agents do not arrive at a thorough understanding of their universal substance, which contains both laws.[45]

The Departed Spirit

In addition to fate, the religion of the underworld also believes "in the Fury of the *departed spirit*" (363.23) seeking to avenge its death. The Fury is not an additional force, but the departed spirit "is itself the subterranean power, and it is *its* Fury that carries out revenge" inasmuch as "its blood lives on in [its] house" (250.8–10). Therefore, the departed spirit exerts a force on the real world through its family, which is the "immediate presence" (287.34) of this spirit. Here, Hegel neither affirms nor denies the possibility of survival after death. But his analysis seems to reduce the afterlife to family piety.[46] The deceased has actuality only in the family (261.2).

Nevertheless, belief in an underworld prepares the way for Roman law by bringing to consciousness the importance of human individuality. While actually alive, the human person is not recognized as an individual by the Greek city-state, whose political life aims rather at the universal good of the city; even as a family member, "the *individual*

counted and was actual only as the universal *blood* of the *family*"
(261.2). But when detached from the family by death, a person somehow becomes more individual: "as *this* individual, it was the *selfless
departed* spirit" (261.3). Therefore, it is as a spirit in the underworld
that a human being is recognized as individual. What the Roman state
later recognizes as actual, the Greek world recognizes only as deceased
(323.25). Thus in contrast to fate, which is "pure negativity in the form
of universality," the departed spirit is pure negativity "in the form of
individuality" or "absolute essence" as "the *self*" (363.24–25). In its
thought of a departed spirit, the religion of the underworld comes close
to identifying the hidden universal substance with the human self.
However, the self is so honored not when actual or alive, but only when
dead. Human personality is not the living human being, just a shadow
of itself when it is "*this* individual shade" (363.27).

Yet even as a surviving spirit, the individual still is not formally
identified with the universal substance because the individual shade is
separate from universal fate (367.27–28). Nevertheless, Hegel sees in
the idea of a shade the surmounting of natural existence, which is
individual and self-centered; the shade is a "*surmounted this*"
(363.28), or a self that has given up individual existence. As a result, it
should also be a "universal self" (363.28–29) because a real self gives
up its individuality in order to join itself to some universal. But the
shade is only the "negative" surmounting of individuality without
acquiring a positive universal significance (363.29–31). In other
words, it negates its existence, or dies, but it does not become anything
universal. Consequently, the religion of the underworld keeps separate
its two different objects of belief, universal fate and the individual
departed spirit. In Christianity, however, the surmounted individual is
also universal: when Jesus gives up his earthly existence, he lives on in
the Christian church.

Hegel's discussion of this distinction between individual and universal is found in his summary introduction to *PhG* VII. But in his fuller
description of the religion of the underworld in *PhG* VI–A, he seems to
identify them. In this section, one reads that the deceased "has been
gathered from the long series of its scattered existence into the one
completed shape, and from the unrest of contingent living into the
repose of simple universality" (244.8–11). In this passage the individual deceased person is said to be universal.[47] Here, however, univer-

sality refers to the corpse: "this universality to which the individual *as such* attains is *pure being, death*; it is *immediate natural being* [that has] *come to be* [das *unmittelbare natürliche Gewordenseyn*], not the *doing* of a *consciousness*" (244.14–16). The lifeless corpse has become a being like others, a mere natural being without spirit, belonging to "*universal* being" (244.17–18). Its universality refers not to its joining universal substance after death and its survival as a conscious spirit within this substance, but rather to its temporary and helpless existence as a corpse, which remains on earth like other natural beings without spirit.[48] But the departed spirit of this corpse is also called "individual" (363.23–31) because its personality is believed to survive.

Yet even that spirit is "*selfless*" (261.3); that is, it is without a real self because the only self Hegel seems to acknowledge is one with a "present" (363.26) worldly existence. When Hegel attributes a real self to the shade (363.25–26), he is probably thinking of its "Fury" (363.23), which actually exists in the family (287.34–35) insofar as it incites another family member to avenge its death (250.8–10).

Belief in fate and in the departed spirit are the two topics that Hegel selects for mention in his summary review of Greek religion (363.21–33) at the beginning of *PhG* VII. He probably mentions these two topics at this point because *PhG* VII examines the concept of spirit from a new point of view, which looks at spirit as absolute substance in human shape (387.26–27; 405.24–25). Hegel's full discussion (241–64) of the religion of the underworld, however, deals with two other religious topics that need to be examined briefly: "divine law" and "divine knowing," both of which are mentioned in the titles (241.23; 251.7) to their respective subsections.

Divine Law

Divine law concerns burial of the dead, an act that Hegel interprets as recognition of the individual person after death (245.18–19). The struggle between divine law and human law amounts to the struggle between individual personality and universal social order. According to Hegel, divine law in this religion is not an arbitrary decree of the gods but a recognition by the family of individual subjectivity[49] at a time when the state ignores it. The family is the group that recognizes an individual as such. And since the family is "the *unconscious*, still inner concept over against its self-conscious actuality [in the state] . . . the [household] Penates over against the universal spirit [of the political community]" (243.2, 5), divine law must operate as an unconscious law in contrast to self-conscious human law. Thus, Antigone "does not come to the *consciousness* and actuality of [ethical essence], because the law of the family is the *inner* essence *in itself* which does not lie in the daylight of consciousness but remains inner feeling and [a] divine [something] without actuality" (247.18–21).

Of course, when Antigone comes to act, her unconscious feeling becomes actual and knowable, which makes her deed subject to political authority (250.29–32). As a result, an open conflict breaks out between divine law and human law because divine law has encroached upon the public domain. But before this conflict occurs, divine law stands for what is removed from public life and its consciousness. Divine law thus finds an appropriate symbol in the underworld, which represents the hidden individual side of spirit that is recognized only after death. In reality, then, divine law refers to human individuality insofar as it has not yet come into consciousness. Its "divine" character as the "unknown" is not superior to human law, the realm of the known. Both laws derive from substance (241.9–10), the ultimate object of thought, which divides itself into what is consciously known and what is unconsciously felt. From this perspective, unconscious divine law is destined to become conscious human law when groups become aware of the individual person as individual.

This development comes about in the Roman empire, where individual persons have legal status (260.25–32). Divine law thus acquires actuality (260.32–261.1), or existence in the real world, by becoming human law. As such, divine law must give up its divine character. Its symbol of the underworld also becomes ineffective because what it gave refuge to—the value of individuality—is now accepted on earth. Both the human law and the divine law of ancient Greece disappear in favor of the individual self (251.19–23) of Roman law (323.25–26). The self then continues in religious history: it becomes the individual self of Roman Christianity, or the consciousness of self that is separated both from the real world and from universal divine essence. This type of individualism is, of course, the unhappy consciousness, which has already been examined. It could not appear in the Greek world, where the individual belongs by nature to a social group (whether state or family) and to a higher law (human or divine). In the Greek world, individual subjectivity has not yet discovered itself in a conscious way; it remains largely unconscious, ignored by human law and recognized only by divine law.

Divine Knowing

Divine knowing is the other obviously religious topic mentioned in Hegel's titles for the religion of the underworld. Unfortunately, it is not easy to find texts that indicate its exact meaning. It very likely refers to oracles and the like, and thus to what is known to the gods but is hidden from ordinary human knowing. Moreover, it does not seem to correspond to divine law alone. Anyone acting on behalf of one law, whether human or divine (255.1–3), offends the other law and suffers its revenge (255.3–7) because what is hidden from one gender's knowing is nevertheless actual (255.8–17) and active in the other gender. Whether man or woman, a character knows only its own law and so does not know the other law; action according to one law transgresses the other (256.24–28).[50] The gods, however, know what a human individual ignores. If divine knowing refers to what a given human agent does not know, then it must refer to the law that is ignored, whether that law be human or divine (255.1–3). Therefore, divine knowing does not correspond to divine law alone.[51] It does however resemble divine law in one respect: just as divine law is unconscious knowing in contrast to self-conscious human law, both laws show themselves to be ignorant—that is, not conscious—of the other law. Thus divine knowing, like divine law, represents something that has not yet come into human consciousness.

Faith

Finally, the religion of the underworld is a faith; "it is faith in the frightful unknown night of *fate* and in the Fury of the *departed spirit*" (363.22–23). Both fate and the departed spirit are "essence posited in the element of pure consciousness beyond actual [consciousness]" (287.33–34), and so they meet Hegel's definition of faith. But this statement needs to be qualified in the case of the departed spirit because Hegel also writes that "consciousness of the departed spirit is properly not *faith* . . . but [this spirit] itself has immediate presence; its element is the family" (287.32–35). Thus belief in the departed spirit is faith inasmuch as it looks to an underworld existing only in consciousness; but it is not faith inasmuch as the deceased is a spirit of vengeance in its family (250.8–10). Fate has a similar actuality in the interplay of conflicting forces in Greek life. But as objectified into a transcendent essence, it must be considered an object for faith.

Hegel's statement that faith is "essence posited in the element of pure consciousness beyond actual [consciousness]" (287.33–34) also indicates that both fate and the departed spirit are derived from human thinking. Fate is "pure negativity in the form of universality" (363.24), or pure thought as universal substance, while "the Fury of the *departed spirit*" is substance "in the form of individuality" (363.23, 24–25). Fate therefore resembles both the supersensible inner essence of the world (363.9–12) and the immutable God separated from the unhappy consciousness (363.13–17), while the departed spirit is the emergent idea of human individuality that is not yet recognized in the real world by actual consciousness.

FAITH IN HEAVEN VERSUS THE ENLIGHTENMENT (286–311)

Whereas the religion of the underworld separates universal divine substance from singular human individuality, Christianity brings them together by its belief in an incarnate God who now dwells in heaven: "faith in the nothing[ness] of necessity and in the underworld becomes *faith in heaven*, because the departed self . . . must . . . unite itself with its universality" (364.1–3, 4). This departed self is of course Jesus, who ascended to God the Father after death.[52] What happened to belief in this figure during the age of Enlightenment is the topic one must examine next. Within a longer section called "Spirit Alienated from Itself: Culture" (*PhG* VI–B), which describes Christian Europe[53] up to the Enlightenment, Hegel devotes two subsections to suspicion about Christianity in Europe: (1) "Faith and Pure Insight" (286–92), which combat one another in (2) "The Enlightenment's Struggle with Superstition" (293–311); this struggle ends in a victory for the Enlightenment, or for pure insight as opposed to faith.[54]

In Hegel's view, Christianity loses this battle because it "unfolds its content only in the element of thinking without the concept" (364.4–5); lacking the concept that unifies thinking and being, or the universal and the individual, faith cannot keep God and human being together. Consequently, faith "perishes in the *religion* of the *Enlightenment*" (364.6) whose God is a "supersensible, empty *beyond* not to be known or feared" because it is neither "self nor . . . power" (364.8–9). Evidently, such Christian doctrines as the incarnation, the indwelling Spirit, and divine providence and judgment have no place in a religion where God has no relation at all to the real world.

With this lean religion, Hegel returns to the first religion he examines in *PhG*, "the *supersensible* or *inner* [side] of objective existence" (363.10); in the Enlightenment "the supersensible beyond of understanding produces itself again" (364.7).[55] As historical phenomena, the two religions are closely related since the scientific understanding that gives rise to the supersensible inner certainly contributes to the Enlightenment itself. This fact emphasizes the deficiency of Enlightenment religion, which is the product of mere understanding (363.9; 364.7) rather than of spirit; the latter brings together God and creation, while understanding keeps them apart.

Hegel makes these points about Christian faith and the Enlightenment in his summary review of religion at the beginning of *PhG* VII. The fuller description found in *PhG* VI-B contains many other topics, including the following ideas that illustrate Hegel's approach to religion.

Faith in a Transcendent God

Hegel's description of Christian faith and the Enlightenment's "pure insight" begins with some general considerations about their underlying similarity. He regards both as types of pure thinking (286.27–289.20).[56] These introductory remarks are rather important for in them Hegel explains that Christian faith is a type of thinking similar to the rationalism of the Enlightenment. Hegel's account of Christian faith comes very close to identifying this religion with speculative reason. And one would not be wrong to conclude that for Hegel all religion, whether Christian or not, derives from human thinking. Just as the unhappy consciousness found its God through a thinking of immutability, so too faith in heaven is "pure consciousness of *essence*, that is, of the *simple inner* [side of things] and *is* therefore thinking—the chief moment in the nature of faith, which [moment] is usually overlooked" (289.5–7). Faith's pure thinking has divine essence for its object, just as Kant's pure reason considers God to be the concept unifying all reality. What is striking in Hegel's discussion, however, is not so much the presence of a God of reason,[57] which one may expect from any philosopher of religion, but rather the identification of this rational God with the God of Christian faith, on the grounds that faith is nothing other than pure reason or nonempirical thinking.

More specifically, faith looks to a world beyond this one, to "the unactual world *of pure consciousness* or of *thinking*" (286.29). This looking to something beyond the empirical world is what constitutes faith. When religion "still has the determinacy of opposition to actuality as *this* [world] in general, and to the [worldly actuality] of self-consciousness in particular, it is therefore essentially only a [*believing* or] *faith*" (287.38–288.1) because its object is unknowable. Such belief in another world is a "flight" (287.26) beyond this one, perhaps not in the sense of a fearful seeking after security, but at least in the sense of an "elevating" (287.2) above the earth, similar to the flight of birds.

Of course, even the most rigorous thinking also goes beyond empirical data. For example, scientific laws are not given to one's senses but are discovered by insights into the data. Consequently, any essence known to thought differs from what is immediately given to sensation. But one can safely say that an essence is real when it refers to the empirical data in question. As applied to God, this principle should lead to a God who is the essence of our world. Faith, however, does not think of God in this way. Rather, it views God as a transcendent essence equivalent to another world, namely heaven; according to Hegel, that is its mistake. Faith fails to make the transition from essence to existence and so for it, God's essence is separated from earthly existence. What prevents faith from unifying its thought with the real world is its inability to develop for itself a dialectical way of thinking. Its thought does not have the ability to move between opposites.

Instead, its thought has an objective "immediacy" (289.7) imposing itself as "*essence*, that is, pure thought" (289.8) elevated above the world or detached from it. This "*immediacy* . . . gets the meaning of an objective *being* which lies beyond the consciousness of the self" (289.8–9, 10–11). This immediate object of thinking, which is so overwhelming that it seems to constitute another world, is what makes thinking slip into imagination and accept its object as a world beyond this one: "it is through this meaning, which the immediacy and simplicity of *pure thinking* gets in *consciousness*, that faith's essence falls away from thinking into *images* and becomes a supersensible world, which is essentially *other* than self-consciousness" (289.11–15). If on the one hand faith is a thinking, on the other hand it is a naive sort of thinking; "consciousness merely *has* these thoughts but does not yet *think* them, or does not know that they are thoughts, but [rather] they are for it in the form of *imagination*" (289.31–33). In other words, its thinking is strong enough to produce a supersensible essence but not strong enough to recognize that this essence is a thought referring to the real world. And without this recognition, its thought appears to be an independent God dwelling in a supersensible heaven.

If my interpretation of this point is correct, then the idea of a "beyond" arises from a pure thinking that is not integrated with the real world. But Christianity's pure thinking of a beyond is not intended as a mere thought because Christianity thinks of it as real and actual. Thus, according to Hegel, Christian faith has its divine essence "in the form of a *common actual* [being], of an actuality which is only elevated into another element, without having lost in this [element of thinking] the determinacy of an actuality not [reconstituted by] thought" (287.6–8). What does Hegel have in mind here? The divine essence that is "indeed beyond actuality yet [also] actual essence" (287.15–16) can be interpreted as a supernatural essence whose "actuality . . . is . . . only an actuality of *pure*, not of *actual* consciousness" (287.22–23). In other words, divine essence is thought to have a nonempirical actuality.

But in Hegel's writings, the word "actual" usually refers to the world of experience; and so the transcendent God who is "indeed beyond actuality yet [also] actual essence" (287.15–16) is difficult to comprehend. This problem arises not from an inconsistency in Hegel's thought but from an inconsistency in faith itself. On the one hand, faith recognizes the actuality of God insofar as God is incarnate and is Spirit in the church (290.12–14). In this sense, God has a human actuality. But when faith attributes to God a divine actuality beyond the human one, making God an "actual essence . . . beyond actuality" (287.15, 16), it thinks of divine essence as having its own divine existence. Faith then "falls away from thinking into *imagination*" (289.13–14), which looks upon thought in "the manner of sensory being" (308.19) with independent existence. When consciousness treats its thought as though it were a sensory being, it makes its thought into an independent actuality separate from itself, and thus into "a supersensible world which is essentially *other* than self-consciousness" (289.14–15).

This kind of thinking is what Hegel means by religious "imagination"; it results in a transcendent God whose actuality is not that of the world and human being but a nonempirical divine actuality. In this case, faith does not have a true thought of God, but remains "still in the sphere . . . of actuality" (286.34–35), applying it crudely to its thought "without having become master over it [that is, over actuality] through the mediated movement [of thinking]" (287.3–4). Thus, its "essence's actuality is . . . indeed elevated into the element of thinking but for this consciousness does not yet count as a thought" (287.22, 23–25) because faith views its God not as a thought but as a supernatural being.

Hegel does not explain here what actuality God has. But in the light of his later system, his meaning seems to be not that divine essence has no actuality, but that its actuality is the world, and is to be developed from within the thought of God rather than imported into this thought from without. When a thought is taken for an actuality, real being is imposed on a pure thought. Thinking then is not yet master over actuality because its thought is not intrinsically actual. Imagination is this type of crude thinking, an intellectual "elevation not yet completed in itself" (287.2).

When faith's transcendent God takes on a real human actuality (290.12–14), faith remains imaginative because the prior transcendence of God is not eliminated. The Son and the Spirit remain as divine persons who preserve their transcendent nature, however much they mingle with the human world. Thus, Christianity does not overcome the initial transcendence given to God by its imagination. Christian faith remains imaginative and never becomes a completed thinking.

Yet imagination is useful to religion. Indeed, it helps differentiate Christianity from the Enlightenment. Possessing an (alleged) actuality of its own through imagination, divine essence resists human thought, at least as far as faith is concerned. Faith lets its object alone because the object is presumed to have an independent existence transcending all thought. In contrast to this respectful attitude, pure insight is the "*negativity* . . . that consumes every objective essence said to be over against consciousness and makes it into a being of consciousness" (288.19–21), that is, into a thought. For pure insight, "objectivity has the meaning of a merely negative content surmounting itself and returning into the self, i.e., only the self is properly its own object, or the object has truth only insofar as it has the form of the self" (289.17–20). In other words, pure insight converts everything into thought; conversely, for pure insight nothing is true until put into the form of thought. Pure insight thus transforms everything into its own thinking. Therefore "its own object . . . is only the *pure ego*" (288.34); "consequently it has at first no content in itself, because it is the negative [subjective] being for self" (288.37) transforming any content whatever into the pure ego's own form of thought. As pure insight, thinking has no intrinsic content; it is empty subjectivity and nothing more. As a result, its ultimate object can have no necessary content either (for this would impose a necessary content on subjectivity) and so the Enlightenment's God is an "empty *beyond* not to be known or feared" (364.8–9).

But as faith, thinking does have a content (289.1), and this statement is true for Hegel not primarily because faith receives a revelation in history, but because faith is a thinking that attributes actuality to its pure thought. Faith begins with its own thinking and considers it to be the transcendence of God. What really happens is that faith takes the "*immediacy*" of its "*thinking*" as "an objective *being* that lies beyond the consciousness of the self" (289.7, 9, 10–11). Therefore, "faith's [divine] *essence* falls away from thinking into *imagination* and becomes a supersensible world which is essentially *other* than self-consciousness" (289.13–15). From this perspective, the basic difference between faith and pure insight is that the former takes its thinking for an independent actuality, while the latter takes it merely as subjective thinking without any necessary content of its own. Faith and pure insight are therefore divergent forms of pure thinking, with pure insight being the negative (288.19) process (288.32), and faith the "positive *repose*" (288.29) in essence as its object (288.35–36), "the *positive universality* of *being-in-itself*" (288.24–25). Put another way, while faith rests in God, pure insight is a restless thinking that recognizes nothing superior to itself. Hegel contrasts these two types of thinking very neatly in the following way: "pure insight consequently has at first no content in itself, because it is negative being-for-self; to faith in contrast belongs the content, without insight" (288.37–289.1).

Both of them are different moments of an alienated consciousness (288.29–30), or of pure thinking separated from the world. For it is not only faith that is alienated from the world; pure insight and the Kantian transcendental ego also have no intrinsic connection to empirical reality. But only faith posits another world, by attributing independent actuality to its own thought. The true "element of faith" (288.23–24) however is not this other world, but pure thinking, "this form of simple reflection into self" (288.23) that in its negative dissolving mode is pure insight itself. Faith is pure thinking as objective, having "the inner *essence* for [its] object" (288.36), whereas pure insight is the same thinking as subjective, the *"pure ego"* (288.34) that negates all objectivity through its conceptual thinking. Each type of thinking needs the other, in order to complete itself.

Faith in a Divine Trinity

Hegel's discussion of faith in heaven also contains three paragraphs on the Trinity (289.27–290.15). How this Trinity is related to human thinking is another topic that one needs to examine with some care.

Divine essence as a Trinity preserves the transcendence that has just been examined. In faith in heaven *"religion . . .* does not yet step forth as it is *in and for itself"* (287.27–29) because divine essence is not yet integrated with human subjectivity. Faith in heaven is, after all, one of the religions of consciousness, in which the divine object of human thinking does not yet include the thinking subject. Like the unhappy consciousness of Roman Christianity, faith in heaven still remains separate from God. It knows God only in thought and so includes neither the actual world nor itself as real in its concept of God. Indeed, the very term "heaven" suggests a distance between God and the actual world; faith in heaven is faith in a transcendent God. As the "absolute object . . . in *believing* consciousness" (289.27, 28), the three divine persons are transcendent "essences . . . in and for themselves . . . spirits remaining by themselves" (289.32–33).

For Hegel, however, the three divine persons are "changeless eternal spirits, whose being is to think the unity which they [themselves] constitute," only when "taken back by thinking out of the changing . . .

actual world" (290.8–10) to which they really belong. The actual world supplies the triplicity of God, or the internal differentiation that makes God the Trinity. For Hegel, the divine differentiation found in this faith is "nothing other than the real world elevated into the universality of pure consciousness" (289.29–30) or thinking, so that "the articulation of the [world] constitutes the organization of [divine essence]" (289.30–31).

In what way does the real world provide faith with a trinitarian structure? The system of logic, nature, and spirit provides an easy answer. Here, however, Hegel seems to have in mind a narrower application of this triplicity, namely the social world of Christian Europe. His comparison of God's eternal substance to the universal power of the state (289.38–290.2) suggests that faith in heaven takes its Trinity not from a metaphysical system but from a social organization. He also mentions that the Trinity does not imitate the alienation of the social world (289.31–32), where individuals are alienated from the universal power of a monarchical government; this comment again indicates a comparison between religion and society.

On the other hand, Hegel's horizon goes beyond the social world. In a Jena manuscript preceding *PhG*, one finds the tripartite scheme of essence, nature, and spirit.[58] And in *PhG* VII, the Trinity originates in God's eternal essence in order to unfold itself in individual natural existence and then in the universal spirit of the church; such a view corresponds to the true content of speculative philosophy (407.1–7). Divine differentiation thus means the wider world of logic, nature, and spirit. This wider scheme expresses itself in the real social world as well as in religion. If the Trinity imitates the structure of the social world, it also imitates the metaphysical system on which the social world is based.

Since the three divine persons imitate the movement of this real world from universal substance to individual existence and finally to spirit, their true character lies not in a changeless eternity, but in a movement from eternal substance into human existence. The pretemporal Trinity then appears as the economic Trinity of Christian revelation. The "simple eternal *substance*" of "*absolute essence*" moves into the "*being for [an] other*" of natural existence, where it becomes an incarnate "*self*" that finally reaches its goal of "spirit" when by self-sacrifice it returns to divine substance, "its first simplicity" (290.1–7). The simplicity is again the universality of divine essence, so God is now universally present as the spirit of the church. By sharing in the humanity of both Jesus and the church, the Trinity participates in human actuality: "the renunciation [or incarnation] of this [divine] substance, and then its spirit, has . . . the moment of actuality and thereby makes itself partake of believing self-consciousness" (290.12–14). Indeed, these movements are necessary because when divine substance moves into natural existence and human being (290.2–5), it is only "realizing its concept of being spirit" (290.2). The true concept of divine spirit thus refers to its becoming human.

Spirit in the pretemporal Trinity must also reflect this meaning, which implies that the Trinity apart from human being simply foreshadows its missions to humanity. If the pretemporal Trinity consists of "changeless eternal spirits" (290.9), they still do not conform to the concept of spirit that comes from the passage from pure essence into human existence and back to universal essence (290.2–7). In other words, the pretemporal ("immanent") Trinity is the logical preparation for the ("economic") Trinity in its work for human being.

But these truths are not understood by faith, whose thinking is not conceptual but imaginative. Its Trinity is "imagined as spirit" (290.7) but not comprehended. For Hegel, the Trinity is the necessary movement from logic to nature and spirit. For faith, however, the trinitarian distinction of persons is "a restful [unrelated] diversity and their movement [of differentiated unity] a *happening*" (289.26–37). Faith does not explain how three persons constitute one God; its Trinity is not a conceptual unity. For faith, then, the Trinity does not have a necessary urgency in its missions to the world or in its internal pretemporal constitution. Consequently, its existence as the world and spirit is easily abstracted into a transcendent God, who remains an object over against the believing human subject.

Faith as Trust

Trust in God is another theological topic that Hegel discusses in his treatment of Christian faith in heaven. The presence of this theme is good evidence for surmising that by "faith in heaven" Hegel means Protestant Christianity.[59] Furthermore, his analysis of trust contains more evidence for the thesis that he interprets religion as a product of human intelligence.

Faith finds God by its own thinking: "what is absolute essence for it is a being of its own consciousness, its own thought, a [something] produced by consciousness" (297.27–28). In this respect, faith resembles pure insight, which also produces its object and feels at home with it (297.22–25). But while pure insight knows it produces its ideas, faith does not; it considers its thought as another being it can trust. This trusting in God is a religious equivalent for thinking's recognition of itself in its ideas. God is the substance that human thinking thinks; as an awareness of this substance, faith "does not posit itself as lost in it and negated, but rather trusts it, which means [that faith] finds itself *in it as this*[60] [individual] consciousness or as *self*-consciousness" (297.32–34). According to Hegel's argument so far, religious faith finds itself in God because God is an object produced by faith's pure thinking.

But Hegel then uses an example that suggests that for faith God is not merely an object of thought but a living person: "[He] whom I trust [has] a *certainty of himself* which for me is the *certainty of my*self; I know my [own] being for myself [i.e., my subjectivity] in him [and know] that he recognizes it and [that] it is [an] aim and essence for him" (297.34–36). This analogy of God to a living person must hold only for faith, not for Hegel, who continues his discussion with impersonal terminology: "faith however is trust, because its consciousness *relates* itself *immediately* to its object, and so views also this, that it is *one* with it [and] in it" (297.36–298.1). Undoubtedly, one is to understand this immediate relation of faith to its object in light of an earlier passage, which states that divine essence is immediately present in human thinking because such an essence is a pure thought (289.7–8). Since this essence is the immediate object of faith and present in its thought, faith naturally feels at home with it. In the same way, pure insight "knows itself in its object of insight" and knows "this unity of the object and itself as *self*" (298.7–8, 11–12). Such a similarity between trusting faith and pure insight shows that the former is simply a variant of the same thinking found in the latter. Faith is a thinking of "inner *essence* as essence" (288.36), not a relation to an actual divine personality.

Hegel also explains why faith feels itself to be a new creation in the

God it trusts: faith feels like an "*other*[61] self-consciousness" (298.3) because in God faith is "*essential* consciousness" (298.6), "alienated from its particular individuality, namely its naturalness and contingency" (298.4–5). This "essential consciousness" must be consciousness of essence, or a pure thinking of divine substance, because Hegel writes that this consciousness is "like pure insight" (298.6). When faith is this pure thinking of its thought, it inevitably feels liberated from its individual empirical existence.

There is not much doubt, therefore, that for Hegel Christian faith is a thinking of divine essence. It is faith rather than knowing only because in its own mind it "indeed does not appear that absolute essence itself is produced by" thinking, which is the intellectual "doing of faith" (298.15–16). Nevertheless, a consideration of the Trinity proves that human consciousness is indeed active in producing its thought of God. Since "faith's absolute essence is essentially not the *abstract* essence which is beyond believing consciousness but . . . the spirit of the community, [or] . . . the unity of abstract essence and of self-consciousness, . . . it is [therefore] *not without* being produced by consciousness" (298.16–22). Here, Hegel probably means that because the community knows God's presence, it therefore produces this presence in its knowing. But Hegel does not mean that God is merely a subjective thought existing only in consciousness. The universal substance that is known by thought is also the substance of thought (and indeed thinks itself through human thought), as Hegel shows in his *Logik* and in *PhG* VII. Here, he only alludes to this higher point of view when he writes: "as essential as the producing [by consciousness] is, it essentially is also not the only ground of [divine] essence but is only a moment. The essence is at the same time in and for itself" (298.22–24).

However, Hegel does not pursue this idea in his section on the struggle between superstition and the Enlightenment. His main concern is to point out that faith produces its object. From this aspect of faith he draws a logical (and polemical) conclusion: the essence worshipped by faith is not an alien being but is rather a pure essence thought by consciousness itself. The Enlightenment is therefore silly when it claims that "for consciousness something absolutely *alien* and *other* was substituted for essence through a hocus-pocus of tricky priests" (298.32–34). On the contrary, there can be no "deception and fraud . . .

where [consciousness] possesses *itself* in its object, inasmuch as it both finds itself therein and produces *it*" (299.3, 5–6). Because consciousness is thinking its deepest self when it thinks of God and is able to entrust itself to this thought arising from within itself, deception by an outside agent is impossible; "in the knowing of the essence in which consciousness has the immediate *certainty of itself*, the thought of deception falls completely away" (299.13–15). By feeling itself present in its thought of God, faith knows with certainty that it is on the road to truth.

But whereas faith experiences its closeness to God as trust in a higher being, for Hegel this phenomenon has another explanation: in faith, human consciousness is thinking its own substance. This interpretation seems evident enough, given the identity Hegel insists on between faith and pure insight (298.12–13, 6–12; 297.21).[62]

Faith and Empirical Knowing

A fourth topic to consider is the relation of faith to sensory or empirical knowing. Hegel discusses this point in a complicated treatment of how the Enlightenment misunderstands Christian faith. In this discussion, one finds confirmation for the thesis that religious faith derives (at least for Hegel) from human thought. After seeing how Hegel examines trust in God as faith's presence in its own universal thought, one is not surprised to find Hegel insisting that faith knows God by pure thinking rather than by sensory knowing.

Faith's "*absolute essence* . . . is pure *thinking* . . . posited as object or as *essence*" (299.24–26). God is essence, and essence is known by thought. Even though in its worship faith uses sensible images to represent God (300.2–7), "what it worships is for it by no means stone or wood or bread-dough or any other temporal sensory thing . . . but in itself is for it only the essence of pure thinking" (300.12–13, 17–18). Now since this God of faith is pure thinking in the form of an object "*imagined*" (299.29) as though it were distinct from consciousness, the question of how faith knows its object is already answered: God is immediately present to a thinking that elevates itself to the universal substance of all things.

But since this thinking produces its object, God is immediately present only through thinking. Hegel explains: "this essence is immediate for it as pure thinking consciousness; but pure consciousness is just as much a *mediated* relation of [subjective] certainty to [objective] truth; a relation which makes up the *ground* of *faith*" (300.20–23). The "truth" Hegel refers to here must be the pure object of thinking, divine substance itself, which is mediated by thinking subjectivity. A thought is produced by a thinker; that is how divine substance comes to be immediately present in a human mind.[63]

However, the Enlightenment does not acknowledge this intellectual character of faith because it does not understand the nature of its own thinking, which is no different from that of faith. Even though it is pure insight, the Enlightenment "does not yet know itself . . . [as] this pure mediated movement" (300.31–33) of thought. Influenced by the empirical knowing (299.33–36) that it converts into ideas, the Enlightenment cannot grasp the *a priori* intellectual nature of faith. And so it interprets faith as an empirical knowing, too—"a contingent *knowing of contingent* events" (300.24)—and claims that faith's certainty rests on "*individual historical witnesses*" (301.1) and on the "circumstance of the preservation of these witnesses—preservation through paper on the one hand, and on the other hand through the skill and honesty of the transmission from one paper to another, and finally on the correct interpretation of the sense of dead words and letters" (301.4–8). Here, one finds the familiar view that faith is historically transmitted and that without such transmission there would be no Christianity. Strongly emphasized in this view is the empirical character of Christian faith, which is thereby made to conform to the sensory mode of knowing the Enlightenment cherishes.

According to Hegel, however, this view of Christianity belongs to the Enlightenment rather than to faith. Therefore, "when faith also wishes to give itself from historical [things] that kind of grounding of which the Enlightenment speaks, or at least [a historical] confirmation of its content, and seriously opines and acts as though it depended on that, then it has already let itself be seduced by the Enlightenment" (301.16–20). And the reason why faith should not be so seduced is that it originates not in empirical knowing but in an *a priori* thinking of divine substance: "[faith] is in its certainty [a] naive relation to its absolute object, a pure knowing of it . . . [a] consciousness of absolute essence . . . [and] this consciousness is the self-mediating ground of its knowing; it is the spirit itself which is the testimony of itself" (301.10–

15). Spirit testifies to itself because absolute essence mediates itself through pure thinking. Of course, faith does not really know where its object comes from; it does not yet know itself as "the *knowing* universal [substance] ... absolute *spirit* which ... as [human] self-consciousness ... is the *knowing* of itself" (300.25–27). Here, absolute spirit "is only absolute *essence* in abstract pure consciousness, or [in] thinking as such" (300.26–27); God is in the form of an object. Faith knows itself only as a consciousness of divine essence, rather than as divine essence knowing itself in human thinking.

The passages contain a definite understanding of faith that one should not let slip away. In Hegel's view, Christian faith is grounded not in history but in pure *a priori* thinking of divine essence. This consideration does not mean that Christianity is independent of history, but only that history is not its primary source. When Hegel writes that "the ground of knowing ... is the *knowing* universal" (300.24–25), he surely means that universal divine substance posits itself as human knowing, as his *Logik* maintains. Christianity, however, takes God as an essence other than human being, and so Christian faith interprets its pure knowledge of God as the effect of divine spirit acting upon human spirit. But for Hegel, the immediate origin of this knowledge is divine essence as human thinking.

Of course, the ultimate logical origin is the object itself—divine essence, which differentiates itself into human thinking. But in *PhG*, Christianity has not yet been studied from this point of view. Faith in heaven, the current topic, occurs in *PhG* VI. Not until *PhG* VII is Christianity studied from the point of view of "absolute essence *in and for itself*" (363.7), or divine substance as including human existence and human thinking.[64]

Victory of the Enlightenment Over Christian Faith

A fifth topic to consider is faith's defeat by the Enlightenment, whose version of religion succeeds in replacing Christian faith in heaven. The Enlightenment has a religion of its own that separates God from everything finite. As a result, God becomes an empty essence with no determinate qualities, for determinacy means finitude (303.4–8). In addition, because finite being itself has no relation to God, it becomes independent and absolute in its own right (303.16–19). This interest in worldly being distinguishes the Enlightenment from Christian faith; but inasmuch as the Enlightenment posits a God beyond the world, it also has a faith of its own, which resembles that of Christianity.[65]

In maintaining that God is unknowable, the Enlightenment appeals to Christianity's reverence for God's transcendence, "unsearchable in its ways and unattainable in its being" (308.6). Therefore Christianity is already disposed in part to agree with its adversary. Furthermore, Christianity also agrees in principle with the Enlightenment's respect for the world because faith in a transcendent God implies that the world is independent of God: since faith "is this divided consciousness of having a *beyond* to *actuality* and [also] a [world] pure[ly on] *this side* of that beyond, so in fact is there in faith *also* this view of the sensible thing according to which it *counts in* and *for itself*" (308.10–13). Therefore Christian faith in God is already similar to Enlightenment Deism. What distinguishes the two is Christianity's belief in a divine Trinity known through the incarnation of God. But when faith gives up its heavenly Trinity, it loses its distinctive doctrine and is left with an empty divine essence, which makes it resemble Deism.

This abandonment of traditional doctrine comes about when faith realizes that its Trinity is based more on sensory imagination than on pure thinking. Hegel does not mean that the Trinity is deficient because it presupposes a link between divine essence and the empirical world. That is a desirable point of view, and one that Hegel himself argues toward. His criticism is rather that faith's thinking of divine essence is not rigorous enough. Since the three divine moments are not unified by a concept with a necessary articulation, they are "a series of independent *shapes* and their movement a *happening*, that is, they are only in *imagination*, and have the mode of sensory being in themselves" (308.17–19). According to Hegel, then, the traditional understanding of three distinct moments in God and of their contingent movement toward the world is nothing but an imitation of the separateness and contingency of sensory things. Therefore, Christian faith fails to preserve the priority of divine essence (which must show necessity, in Hegel's view of it) over the sensory world.

When "the Enlightenment illuminates that heavenly world with mental images of the sensible [world]" (310.16–17), faith in heaven is convinced by its opponent and agrees that its most cherished doctrine (the Trinity) derives not from pure thinking but from imagination, which thinks in a sensory way, or which mixes thinking and being.[66] Persuaded by the Enlightenment's argumentation, faith surrenders its heaven. Consequently, "faith has thereby lost its content" (310.22) and has only "an empty *beyond*" (310.30–31) for its God. When it gives up the Trinity, faith loses not only the determinate content of God but also God's entry into the world through Christ and the Holy Spirit because divine determinacy includes the doctrines of the incarnation and the church. Without the divine Trinity, then, Christian faith transforms itself into the religion of the Enlightenment: "faith has thereby in fact become the same as the Enlightenment, namely the consciousness of the relation of finite being in itself to the unknown and unknowable absolute without predicates" (310.33–35). Faith in heaven has now lost its determinate object; "insofar as it finds only the empty [divine essence] when it goes beyond the finite, which is [now] the only content [it has], it is a *pure yearning*" (310.30–31) like the unhappy consciousness.

This abandonment of trinitarian doctrine seems to be contained in the very principle of faith, according to which it is a pure thinking of divine essence. When God is known by a pure thinking elevated above the world, divine essence has a transcendence that cannot be plausibly linked to the real world anyway. Separation between God and the world can, however, be overcome by a position that thinks of finite actuality as "a *moment* in the spiritual movement of essence itself" (308.22). With this remark, Hegel indicates his own solution to the Enlightenment's critique of Christian faith in heaven.

CONCLUSION

When the actual world is not included in a concept of God, religion is left with a transcendent essence that is more properly an object of faith than of knowing. Since the Enlightenment's God is beyond the world, it too is an object of faith rather than of knowing.[67] In this respect, it resembles all the religions described in this chapter: the supersensible inner of understanding, the unhappy consciousness of Roman Christianity, the Greek religion of the underworld, Christian faith in heaven, and the Enlightenment's Deism. All of these religions believe in a beyond. Furthermore, in Greek religion and in Christianity, one sees the beginnings of an integration between this transcendent divine essence and human individuality. But neither the departed spirit of Greek religion nor the risen Jesus of Christianity is an actual human being living in this world; both have their life only in the beyond. Living human being is still separated from its transcendent God, and this distance is one of the reasons for the unhappiness of the unhappy consciousness. This consciousness is that of the individual thinker isolated both from the actual world and from its transcendent God. Later, this consciousness discovers itself in its pure thinking of God; it feels itself accepted by divine substance, and so is trusting faith, or faith in heaven.[68] Nevertheless, its positive relation to divine substance is found only in its pure thinking, which is still opposed to its actual existence in the world (287.38–39).

Finally, because Christian thinking has after all no firm grip on the beyond, it loses its ability to link human being with God and so comes to resemble the Enlightenment's Deism. The latter is nothing other than the supersensible inner of understanding (364.6–7), a religion of divine substance without a self (363.9–12)—that is to say, of God without a human self. Thus the religions of faith end where they began, namely in a transcendent God separated from human being.

NOTES

1. Although angels offer another possible transitional form between God and human being, Hegel has in mind here (in his analyses of faith in the underworld and in heaven) deceased *human* beings who survive in another world. Angels do, however, appear later on in *PhG* as intermediate shapes existing between God and human being. In *PhG* VII's analysis of the pretemporal Trinity, angels occur as a differentiation of divine essence on its way to human existence. In Hegel's view, angels are imaginative anticipations of actual human existence.
2. The term "supersensible inner" is my wording and is derived from Hegel's description of a "Bewußtseyn des *Uebersinnlichen* oder *Innern* des gegenständlichen Daseyns" (363.9–10) at the beginning of *PhG* VII. This brief description refers to the fuller discussion in *PhG* III, pp. 82–102.
3. See the notes to *PhG* 82–102 in *GW* 9: 495–97.
4. The arrangement of religions in *PhG* depends of course on the chapter divisions of the entire work, which follow a logical order of different types of consciousness rather than a chronological order of historical

appearance. Only *within* each type of consciousness (e.g., "Die Religion" in the whole of *PhG* VII) does Hegel observe a chronological sequence corresponding to historical fact.

5. One of the best contemporary interpreters of Hegel refers to this chapter when he writes: "there remains much in the *Phenomenology* which is enigmatic ... one at times [is] only sure that he is saying something immeasurably profound and important, but not exactly what it is. (I am in this position, despite help, regarding the two intelligible worlds in the section of Force and Understanding.)" See J. N. Findlay, "Foreword" to the *Phenomenology of Spirit* by G. W. F. Hegel, trans. A. V. Miller (Oxford University Press, 1977), pp. xii, xiii.

6. For analyses of the entire chapter, with emphases different from my own, see Lauer, pp. 70–89; Kainz, 1: 69–82; Hyppolite, pp. 116–36; Solomon, pp. 363–85.

7. Solomon adds that Hegel also had in mind Roger Boscovich (p. 375) and the discovery of electromagnetism after Newton (pp. 369–70).

8. In this respect, Hegel continues a great philosophical tradition—one represented by Spinoza, for example, who thought of God as the one substance underlying the real world of minds and bodies. See Frederick Copleston, S. J., *A History of Philosophy*, vol. 4: *Descartes to Leibniz* (Paramus, NJ: The Newman Press, 1958), pp. 216–17. Even Hegel's triad of logic, nature, and spirit is part of this tradition; Spinoza himself divides divine substance into extension and thought.

9. *PhG* VII.

10. Hyppolite refers to the inverted, second supersensible world as the first supersensible's manifestation in the phenomenal world of experience (pp. 132–34). As a result, the phenomenal world is now seen as a manifestation of the supersensible (p. 122). Conversely, the supersensible then becomes the absolute concept or the relation between essence and real existence (p. 125). As an interpretation of Hegel's own system, Hyppolite's view is, of course, correct. But as an interpretation of the consciousness Hegel is describing, it seems to go too far too early. Hegel does indeed say that the inverted supersensible world repels from within itself the empirical world (97.28–29). Yet he also calls this position "superficial" (98.27) since the inverted world is based on "imagination" (98.7–8) rather than on a concept. And even understanding does not pursue the conceptual relation of the empirical world to the inverted supersensible world. Instead, in the object as a synthesis of differences, it discovers its own subjectivity (100.35–101.2; 101.30–33). Only *"for us"* (101.24–27), i.e., for Hegel and such comprehending readers as Hyppolite, does the pure concept of infinity (and its application to the imagined repulsion of

the appearing world from a supersensible inner) emerge at this point in *PhG*.

11. For an excellent discussion of the inverted world's importance, see Hans-Georg Gadamer, "Die verkehrte Welt," in Gadamer's *Gesammelte Werke*, vol. 3 (Tübingen: J. C. B. Mohr, 1987), pp. 29–46.

12. As these texts indicate, Hegelian "contradiction" is often meant as otherness, difference, or logical opposition.

13. As my chapter V shows, Hegel understands these examples in a way that seriously diverges from the way Christianity understands them.

14. As Kainz points out, "the 'infinite Concept' ... [is] true speculative philosophy in the Hegelian sense, which reestablishes unity amidst dialectical oppositions" (1: 143 n. 20).

15. Hegel therefore thinks of God's infinity as necessarily creative, and then (from its triple relation to creation) as Trinitarian. His understanding of divine infinity is clearly different from that of Aquinas, for whom the nature of God is infinite perfection apart from its differentiation into three persons and apart from its relation to a world.

16. A similar tendency appears in the earlier portrayal of the first supersensible world, where differences are attributed to understanding (94.33–35) as analytic rather than to the object itself. Subjective explanation is held responsible for the movement (95.18–24, 35–39) that creates differences (95.27–35) in the object. The subsequent attempt to posit movement in the object itself then leads to the inverted world, which now points back to subjectivity.

17. For other discussions of the unhappy consciousness, see Hyppolite, pp. 184–208; Kainz, 1: 95–98; Kojève, pp. 66–73, 155–57; Lauer, pp. 117–24; Solomon, pp. 465–70, 616–22.

18. Solomon would extend it to the Reformation (p. 470) and "secularized Protestantism" (p. 619), but this interpretation is unlikely because Hegel places monastic renunciation near the end of the chapter (*PhG* 131.15–16). Hegel's discussion of the unhappy consciousness therefore concludes with the Middle Ages.

19. It combines within a single human type the two separate consciousnesses of master and slave (*PhG* 121.31–39), which respectively stand for a universal thinking willing to give up its individual natural existence (the master), and attachment to individual existence at any price (the slave).

20. With good reason, Hyppolite claims that "the unhappy consciousness is the fundamental theme of *Phenomenology*" (p. 184), whose main concern is the relation of individual subjectivity to its universal substance (p. 340). The unhappy consciousness is "the pain of a self which does not arrive at unity with itself" (p. 184).

21. By its knowing of the universal it resembles the master. But this knowing is not its self-knowing since what is universal is considered beyond it. Seeing itself only as individual, the unhappy consciousness retains only the self-knowing of the slave. Interpreters like Hyppolite (pp. 191, 204) and Kojève (pp. 67, 99) rightly draw attention to the correspondence of master and slave to God and the unhappy consciousness. Kojève in particular exploits this parallel throughout his commentary. One should not, however, assume too easily that Christianity is accounted for by ancient slavery. Hegel views both slavery and Christianity as developments of the same underlying factors, namely consciousness of self as individual and consciousness of universal essence.

22. See also *PhG* 125.1–6, where Hegel says that the unhappy consciousness does not know God's human shape in and for itself.

23. Relevant to this movement is Kojève's understanding of Christian immortality: "the ultimate motive for the ideology of 'two worlds' . . . is the servile desire for life . . . sublimated in the desire for an *eternal* life" (p. 183). Since Hegel never makes this point so explicit, one wonders whether Kojève is interpreting Hegel correctly here. In general, the Christian desire for immortality is not necessarily a slavish desire for life at any price; it can also be understood as an intellectual desire to know God. That in fact is the interpretation Hegel gives to it later in *PhG* (419.1–2). For him, Christianity does not cling to the life that it knows "but consciously gives itself up" (400.27). Hegel, I think, would agree with Kojève that there is no life beyond this earthly one. But I do not think that Hegel would accept Kojève's reduction of Christianity to the slave's preservation of natural existence because that is precisely what Hegel sees Christianity giving up.

24. By appealing to Hegel's earlier religious writings, Hyppolite attributes the touching of God by individual human being (*PhG* 123.1–3) to a middle period of the Old Testament: David, the prophets, and the wisdom of Solomon (Hyppolite, pp. 185–87, 193–94). This claim is plausible since Christianity does arise within Judaism. According to Hegel's *Philosophy of History*, trans. J. Sibree (1899; reprint ed., New York: Dover Publications, 1956), pp. 329–30, Roman monotheism derives both from Stoicism and Skepticism on the one hand and from Oriental or Jewish religion on the other. In *PhG*, the unhappy consciousness follows upon Skepticism and Stoicism, and could easily have drawn upon Hellenistic Judaism as well.

25. More precisely, a "threefold way" (123.11) of linking the two; see my next paragraph.

26. There is much truth in Kojève's remark that "Hegel sees the origin and

basis of Christianity in the idea of *individuality*, discovered by the slave" (p. 155). Furthermore, according to Kojève, since the slave's individuality is not recognized in this world, it is projected into an individual incarnation of God (pp. 155–56) until such time when it is recognized by the real social world (pp. 156–57). In my reading of Hegel, however, the goal of human individuality is to comprehend itself within God; the comprehension is embodied in a humane social order. For Hegel, then, the social world belongs to the existence of universal divine essence.

27. Solomon (p. 618) does not interpret these works in this way because he thinks the joy of reconciling oneself to God (*PhG* 123.21–22) must refer to Hegel's own position. But since Hegel refers to joy again when he examines Christianity as the "manifest religion" (407.9), and for the same reason as in his chapter on the unhappy consciousness, namely, because the human self sees itself in God (407.9–13), one can surely interpret (despite Solomon, p. 618 n. 84) spirit's joy here (in the unhappy consciousness) as referring to Christianity, which announces "good news of great joy" (Luke 2:10). This joy later disappears because the unhappy consciousness continues to worship a transcendent (though incarnate) God separate from it.

28. Perhaps an allusion to the Catholic idea of grace as an internal supernatural help.

29. Despite these clear allusions to the Eucharist, Hegel also seems to envision a wider object. His insistence on labor ("Arbeit," 126.31; 127.1, 5, 13, 21) would be more appropriate to the workaday world (Solomon, pp. 470, 619) than to the Eucharist. Thus, he refers to a "sanctified world" (127.9), which is holy because the incarnate God's individuality has "the significance of all actuality in general" (127.11). Hyppolite mentions both the world and the sacramental elements of bread and wine (*Structure*, p. 203; 1: 185 n. 41 of his translation contains more nuance, referring to the work performed by Crusaders back from the wars). Perhaps the sacrament is a symbol of the sanctified world, or perhaps they are not related at all but are two distinct aspects of Christian life. This interesting question needs further study.

30. In Hegel's view, they can be unified only by the concept of human being as the real existence of divine essence.

31. This takes place via the acceptance of both the advice and decisions of a mediator (130.11–14), whom Baillie (p. 265 n. 1) identifies as the priest.

32. Hegel may be thinking of the three monastic vows in this paragraph (130.9–24), but the allusion is not entirely certain. Giving up one's will

(130.9–15) could refer to religious obedience, while giving up one's possessions and their enjoyment could easily designate religious poverty (130.16–24). But since there is no clear indication of chastity, Hegel's description might instead refer to obeying the clergy (130.9–15), donating one's property to the church (130.22–23), and practicing the various mortifications (130.23–24) found in medieval Catholicism. He would then have in mind the ordinary people and the monks of medieval Catholicism.

33. By speaking in Latin (see Hyppolite's translation, 1: 190 n. 52; Baillie's, p. 265 n. 2).

34. In the passage quoted, consciousness is "simple and thereby immutable consciousness" (122.21). A simple thing is always the same; immutability follows from such simplicity. In previous pages, Hegel has already noted the simplicity of consciousness. The *"pure ego"* (107.22) certain of itself knows itself as a "simple essence" (107.21–22); thus the stoical self-consciousness has "the simple thought of itself" (119.6). Then in the unhappy consciousness, this internal simplicity becomes an immutable object, the transcendent God of antiquity. In Hegel's own system however it is universal human thinking, which he interprets as the empirical appearance of God.

35. A good example of such a divine object may be found in Augustine's Platonism. See Saint Augustine, *On the Free Choice of the Will*, trans. Anna S. Benjamin and L. H. Hackstaff, Library of Liberal Arts (Indianapolis: Bobbs-Merrill, 1964), pp. 40–71 (Book II, # 20–155), which proves the existence of God by appealing to the "true and immutable rules of wisdom" (p. 62, # 119), in which human consciousness participates imperfectly.

36. In this passage (122.21), "immutable consciousness" clearly refers to human being. The same phrase is used of God elsewhere: the incarnate "immutable consciousness *renounces* its shape and *gives* it *up*" (128.8–9) in the Eucharist. The language of this text suggests the real existence of a divine consciousness beyond human being; but one must be wary of such an interpretation since Hegel has already identified the "immutable consciousness" (122.20–23) with human being. The same phrase in 128.8–9 may simply mean that the immutable God as incarnate has a human consciousness. Since the overall meaning of *PhG* places divine consciousness in human being, such passages as 128.8–9 are best interpreted in light of this overall meaning whenever possible.

37. Probably through its pious thoughts and devotional works, by which the unhappy consciousness unites itself in spirit to God. Hegel merely says

that the incarnate God is present through consciousness rather than through itself (125.3–5).

38. "All reality" makes reason universal thinking and therefore brings religion back to human consciousness.

39. In *PhG* VII, "spirit" refers to divine essence in human form. The difference between these two views of spirit lies in their different applications of universality. As pure essence, the universal is divine substance; as an existing social essence, the universal is political society in a broad sense. Thus Hegel can easily interpret society (in the *Philosophy of Right*) as the worldly existence of God. Furthermore, both kinds of universals—pure divine substance and empirical social groups—also have a singular existence through the universal thinking of real individuals. Such thinking connects them to the universal and allows the universal to appear in them. Thus a universal society expresses itself through its individual members, and universal divine substance appears as an individual incarnation of God. Hegel has a coherent concept of "spirit" that functions on more than one level.

40. Hegel uses "Sitte" as an equivalent of the Greek word "êthos" in an article dated 1817: "Ueber Friedrich Heinrich Jacobi's Werke," in *Sämtliche Werke*, Jubiläumsausgabe, 6 (Stuttgart: Fr. Frommanns Verlag, 1956): 331. And in *PhG*, he links "Sittlichkeit" to one of the meanings of "êthos," namely "character" (e.g., *GW* 9: 324.8–10). A person's character in Greek tragedy illustrates an ethical law imposed by nature. In this way, individual behavior is the expression of a universal substance. This way of looking at human individuality is clearly analogous to Hegel's concept of absolute spirit as the individual human existence of universal divine substance.

41. Lauer calls "Sittlichkeit" "The Norm of Immemorial Custom" (p. 179). This rendering expresses well the idea that a Greek man or woman does what the tribe expects of him or her. One should not forget, however, that cultural expectations in Greece were also based on gender, a division of nature that is prior to custom.

42. For discussions of the whole section, including both Greece and Rome, see Hyppolite, pp. 323–63; Kainz, 2: 13–35; Kojève, pp. 99–107, 184–93; Lauer, pp. 179–90; Solomon, pp. 534–52.

43. Kojève (p. 188) points out the role of Alexander the Great in effecting the transition from Greece to Rome. In the figure of this conqueror, individuality imposes itself on the public domain. In Rome itself, individuality has legal status. Solomon explains it well: "citizenship is open to any individual who . . . happens to live within the far-flung borders of the empire" (pp. 549–50).

44. See Hegel's *Philosophy of History*, pp. 289–90; 316–17. Kojève (pp. 116, 189–91) finds in private rights to property and capital the material basis for the intellectual movements of ancient Rome that Hegel analyzes: stoicism, skepticism, and the Christian otherworldliness of the unhappy consciousness. But since these intellectual systems (described in *PhG* IV–B) appear before any mention of private property (VI–A–c), the latter cannot be the basis for the former in Hegel's view.

45. In contrast to the limited knowing of a Greek character is the unlimited knowing of "Moralität," the moral philosophy of German idealism, in which every individual is potentially capable of thinking all reality in a general way. See Hegel's introduction to "Die Moralität," *PhG* 324.5–17. The natural factor that limits ethical knowing in Greece is then overcome by thinking, through which an individual person can surmount the ethical law of his or her gender imposed by nature. Therefore, the distinction between "Sittlichkeit" and "Moralität" is between "objective and social" morality on the one hand and "subjective and personal" morality on the other, as T. M. Knox indicates in his translator's preface to Hegel's *Aesthetics*, 1: xiii. However, Kantian subjective morality must also be understood as a universal thinking open to everything objective. Lauer correctly calls "Moralität" a "rational reflection" (p. 180).

46. Kainz compares Greece to Christianity, which "idealizes the individual more fully, and ascribes greater significance to him. . . . The Christian idea of the self-conscious disembodied soul in heaven contrasts markedly with the Greek idea of the melancholy 'shade' in . . . Hades" (Kainz 2: 17 n. 17). This comparison (in itself correct) does not apply to Hegel's own view, which seems uninterested in an afterlife beyond the earth. Kainz's Christian interpretation also appears in his analysis of *PhG* 244.39–245.17, which he applies to the " 'shade' . . . spiritually transformed through the conscious deeds of the individual family members." I think that Hegel's text refers to the earthly corpse rather than to the surviving shade; see below, n. 47.

47. Kainz rightly notes the difficulty of "this rather startling idea" (2: 16 n. 15) and proposes that the deceased person becomes universal in a nonempirical afterlife. The suggestion is reasonable; however, since Hegel himself refers to the "*universal* being" (244.17–18) of the earth, it seems better to look for the universality of the deceased person in the corpse that returns to dust (see above, n. 46). In 363.26–28, the shade is clearly separated from universal fate. As nonempirical it is only potentially universal (363.28–31).

48. Hyppolite says that "the family . . . raises the dead person to the universality of spirit" (p. 333). While it is true that the whole point of burial for

Hegel is to do something spiritual or human for the corpse, the universality that results is not spiritual because the corpse is returned to the earth. This is the universality that Hegel's text insists upon. However, since burial by a family member is an expression of family solidarity, which itself is a kind of spiritual universal, the latter may be implicit in Hegel's description.

49. Solomon correctly states that "Antigone represents the losing battle against the breakdown of . . . family-tribal society" (p. 548). But one must not forget that she also represents an early recognition of individuality, which wins many victories later on.

50. Thus, ignorance and guilt are necessary features of the Greek ethical world. Transgression may well be an oversight or an unwitting trespass, but the individual is nevertheless held accountable for it.

51. In his lectures on art, Hegel explains that each character can appeal to a different kind of god: Antigone "worships . . . the underground gods of Hades . . . the inner gods of feeling, love, and kinship, not the daylight gods of free self-conscious national and political life" (G. W. F. Hegel, *Aesthetics*, trans. T. M. Knox, 1: 464). Apollo is the best example of these daylight gods who protect the masculine domain of public life. Human law, then, has its gods also.

52. In itself, "faith in heaven" could refer to belief in the whole heavenly realm consisting of God, angels, and saints. However, Hegel does not mention angels in this section of *PhG*, and the only human individual he refers to, as far as I can discover, is the incarnate God of Christianity (290.2–15).

53. Kainz (2: 55) identifies Roman Catholicism as the specific variety of Christianity Hegel has in mind here since the distinction between religious faith and secular insight corresponds to Hegel's description (*Philosophy of History*, pp. 421–22) of the Catholic separation of religion from secular interests. In Kainz's commentary, the unhappy consciousness is Judeo-Christianity (2: 55), while Protestantism appears as the Christian community of *PhG* VII (2: 56). In my scheme, however, the unhappy consciousness (which may well contain elements of Judeo-Christianity) must refer to Roman Catholicism because the text clearly contains allusions to medieval Christianity. The Christian community of *PhG* VII must be the early New Testament community, which comes immediately after the incarnate God portrayed earlier in the same chapter. That leaves Protestantism as the likely source for faith in heaven. The best reason for identifying it with Catholicism is not the separation of religion and secular life (which is not a major issue here) but the character of its opponent: the Enlightenment Hegel describes is largely French, and it

leads to the French Revolution (the "Absolute Freedom and Terror" of *PhG* 316–23). Consequently, one expects the corresponding faith in heaven to be Catholic. But the positive description of that faith resembles Lutheranism more than Catholicism; see below, n. 59, for evidence and a proposed explanation of this incongruity.

54. See Hyppolite, pp. 404–34; Lauer, pp. 199–209; Kainz, 2: 54–78; Kojève, pp. 133–41; Solomon, pp. 552–59.

55. The supersensible inner begins with a determinate content of scientific laws that Hegel then reduces to the simple assertion that everything is different and subject to law (92.16–19). Thus the supersensible inner is as empty as the God of the Enlightenment.

56. After considering their similarity, Hegel examines each one according to three aspects: (1) *"in and for itself"* (289.24) in "the element of pure consciousness" (289.21–22); (2) in relation to "the *actual* world opposed to pure consciousness" (289.25); and (3) in relation "to each other within pure consciousness" (289.26). Faith in its first aspect is faith in the divine Trinity (289.27–290.15), and in its second aspect it is worship (290.16–37). Pure insight in its first aspect is the restless omnipotent self that aims to convert everything into its own concepts (291.5–11); in its second aspect it aims to universalize pure insight by bringing everything into a single concept accessible to everyone (291.12–292.10). The third aspect is common to both faith and pure insight; it is their mutual conflict as described in the subsection called "The Enlightenment's Struggle with Superstition" (293–311).

57. "God of reason" is a traditional phrase indicating that thinking knows God without being aided by a further divine revelation. Hegel for his part uses "reason" in a limited empirical sense when he writes in *PhG* VII that reason has no religion (363.18–20).

58. *GW* 8: 282.15–283.16; 286.9–15.

59. Hyppolite thinks that faith in heaven must be Catholic, both because it has a sensory element (p. 410) and because the Enlightenment Hegel describes is the French variety (p. 415), as allusions to Voltaire (p. 419) and Diderot (p. 420) prove. The second of these two reasons is correct, but the first is debatable. When faith thinks of God as a being beyond the world, its thought is not peculiarly Catholic. What is Catholic in Hegel's view is the mixture of sensory forms with divine being, such as in the Eucharist; see his *Philosophy of History*, trans. Sibree, pp. 415–16. But what faith in heaven "worships is for it by no means stone or wood or bread-dough, nor any other temporal sensory thing" (*PhG* 300.12–13), and this conscious distinction between inward thought and outer thing is Lutheran rather than Catholic, according to Hegel's *Philosophy of History* (pp. 415–16).

Consequently, faith in heaven has more than a touch of Lutheranism. And, of course, the terms "faith" and "trust" sound more Lutheran than Catholic, especially in the Germany of Hegel's day. Finally, a symmetrical order is obtained when one identifies the unhappy consciousness with Roman Catholicism and faith in heaven with Lutheranism. But the weighty objection remains: the action of the Enlightenment that Hegel describes undoubtedly takes place in France. Is it possible that Hegel was defending his own Lutheranism against the French Enlightenment? Such a theory would explain why an apparently Lutheran faith is confronted by the *philosophes*.

60. Faith is not simply a general trust in God but more specifically a trusting in God as one's personal savior.

61. Hyppolite (p. 425) takes this other self-consciousness to be God present in the soul. One must, however, distinguish faith's point of view from Hegel's. For faith, God is present in the human soul as a divine self. But for Hegel, God is present as the human self's thinking of divine essence, or (in *PhG* VII) as essence knowing itself through human being.

62. According to the *Logik*, the human self is the highest development of divine essence. But this point is unknown to faith, which deals not with absolute essence in and for itself, but only with its discovery by pure thinking.

63. Of course, this point applies only to the *immediate* production of the thought. As the *Logik* and *PhG* VII's trinitarian theology show, human thinking is itself the product of divine self-differentiation. God therefore is the ultimate source of one's thinking; divine essence produces its own presence in the human mind.

64. Hegel alludes to this higher point of view in his analyses of both faith in heaven (289.22–24) and the unhappy consciousness (125.1–6).

65. Deism is the well-known religion of the Enlightenment. Kojève (pp. 137–38) rightly sees it as bringing the Christian God to the limit of transcendence.

66. The quoted passage may, however, refer to worship that uses sensory forms rather than to a doctrine that gives a sensory existence to God. Both concepts may be intended, too, because belief in God's incarnation justifies the use of sensory objects in Christian worship. Here, I apply the passage to doctrine in order to account for the transformation of trinitarian faith into Deism.

67. Hegel's early work *Glauben und Wissen* explores this problem in the philosophies of Kant, Jacobi, and Fichte, all of whom follow the Enlightenment in this respect. They limit the scope of reason and leave the

supersensible to a kind of philosophical faith. See *Glauben und Wissen*, *GW* 4: 323.4–9, 13–17.

68. This difference between the unhappy consciousness and faith in heaven probably corresponds to Hegel's view of the difference between Roman Catholicism and Lutheranism. For him, Lutheranism advances beyond Catholicism by interiorizing a conscious relation to God. See Hegel's *Philosophy of History*, pp. 390–91, 415–16.

CHAPTER III

MORALITY

CONVERTED BY THE Enlightenment, faith no longer has a heaven with a determinate God; the divine object it believes in is acknowledged to exist but is nevertheless empty for knowledge because its essence is considered unknowable. Faith loses its former character and comes to resemble the Enlightenment—but not entirely: whereas the Enlightenment is *"satisfied"* (310.36) with its empty beyond, faith is not. Unwilling to accept such an empty ultimate object, faith is the *"unsatisfied* Enlightenment" (310.36), which in German idealism produces a new shape of religion called "Morality" (*PhG* VI–C).

This final division of Hegel's sixth chapter has a twofold religious significance. First, it contains "the religion of morality," which in contrast to the Enlightenment "restores . . . the absolute essence" as "a positive content" (364.10–11). Hegel is undoubtedly referring here to Kant's religious postulates of a divine mind connected with an ultimate goal for both the individual self and the entire world. Together, these three postulates of a God, of individual salvation, and of a cosmic transformation constitute a philosophical justification for Christian faith. Hegel describes Kant's postulates in a subdivision called "The Moral World-View" (*PhG* VI–C–a), and criticizes them in another subdivision called "Transposition" ("Die Verstellung") (*PhG* VI–C–b).

Even more significant for religion, however, is the third subdivision: "Conscience. The Beautiful Soul, Evil and Its Pardon" (*PhG* VI–C–c), which apparently refers to Fichte and his disciples. In his review of religions at the beginning of *PhG* VII, Hegel uses conscience for the transition from "Die Moralität" (*PhG* VI–C) to "Die Religion" (*PhG* VII), where "the self-consciousness of spirit" (363.8) begins. Thus, conscience—and especially its final section, "Evil and Its Pardon"—is the source (according to 364.14–23) for "the *concept* of religion" (367.32) used by *PhG* VII. In "Conscience," one finds the shift from the religions conscious of a transcendent God to the religions in which human being is conscious of itself as a development of divine substance.

In broad outline, then, Hegel's discussion of morality has two main parts: Kant's religious postulates, and the analysis of conscience in Fichte and his disciples.[1] Before I examine them in detail, I provide some general remarks that may help to put them in a clearer context.

In relation to what has gone before, morality is an intelligible step forward. As the knowing[2] of all being through universal thinking (324.12–13, 19–20), morality continues the Enlightenment's pure insight. As a result, it comes close to the ideal of reason reached in thought by the unhappy consciousness. At the end of its development, this unhappy consciousness became "the certainty . . . of being in its individuality absolutely *in itself*, or all reality" (131.30–31). This ideal seems to be very close to absolute knowing. Human consciousness, however, cannot be absolute if something lies beyond it—namely the divine beyond acknowledged by the religions examined here, and even by the Enlightenment itself. Such a beyond is also retained by Kant's postulates, which leave room for faith[3] because for Kant human knowing is limited and cannot be absolute.

Conscience, however, goes further and absorbs even this beyond; in Fichte and his followers, the self "no longer sets outside itself its *world* and its [i.e., the world's] *ground*, but lets everything die away in itself, and as *conscience* is spirit *certain*[4] *of itself*" (240.19–21) because it now supposes itself to contain everything, including the divine ground of the world. It is, in fact, through human knowing that God appears at the end of conscience's development, when evil is pardoned: "it is God appearing among those who know themselves as pure knowing" (362.28–29). Hegel probably means that God appears not only *in* human knowing but also *as* human knowing, for *in* human knowing God could still remain an object beyond the knower. If, however, God appears *as* human knowing, pure knowing can then be interpreted as the actualization in human being of divine essence itself. Spinoza's divine substance would then be intrinsically linked to its modification as human thought.

The point of view of *PhG* VII then becomes intelligible: religion is both "the absolute essence *in and for itself*" (363.7) and the "self-consciousness of spirit" (363.8) because the absolute essence is understood as having developed itself into human knowing, hitherto considered to be God's opposite. By absorbing in this way the beyond that neither the Enlightenment nor Kant succeeded in eliminating, conscience thus prepares the way for a new treatment of religion. For the same reason, it also fulfills the Enlightenment's desire to bring everything into its pure insight, including the divine beyond.

Consequently, one must have a good grasp of what happens in the section on conscience in order to comprehend the point of view of *PhG* VII, Hegel's chapter on religion. First, however, one must examine Kant's attempt to preserve a divine beyond. The affirmation of such a beyond makes Kant's moral postulates a religion of consciousness, similar to those I discuss in my chapter on faith. Obviously, Hegel has to deal with the Kantian religion of consciousness before examining religion as the "self-consciousness of spirit" (363.8).

KANT'S MORAL RELIGION (324–340)[5]

Hegel's term "religion of morality" (364.10) refers both to his description of "The Moral World-View" (324–332) and to his criticism of it as a type of speculative "Transposition" (332–340). These chapter subdivisions[6] cover the same material, namely Kant's[7] practical reason with its postulates of God, personal immortality, and a final aim for the world. The "religion of morality," therefore, is not the living faith of a church but a system of ideas providing a philosophical justification for religious faith.

"The Religion of Morality" (364.10–16)

In his introduction to *PhG* VII, Hegel summarizes this religion of Kant in allusive language that is rather difficult to decipher. The passage reads as follows.

In the religion of morality finally this is produced again, that the absolute essence is a positive content, but it [this content] is united with the negativity of the Enlightenment. It [this content] is a *being*, which also is taken back into the self and remains enclosed in it, and a *differentiated content* whose parts are just as immediately negated as they are [positively] set up. But the fate into which this contradictory movement sinks is the self conscious of itself as the fate of *essentiality* and *actuality*. (364.10–16)

What does Hegel mean? "Absolute essence" must refer to divine essence as duty because duty is absolute essence in the earlier discussion of morality: "self-consciousness knows duty as the absolute essence" (324.30). This meaning also gives Kant's absolute essence a "positive content" (364.11) lacking in the empty beyond of the Enlightenment (364.6–9). Furthermore, it explains how absolute essence "is united with the negativity of the Enlightenment" (364.11–12), namely with pure insight's critical ability, since duty appears as the "pure consciousness" (324.31) of reason.[8]

Hegel then continues his description of morality's absolute essence by calling its content "a *being* which [is] nevertheless taken back into the self and remains enclosed in it" (364.12–13). These words may refer to God as the postulated harmony of duty and real existence (340.5). All the postulates begin with human awareness of pure duty, which calls for its practical realization. From this demand of duty to actualize itself in sensory being, Kant infers the various postulates of practical reason. Since God as the connection of duty and being is postulated by the self, one also has an explanation for how this being is "taken back into the self and remains enclosed in it" (364.12–13) as a mere postulate or thought.[9] Kant's God is affirmed as a being independent of consciousness (its independent existence is part of its positive content) yet also as one subject to human thinking.

Further, Kant's absolute essence is not simply a being but also has "a *differentiated content* whose parts" (364.13)[10] must be the various "postulates" (328.25) about God—for example, that God is a holy lawgiver (337.26) or again the bestower of grace (336.36–37). These postulates are "negated as soon as they are set up" (364.13–14) because they contradict some feature of practical reason itself. In his longer analysis of Kant in *PhG* VI–C, Hegel calls this inconsistency in argument a "Verstellung" (332.13) or a transposition that changes a position previously adopted. In Hegel's view, Kant's moral philosophy is a "contradictory movement" (364.14–15) that constantly negates its initial concept.

Weary of its own restlessness, human thinking then "sinks" (364.15) into itself through Fichte's theory of conscience, which accepts "the self conscious of itself as the fate of [divine] *essentiality* and [empirical] *actuality*" (364.15–16). Here, the self appears to abandon its attempt to know divine essence and the real world. And the way to this position (occupied by Fichte) was prepared by Kant, whose moral philosophy Hegel judges to be a failure because it never produces any firm affirmation about God.

Such is Hegel's view of Kant in his brief summary of religion at the beginning of *PhG* VII. Interpreting this text has not been easy, and the correctness of the interpretation proposed here depends on how coherent it is with Hegel's longer analysis of Kant in *PhG* VI–C–a ("The Moral World-View") and VI–C–b ("Transposition").

Hegel begins his treatment of Kant's "Moral World-View" by examining its point of departure, namely moral self-consciousness. His analysis then quickly turns to the role of nature in morality, a topic related to the "*being*" (364.12) mentioned in the brief summary just examined.

Two Views of Nature (324.30–325.37)

In Kant's moral thinking, "self-consciousness knows duty as absolute essence; it is bound only through [duty] and this substance is its own pure consciousness" (324.30–31). Duty is reason itself, aware of a rational good; in duty, reason is accountable only to itself. Furthermore, because duty is practical reason, it aims to act or to realize itself in actual reality and thereby create a harmony between itself and sensory existence. Though "duty counts as essence" for moral consciousness, this consciousness also "is *actual* and *active*, and fulfills [its] duty in its actuality and act" (324.25–27) because rational duty acquires being and actuality through its implementation in sensory existence. Even then, however, "duty makes up its unique essential aim and object" (325.5–6) so that, as Hegel later says of Kant in his lectures on the history of philosophy, "for the will [there] is no aim other than the

[aim] created from itself, the aim of its freedom."[11] In other words, by carrying out its own purposes, practical reason implements itself; thus it is free.[12] Nature or actual existence is the pliable material that it shapes.

But because duty derives from thinking rather than from nature, the world of nature—the realm of actual existence or sensory reality—is not only "an actuality completely *without significance*" (325.6),[13] but also "an independent whole of laws proper" to itself (325.12) and opposed to moral thinking. Moral self-consciousness and nature are separate and distinct, with no intrinsic relation between them; each is free of the other and acts independently and without regard for its opposite (325.7–15).[14]

Thus, Kant makes "conflicting presuppositions" (325.24) about nature. Although he maintains "the complete dependence and non-essentiality of nature [as against] the consciousness of the exclusive essentiality of duty [alone]" (325.21–22), he also discusses "the complete *indifference* and proper *independence* of *nature* and of *moral* aims and activity against one another" (325.19–20).[15] In the first place, Kant has duty thinking of nature as a pliable material, capable of being shaped by the moral aims of consciousness and thus of giving existence to those aims. But in the second place, Kant makes nature a powerful antagonist of morality, an opponent capable of resisting the moral goals of practical reason. The second point of view arises from duty as pure reason that respects only itself or that knows its pure consciousness as absolute essence and substance (324.30–31). As a result, what is not moral (namely nature) is considered to be positively immoral.

This conflict in Kant's view of nature affects his moral religion. If nature is pliable to morality, conscious duty will assert its mastery over natural existence and achieve the harmony of duty and being;[16] "pure duty and the knowing of it as essence" will then be found "only in" moral human consciousness (339.35, 36) rather than in a God beyond it. But if nature is viewed as resisting morality, then their harmony is to be found not in the actual moral self but (if this harmony is to exist at all) "only as the *beyond* of actual being and consciousness" (339.34–35). Thus, "the setting apart of the moments of the *self* and the *in-itself*" (340.3–4) is created, which is "the basic contradiction" (332.26) permitting the construction of Kant's postulates: how can moral reason be absolute if contrasted with a moral "in-itself" beyond consciousness? This contradiction, however, depends on the two different views of nature that Hegel discerns in Kant. If nature obeys morality, duty can attain its goals, and one can consider as absolute practical reason as it now exists in human being. But if nature opposes morality, practical reason is frustrated and hardly absolute. It must then postulate its fulfillment in a beyond, in an absolute goal that motivates earthly consciousness.

Yet if nature and morality were completely opposed to one another, the result would be an eternal dualism rather than a postulated harmony. There must be some ground for expecting them to come together in harmony, and that ground is the first view of nature as the pliable material for morality aiming to actualize itself in real existence. But this realization cannot be attained because nature is also thought of as opposed to morality. Consequently, the unattainable harmony is postulated as existing beyond the actual self.[17] In this way, Kant's religious postulates rest on the conflicting assumptions that morality can shape nature, but not the nature that we now know. Kant's concept of morality is therefore incoherent.

The general idea behind Kant's religious postulates, as well as Hegel's criticism of them, has been explained. But because little has been said about the postulates in detail, my summary of Hegel's analysis continues by examining the specific religious postulates Kant constructs.

Eschatology (326.1–34)

The first postulate is about "the harmony of morality and of objective nature, the ultimate aim of the *world*" (328.16–17). For Kant this aim is equivalent to Christianity's "kingdom of God,"[18] and his argument resembles the traditional view that a better world is desirable but not attainable in this life. Kant begins his own argument with the experience of nature as an irrational force indifferent to the happiness of moral consciousness, whose aims are never actualized in real existence with any consistency (325.27–37). On the other hand, because practical reason is driven to act, "moral consciousness cannot renounce [the] happiness" (326.1) that would result from the unity of morality and nature (326.20–22). In other words, morality continues to seek its frustrated goals.

The same idea is expressed in different language as the unity of universal and individual, and more specifically as the unity of universal moral thought with its individual actualization in nature, which contains "the side of *individuality* as against the abstract aim" (326.14–15) of universal thought. Even as *"pure duty,"* a moral aim "essentially . . . contains *individual* self-consciousness" (326.3–4) because morality aims to be universal "duty fulfilled . . . as realized *individuality"* (326.13–14). All Hegel means by these phrases is that the abstract goals of morality seek real existence by being put into practice or harmonized with the individual bodies of nature. Moral goals contain "the *thought* of *actuality"* (326.19) because they are oriented toward action.

Consequently, the "harmony of morality and nature, or . . . of moral ity and happiness, is *thought* as necessarily *being*, or it is *postulated"* (326.20–23) as the goal of moral action; "something which is not yet actual is thought [as] *being"* (326.23–24) and more specifically as "demanded *being"* (326.26). This "demand of reason" (326.33) is made according to the "concept of morality itself, whose true content is the *unity* of *pure* and *individual* consciousness" (326.27–29) or of morality and existence. But because of "the experience of the disharmony" (326.16) between nature and duty, such a unity is postulated by Kant as a distant goal rather than simply expected as the normal result of every moral action. Because morality and nature are opposing forces their harmony can exist only in thought, as a desired aim resembling the expectations of Jewish and Christian eschatology.

Immortality (326.35–328.15)

A second postulate arises when the idea of the first one is applied to individual persons, who within themselves aim to harmonize their moral or rational side with their natural animal sensory side. In this goal of individual moral perfection, "the harmony of morality and of sensory will" is postulated as "the ultimate aim of *self-consciousness"* (328.17–18). This sensory will is of course affected by nature; it consists of *"drives* and *inclinations"* with their *"individual aims"* that are opposed to the universal intellectual aims of "the pure will" (327.4–

6).[19] The opposition of these two aspects of human being is overcome in principle when "sensory existence is *conformable* to morality" (327.25–26). But like the first postulate's unity of morality with all of nature, the same unity in individual human being occurs only in theory; it "too is a *postulated being*; it does not *exist*; for what *exists* is . . . the opposition of sensory existence and of pure consciousness" (327.26– 28). Thus the second postulate, like the first, posits a state of being that is beyond the actual world.

Furthermore, the distance between any actual self and its postulated future harmony consists of an infinite time: morality's "*completion* . . . is *postponed* into the *infinite*" (327.34–35) because no actual harmony is conceivable between the two opposing principles of morality and sensory existence. From the infinite time needed to effect this future harmony, Kant infers the immortality of the soul as a postulate of practical reason. And this immortality of course contributes to the religious character of Kant's moral world-view.[20]

God (328.16–331.10)

Kant's third postulate concerns the existence of a divine consciousness outside human being. This divine consciousness corresponds to more than one postulate, however; Hegel refers to "postulates" in the plural (328.25) when introducing Kant's argument for the existence of God. The set of postulates about a divine consciousness neatly follows the two earlier postulates of ultimate aims for the world in general and then for individual self-consciousness. The first postulate has the "form" of a harmony "*in itself*" and outside human consciousness; the second is a harmony "*for itself*" or intrinsic to consciousness; and the postulates concerning God unify both of these aspects (328.25–26) because divine consciousness is both "in itself" as an object outside human consciousness and "for itself" simply as an individual consciousness (339.11–13).

One could then argue toward the existence of God by postulating a cause for the harmony the first postulate requires.[21] But God would then be needed only in the future. Kant's argument, therefore, looks to the present situation of moral consciousness faced with harmonizing itself with nature, and specifically with nature as a multiplicity of beings and events. Thus, "moral consciousness is as the *simple know-ing* and *willing* of *pure* duty related to the object opposed to its simplicity—to the actuality of the *manifold* case[—]and thereby has a manifold moral *relation*" (328.27–30). Here again, one encounters the Kantian difference between thinking and being. This time, however, being is considered in its aspect of a manifold content for moral thought: thinking itself is simple and pure, an immaterial synthesis, whereas actual existence contains material multiplicity.

From this multiplicity arise "*many duties*," but "for moral consciousness [there] counts in them only *pure duty* in general; the *many duties* as many are *determinate* and consequently as such [are] nothing holy for moral consciousness" (328.33–35). However, if moral consciousness is to act in a manifold world (328.36–37), these duties "must be considered as being in and for themselves" (329.1) or as absolutely valid for consciousness. But they are not valid for *human* consciousness "for which only pure duty is pure in and for itself, and holy" (329.3). Yet "since they . . . can be only in a moral *consciousness*" (329.1–2), which is also a consciousness of the manifold actual world, "it is thus postulated that there is an *other* consciousness which makes them holy or which knows and wills them as duties" (329.4–5). Thus, Kant postulates a divine consciousness from the need to justify duty as manifold or multiple.[22]

But since multiplicity arises from sensory actuality, as opposed to the simplicity of pure duty, the postulate of divine consciousness is made for the same reason as the first two: human reason is unable to master the sensory world, so a harmony between them is postulated outside of human morality. In fact, Hegel writes of this divine consciousness that "its concept [is] thus the same as the concept of the harmony of morality and happiness" (329.12–13); both concepts suggest "the separation of . . . moral consciousness from actuality" (329.13–14), which then have to be harmonized outside the actual world. The only difference is that in the first two postulates actuality gives duty its being or existence, while in the third postulate actuality gives duty its determinate content (329.16–20). And because duty is only for a moral *thinking*, which as determinate cannot be human since determinacy is not holy for human morality (whose determinacy arises from nature and not from thinking), so too must these determinate duties be for a thinking other than human, or for a divine consciousness (329.18–22). While the first two postulates demand only duty's actual being, the third one differentiates it into determinate multiple being.

Now insofar as determinacy is already found within actual existence, there is no need to posit a divine consciousness of it; the need arises only because being gives determinacy to *duty*, which supposes thought. Consequently, there is posited a thinking of determinate duty by a divine moral consciousness whose object is the harmony of duty and determinate being. Thus, God is the world's ultimate aim—the harmony of duty and being—"posited as [a] consciousness" (329.18–19) harmonizing duty and *determinate* being.

By bringing together duty and determinate actuality, divine consciousness of course unites duty and indeterminate being as well. Perhaps this is why God is also said to be "the lord and ruler of the world, who produces the harmony of morality and happiness" (329.22–24). No other explanation is given for the production of the world's ultimate aim. It is a point that Kant cannot be too precise about, since the realization of this aim is unthinkable.[23] In any case, God is now linked to Kant's first postulate as cause to effect. Like the postulate of determinate moral thinking, these postulates give Kant's God the "*determinate content*" (364.13) referred to in *PhG* VII.

Other postulates follow. Initially, God was postulated as the moral knowing of determinate human duties. Now even one's pure knowing of duty is shifted onto God because the sensory side of human existence makes even pure thinking impure. In moral action, human being is "directed to actuality as such and has it for [its] aim, for it wishes to accomplish [something]" (329.31–32). But if actuality has value, then human morality recognizes something "other than pure duty" (329.25), which therefore cannot be pure in human being. Consequently, "*duty in general* falls outside it into another essence, which is the consciousness and the holy lawgiver of pure duty" (329.32–34). God then becomes not only the source of determinate duties but also of pure duty itself.

Next, because duty is holy in God "outside of actual consciousness, the latter consequently stands as the *incomplete* moral consciousness" (330.1–2). Human morality "knows itself as . . . incomplete and contingent; likewise according to its *willing* as . . . affected with sensuality" (330.3–5). Human morality is also incomplete according to its own essence of a duty opposing a sensory will, which leads to the postulate of an infinite progress and immortality. But now, it is incomplete by comparison to God, in whom the opposition between moral thinking and actual being is overcome. Incomplete human being looks upon itself as sinful, and "because of its unworthiness it can therefore look at [its] happiness [as] not necessary but as something contingent, and wait for it from grace" (330.5–7). Here Kant's religion takes on another Christian theme, the justification of sinners by divine grace. Again, there is no proof that such happiness will in fact come about. Instead, Kant proves only that human being is morally incomplete, and that its final happiness—which must be postulated as the goal of its desire to realize its morality—will therefore be undeserved.

Hegel's next paragraph specifies that divine grace is "*imputed merit*" (330.14–15). Human happiness (the first postulate) will then come about when God treats human being as though it had conquered sensuality within itself and were fully moral (the second postulate). Therefore, the postulate of divine grace neatly integrates the first two postulates with the third one, which concerns the existence of a divine consciousness. However, Hegel does not draw attention to the elegance of this conclusion, which is only implicit in his description.

Instead, Hegel explains the relation between grace and merit: even though human "actuality is [morally] incomplete" (330.8), "in [its] thinking it is . . . complete" (330.10) because "for its *pure* willing and knowing duty counts as essence" (330.8–9). When moral consciousness thinks of duty alone or abstractly, it thinks of itself as complete. In its sensuous actuality it is incomplete, but in its abstract thinking of pure duty it is complete. In other words, one might say that its intentions are complete although its achievements are not. But suppose moral consciousness were accepted on the basis of its intentions or its thoughts of duty alone? In that case its acceptance would overlook its incomplete achievement, or would "forgive" its sensory existence for not measuring up to moral duty.

Such an argument seems to be in Hegel's mind because he identifies divine mercy with the thought of accepting human sensuality, or the sensory existence of human being. Having already said of moral consciousness that "in [its] thinking it is . . . complete" (330.10), he continues:

... the absolute essence however is just this thought, and postulated beyond actuality; it is consequently the thought in which morally incomplete knowing and willing counts for complete; [and] hereby also, in that it takes the same [incomplete one] at full weight, [it] does apportion happiness according to worth, namely according to the *merit imputed* to it. (330.11–15)

Here, Hegel describes a thought according to which human being is considered morally complete, even though in actuality it is never complete. This thought is equivalent to a God who overlooks sins and imputes to human beings a merit they do not actually have.

With such a thought, Kant's moral "world-view is . . . completed" (330.16) because in it the two sides of moral consciousness, "pure duty and actuality, are posited in one unity . . . as *moment*[s] or as surmounted" (330.16–17, 18). In the thought of God's mercy toward human being, duty and actuality find their equilibrium "for consciousness" (330.20). Moral consciousness "puts pure duty into an essence other than itself" (330.20–21), namely God, whose separateness from human being is therefore that of an essence "*imagined*" (330.21). Nevertheless God is not simply pure duty, or a holiness transcending human nature, because this divine holiness accepts human sinfulness; in God's mercy, pure duty is "not what counts in and for itself, but rather the immoral counts as complete" (330.22–23). Thus God is thought of as pure duty accepting sensory actuality. Furthermore, consciousness "posits itself as such a one whose actuality, . . . inadequate to duty, [is nevertheless] surmounted, and as *surmounted* or in the *image* of absolute essence no longer contradicts morality" (330.23–26). In the figure of a merciful God, the two sides of human morality come together. Neither side is absolute: not pure duty, because God does not judge human being according to what duty expects; nor sensory actuality, because God's mercy gives it a better judgment than it really deserves.

However, this figure only confirms the suspicion that Kant's divine essence is really a human thought that has not quite understood itself. The acceptance by divine mercy of sinful human being corresponds to the joining of pure duty and sensory actuality, which are the two fundamental aspects of moral human being. Taken separately, God corresponds to Hegel's description of pure duty; divine essence appears in thought when human consciousness "posits pure duty . . . in an essence other than itself, i.e., it posits it as [something] *imagined . . .*" (330.20–21). In other words, God's transcendent holiness is morality's own thought of duty imagined as a separate essence. And when God is said to move toward actuality by accepting sinful human being, this acceptance is imagined as a divine act, remaining within God, so that sensory existence is "surmounted" only "in the *image* of [transcendent] absolute essence" (330.24, 25) and not in actuality. Such a God includes human actuality only in thought. Therefore, Kant's God is human morality with its two aspects of duty and actuality synthesized in human thought, and kept separate from the real world by imagination. Consequently Kant's morality produces a religion of faith, in which God remains distant and transcendent.

Hegel's summary of Kant's moral religion (324.28–330.26) concludes with the postulate of grace, for Kant's "world-view is herein completed" (330.16). What follows in Hegel is a long criticism (330.27–340.8) of that same world-view.

The Concept Imagined (330.27–332.11)

Hegel's description of Kant's God as a "thought . . . postulated beyond actuality" (330.11–12) already seems to be a criticism, implying that what is merely thought is nevertheless affirmed as existing beyond the actual world. According to Hegel, moral consciousness does not see that in its world-view it "develops its own concept and makes it into . . . an object" (330.28–29) beyond itself. By "concept," Hegel here must mean "the concept of moral self-consciousness" (331.12), "the concept" (331.16) according to which thinking and actuality already form a unity prior to any postulates of a beyond.

Since duty intends to act, it has to look upon nature as conformable to morality; otherwise, moral action is not possible. Thus, "actuality in general has essence only insofar as it is conformable to duty" (331.17–18). From this point of view, moral thinking looks upon actuality as a pliable material to be shaped by duty. Therefore, nature has "essence" in moral "knowing" (331.18) because in such knowing nature is potentially moral. Such an essence is not abstract because moral knowing is "in immediate unity with the actual self" (331.18–19); in human being, moral reason is joined to sensory existence. Consequently, a unity of morality and nature already exists in human nature defined by "the concept of moral self-consciousness" (331.12).

Why then does Kant postulate this unity only in such distant objects as a transcendent divine consciousness or in ultimate aims resembling those of Christian eschatology? The answer, according to Hegel, is found in the type of thinking that Kant engages in. Kant's practical reason "knows as pure knowing or as itself only *pure essence*, or the object insofar as it [is] *duty* [or the] . . . *abstract* object of its pure consciousness" (330.32–35). What is rational for Kant is not nature but only pure reason. Therefore, his critique of practical reason does not maintain the *concept* of moral self-consciousness, according to which there is a unity of moral thinking and real existence. Kant's moral consciousness "thus behaves only [in a] thinking [way], not [in a] conceptual [way]" (330.35); it values only the abstract thinking of pure transcendental reason, which gives to consciousness a knowledge of its duty but not a knowledge of the real world.

More precisely, Kant's moral consciousness fails to view nature as the medium in which its duty is to be realized; or if it does, it does not do so consistently. Nature, "the object of its *actual* consciousness[,] is not yet transparent to it; it is not the absolute concept which alone grasps *being-other* as such, or its absolute opposite, as itself" (330.35–331.1).[24] What Hegel is alluding to, of course, is Kant's well-known separation of actual existence or nature from pure transcendental reason. Because Kant's transcendental reason is abstract, "the freedom of pure thinking" (331.3) that is above actual material existence, "nature too has arisen as a [being] just as free over against" pure thinking (331.3–4). If moral thinking fails to comprehend its unity with nature, they will of course be seen as opposites. Then too arises the occasion to unify them in a distant beyond, consisting of postulates that preserve Christian doctrine.

According to Hegel, this postulated unity occurs through imagination. Since moral consciousness knows actual being in a twofold way, as both "the *freedom of being* and its being enclosed in consciousness" (331.5–6), the "object" (nature in general) is known as "a *being* which *at the same time* is merely *thought*" (331.6–7). The abstract being of nature enclosed in thought is then affirmed as the existence of God. Thus "in the last part[25] of its [world-] view the content is essentially posited [in] such [a way] that its *being* is an *imagined* [one] . . . this linkage of being and thinking . . . [is] . . . *imagining*" (331.7–10). Hegel means that Kant's God is a thought whose alleged existence is not the real existence of the actual world but only an existence imagined in thought. Put another way, Kant *postulates* the unity of reason and existence but fails to *comprehend* it as the unity of absolute essence and real existence.

As a result, the postulated harmony does not really contain actual being; at best, it refers to being in an abstract way. As the harmony of nature and morality, Kant's God is merely the abstract thought of nature joined to the abstract thought of duty. This God is therefore a being of pure consciousness alone, or a pseudo-being, since actual being refers to the real world alone. As the pure thought of actual being joined to the pure thought of duty, God can be envisioned as a harmony of nature and morality; in this view of God, however, actual being has lost its actuality in the abstractness of thought. Yet because thought or duty is abstract, it is separate from nature, and so the Kantian God is imagined[26] as a being separate from nature.

One could also say that Kant's idea of a divine consciousness is abstract because it derives from pure transcendental reason, which is separate from the actual world. This interpretation is confirmed by other passages in *PhG*. Kant's God is said to be "the holy essence" (338.9) or divine "other" (338.19) that is the idea of "purely completed morality" (338.20). As duty, it is abstract because it is pure practical reason distinct from nature; in the form of divine consciousness, it still "does not stand in relation to nature and sensory existence" (338.21), so that it is "an unconscious, unactual abstraction" (338.31–32).[27] God's abstractness thus derives from the pure thinking of the transcendental subject which has only an abstract idea of nature. Because it cannot *think* the actual world, all its thoughts (including its thought of God) remain abstract or separated from actual existence. In Hegel's view, Kantian reason is not absolute enough since it does not incorporate natural existence into its rational object. Failing to consider the real world as the existence of absolute essence, it gives God only an imagined existence instead of a real one.

This interpretation also explains why imagining separates God from *human* being as well. Since human being consists of rational thinking in an animal body, it is both intellectual and sensory. Through its sensory body, it belongs to nature, which is excluded from Kant's idea of God. As a result, not only nature in general but human being in particular is kept separate from God, who is an abstract thought "imagined" as an independent being beyond nature.

Kant's religion, therefore, resembles all the others previously considered in *PhG*. It, too, is a religion of consciousness: despite its high level of thinking, it yields only a mental image in which God's being is abstract. The main difference between Kant's religion and those other religions is that his religion "*consciously produces* its object" (332.15) as a postulate of the mind. This religion therefore links the idea of God to human thinking, and so has the merit of joining absolute essence to the rational self (364.10–16). But the real truth about God is concealed from Kant. According to Hegel, Kant's God is only the abstract harmony—postulated in a distant beyond—of universal essence and individual existence. Because Kant fails to comprehend the unity of essence and existence, his moral religion does not reach the concept of spirit, where human being is known as the real existence of universal divine essence.

Kant's religion postulates a God beyond itself. Initially, however, its content is not a divine beyond but rather itself: consciousness envisions its own moral aims and intends to realize them in the natural world, which then "has essence only insofar as it conforms to duty" (331.17–18). Thus, there "*is* a moral actual consciousness" (331.19–20) in the sense that duty can actualize itself in real existence.

Nevertheless, Kant falls away from this initial concept by his separation of sensory existence from thinking, which thereby remains imprisoned in its own abstractness. The unity of reason and existence is, according to Hegel, already actual in moral consciousness, but Kant's treatment of this consciousness dissolves its original unity because abstract thinking cannot synthesize itself with sensory existence. For Kant, the unity of reason and sensuality is a postulated *result* rather than a starting point (327.12–15). Thus consciousness "imagines its content as [an] object, namely as *ultimate aim of the world*, as [the] harmony of morality and all actuality" (331.20–22).

This harmony is already contained in the concept of morality, but since Kant's abstract reason "is not yet the concept which has power over the object as such" (331.23–24), it cannot unify its thought with nature. Rather, it postulates its unity as a future goal. That unity however is really itself, namely "the concept of moral self-consciousness itself, which it makes objective to itself" (331.12–13) in its postulates. It behaves this way because in its own mind it falls away from this concept, and sees itself only as an abstract thinking of duty or pure reason. Consequently, its own concept slips away from its grasp and becomes an "*object*" which it "imagines" (331.22–23), "a negative of self-consciousness . . . beyond its actuality" (331.24, 25). In this way, there arises the mental image of a beyond that is differentiated into the specific postulates of Kant's moral religion. Even though this beyond is postulated "as *being*, yet it is only thought" (331.26).

Since the harmony of duty with actuality has been shifted into the abstract object of thought, what "remains left over" for the actual subject "which as self-consciousness is an *other* than the object" (331.27–28)? Only "the disharmony [between] consciousness of duty and actuality, and indeed its own actuality" (331.28–29). Consequently, "*there is no moral . . . actual* self-consciousness" (331.29–30). Moral actuality exists only in the "ultimate aim of the world" (331.21), an abstract object of thought in which the actually existing subject has no share. Instead, the living subject shares in the immorality of nature. Only in the abstract ideal of thought, imagined as a separate object, is there a harmony of morality with nature.

Nevertheless, the self is not content with this difference between its actual subjectivity and its abstract object, because the latter is the projected completion of the former and thereby takes away from the self its proper unity. The moral self is "one self [and therefore] . . . *in itself* the unity of duty and actuality" (331.35–36), combining its imagined completion and its unfulfilled "self-conscious actuality" (331.38–39). The two sides of the self—its abstract thinking and its actual subjectivity—are now brought together in a further development of the abstract object, in which subjectivity's actual moral deficiency is counted as "completed morality" (331.36–37) by a forgiving God, who remains "a *beyond*" (331.37). In actual existence, nothing is changed; the subject still remains immoral. This actual subject "is however in imagination moral, and is taken at full value" (332.7–8) "by another" (332.11) entity, who is God. The actually immoral subject is then considered to be moral, so that a harmony is finally achieved between its actual existence and its abstract ideal.

Hegel's words refer to Kant's postulate of divine grace, analyzed more fully in 327.37–330.26. God's grace is postulated so that an actually immoral consciousness might consider itself moral. Consciousness has constructed an idea of God out of its own resources in order to overcome the contradiction between its moral thinking and its actual sensory existence. It cannot accept its "*actual im*moral" (332.6) side "because it is also pure thinking and elevated above its actuality" (332.6–7). Thus it transforms its own intended fulfillment into a divine consciousness in which morality and actuality are harmonized (329.11–13, 16–20), and then it takes the additional step of having merit imputed to its own inadequate actual morality by that same God.

Thus, morality resolves its own contradiction. It begins by affirming the existence of a moral self-consciousness (331.15–20) and then denies this point of departure by imagining a moral existence only beyond itself (331.21–26). Its own life is not moral (331.27–29), so that a truly moral self-consciousness does not exist (331.29–30). The contradictory positions are synthesized (331.38–39; 332.8–9) by the image (332.5, 7, 10) of a gracious God who accepts immoral human being as nevertheless moral (332.7–8, 10–11).

Hegel continues to explore this contradiction in "Die Verstellung" (332.12–340.25). Before this section is examined, however, some reminders about his own concept of God seem appropriate. In calling "the moral world-view . . . nothing other than the concept of moral self-consciousness itself, which it makes objective to itself" (331.12–13), Hegel seems to be calling Kant's God a projection of subjective thinking. But this criticism of Kant's religion does not imply a rejection of divine essence itself.

The Concept Correctly Understood

One must be very cautious in assessing this kind of criticism. Hegel himself acknowledges that the subjective origin of a thought does not invalidate its truth. Concerning the divine spirit of the Christian community of faith, he writes: "it is *only through the producing* of consciousness;—or rather *not without* being produced by consciousness; for as essential as the producing is, essentially it is also not the only ground of essence, but is only a moment. The essence is at the same time in and for itself" (298.20–24). In a similar way, Hegel cautions against misinterpretations of the unhappy consciousness's immutable God: "until now only immutability as immutability of consciousness has arisen for us, which consequently is not the true [immutability] but is still afflicted with an opposite, not the immutable *in and for itself*" (123.31–34).[28] Taken together, these two passages indicate a difference between divine essence in and for itself and divine essence as an abstract object produced by consciousness.[29]

But what is divine essence in and for itself? The phrase recurs again at the beginning of *PhG* VII, where Hegel announces that his chapter on religion treats "absolute essence *in and for itself* . . . the self-consciousness of spirit" (363.7–8). Earlier discussions of religion in *PhG*—including the unhappy consciousness, faith in heaven, and Kant's moral world-view—are all "from the *standpoint of consciousness*, which is conscious of absolute essence" (363.6–7). This essence is produced by abstract thinking, which objectifies it into an object beyond the self; so for consciousness this abstract God is other than the actual self.

Although Hegel remains committed to speculation about absolute essence, he criticizes that kind of abstract consciousness whose God is beyond the world. Hegel's own position emerges in *PhG* VII, in which actual human being is not separate from divine substance because "the absolute essence would only have this empty name [of 'absolute'] if in truth there were an *other* for it" (415.23–24). Instead, Hegel understands human subjectivity in its actual existence as the highest development and expression of divine essence. This point of view, set forth in the *Logik*, enables Hegel to surmount the traditional separation between human subject and divine object, or between sensory existence and abstract essence. Hegel's God is not abstract precisely because it exists as the whole material universe along with human spirit, too. Hegel's God is real because its content is the actual world.

Kant for his part recognizes the objectivity of essence inasmuch as universal duty imposes itself on subjective thinking. But this rational essence does not succeed in making itself actual, because of the theoretical separation of reason from nature. This failure to integrate reason with real existence leads to many difficulties in Kant's position. Hegel's criticism of it continues in "Die Verstellung," or "Transposition."

"Transposition" (332–40)

While "The Moral World-View" (324–32) contains Kant's religious postulates and offers critical insights along the way, "Transposition" (332–40) is intended from the start as a severe criticism of Kant's method of arguing. Not all of what Hegel says in "Die Verstellung" can be examined here; its contents are too detailed for a brief treatment. Nor do they need to be examined carefully, for they consist of the same postulates as "The Moral World-View," which has already been discussed. The main difference is that Hegel, in addition to all his previous criticism, analyzes Kant's long argument as nothing but a "transposition" or "Verstellung."

Two common meanings of "verstellen," the verb from which "Verstellung" is derived, are "transpose" (or "displace") and "disguise."[30] Possibly, Hegel alludes to both meanings when he uses "verstellen" or its derivatives.

"Verstellung" is Hegel's term for an indecisive thinking that first affirms and then denies the same proposition. At the beginning of the subdivision on "Verstellung," he describes Kant's moral consciousness in these terms: "consciousness . . . fixes one moment[31] and from there immediately goes over to the other [one] and surmounts the first [one]; but now as it has *posited* [*aufgestellt*] this second [moment] it *also transposes* [*verstellt*] the same [moment] again and rather makes the opposite [one] into essence" (332.28–32). Clearly, the word "verstellen" indicates a negation of some sort, reversing what has just been posited or "aufgestellt."[32] In this passage, "*verstellt*" (332.31) is parallel to "aufhebt," or "surmounts" (332.30), which also has a negative meaning; the two verbs are contrasted with "festsetzt" (332.29) and "*aufgestellt*" (332.31), respectively, both of which suggest positive affirmation. Thus, "verstellen" must indicate a denial or negation of something that has also been affirmed. Another parallel term for "*Verstellen*" (333.1), then, is "contradiction" (332.32), by which Kant's moral consciousness "goes over[33] from one moment *immediately* . . . to the opposite" (333.1–2).

How then should one translate "verstellen"?[34] "Displace" and "conceal" often seem appropriate. Both meanings are suggested by the English term "transpose," which offers a more general meaning along with a good morphological equivalent to "verstellen." Hegel himself explains "verstellt" (338.11) as "anders gestellt" (338.15), which means "put or placed differently"—a general rendering also found in "transpose." The term preserves the logical contrast with what has been "posited" or "aufgestellt" (332.31), as well as suits a passage where neither "displace" nor "conceal" seems to fit: "but in [moral] *acting* itself that position [Stellung] is immediately [changed or] transposed [verstellt]" (333.16–17). Consequently, I prefer to translate "Verstellung" as "transposition" and to let the context provide further nuances.

As indicated above, Hegel uses the term to describe Kant's practice of transposing a position just affirmed, thereby denying it (332.28–32). The positions basically refer to the relative importance given either to the actual moral self or to an absolute essence postulated beyond the self. Kant's indecision wavers between this imagined object "in itself" and the conscious moral subject "for itself."

In the first three paragraphs (332.14–333.35) of Kant's discussion, one finds a convenient description of this problem. According to Hegel, the very postulating of a beyond implicates moral consciousness in a fundamental contradiction. On one hand, "consciousness *itself consciously produces* its object" (332.14–15),[35] carefully thinking it out and giving it a determinate content based on its own human existence. The object, therefore, "no longer goes beyond" (332.21) it as an "alien" (332.16) but is somehow "itself" (332.18). On the other hand, however, consciousness places this object *"outside itself"* as "a beyond" (332.22).[36] Thus, a contradiction in moral consciousness exists, and the whole Kantian "moral world-view is . . . in fact nothing other than the development of this basic contradiction according to its different aspects" (332.25–27).[37] Hegel begins to prove his point by considering "the harmony of morality and nature, the first postulate" (333.10–11).

First, he addresses "the presupposition that there is an actual moral consciousness" (333.8–9). Next, he discusses the movement away from this actual consciousness into a beyond containing "the harmony of morality and nature, the first postulate" (333.10–11). This postulate concerns a "highest good" (334.24) or "ultimate aim of the world" (335.12), an aim that is *"in itself*, . . . not for actual consciousness, not present" (333.11–12) in the empirical world where "*morality*" and sensory "actuality" are "not in harmony" (333.13–14). So far there seems to be no contradiction in Kant's argument, which views moral consciousness as limited by natural existence at the present time and as finding its fulfillment only in a distant future. However, in order to postulate that harmony in the future, Kant has to think of nature both as an adversary of rational morality at the present time and as an ally of it in the future.[38] The object of consciousness then, which is the harmony of nature and morality, is outside the actual present self (whose body belongs to nature) and postulated as existing only beyond the self. Such a beyond is in principle excluded from the real possibilities of the current world.

But moral consciousness can be analyzed from another point of view that has a more coherent meaning; here, the contradiction between the actual self and its beyond comes into view. Since nature gives actual existence to moral aims, it does not limit morality but rather enables morality to fulfill itself. Both components—morality and existence—come together in moral action "for acting is nothing other than the actualization of the inner moral aim" (333.17–18); "acting thus in fact immediately fulfills what . . . was supposed to be only a postulate, only beyond" (333.26–28). Therefore, the object of consciousness, the harmony of nature and morality, is not outside the actual self. Through its reason, the latter already contains morality, and through its natural body is able to transpose its moral aims into real existence. As a result, the human self is the harmony of nature and morality, through its moral action.

And if the harmony of existence and morality occurs in moral action, then "in *acting* itself . . . [there] is immediately transposed [or negated] that position" (333.16–17) of a harmony beyond the acting self. When nature is seen as giving a reality to moral aims instead of interfering with them, a more affirmative view of one's present moral existence is possible. Furthermore, the argument for a postulated beyond loses its force. Evidently Kant's religion requires the view that nature is an enemy of morality, while in the opposing view that nature gives reality to morality there is the basis for another kind of religion, which Hegel considers in *PhG* VII.

There follows a series of conflicting Kantian assertions that illustrate "the basic contradiction" (332.26) between the actual self and a beyond postulated in itself. Discussing Hegel's exposition in detail would be both tedious and unnecessary because the main point of "Transposition" has already been explained, and the particular themes examined in it have already appeared in "The Moral World-View."

In conclusion, Hegel's analysis of Kant is that Kant's "basic contradiction" (332.26) appears to derive from the twofold view of nature (e.g., 339.32–34) held by moral consciousness. Hostile to morality, nature cannot be harmonized with it, and so the harmony must be postulated in an absolute object "in itself" beyond the actual self (339.34–35). But as open to morality, nature can be harmonized with the actual self, whose pure knowing of duty can then be considered absolute (339.35–36).

All the major flaws Hegel finds in Kant's position can likewise be linked to this twofold view of nature. For example, when morality knows its duty as an "*abstract* object of its pure consciousness" (330.34), it views nature as an enemy, which can be overcome only in a postulated beyond. This beyond is obviously a mental image: a postulate is a thought, and a thought affirmed to have real existence beyond the self is what Hegel means by "mental image." Instead of comprehending duty and actuality in a single concept, the two are juxtaposed in a postulate or uncomprehending affirmation.

On the other hand, when nature is viewed as friendly to morality, their harmony is realized in the real world because moral consciousness is then considered able to imprint its aims on sensory actuality. Only with this other view of nature can morality be an absolute law to itself, as well as the principle from which the postulates derive. But if morality is absolute, there is no need for the postulates. The two views of nature then lead again to the "basic contradiction" (332.26) that has just been examined.

They also lead to the "Transposition" that Hegel devotes many pages (332–40) to. Moral consciousness can be absolute only if it controls nature; if it considers nature unmanageable, it postulates this control in a beyond. Each approach transposes or negates the other: when the self is absolute it transposes the importance of a beyond, and when a beyond is absolute it reduces the self. Thus, "Transposition" (like many other themes) appears to derive from Kant's two views of nature. Hegel's criticism of Kant is therefore coherent, founded as it is upon the claim that Kant views nature in contradictory ways.

From Kant to Fichte

Hegel concludes his analysis by showing how Kant's incoherence leads to Fichte. Eventually, consciousness realizes that "placing apart the moments of the *self* and the *in-itself* is not serious" (340.3–4) because the harmony of duty and nature is in the moral self and not somewhere beyond it (340.5–8). Human selfhood now knows that "the placing apart of these moments is a transposition" (340.8–9) of the primacy of moral consciousness. When an imagined object "in itself" is postulated as the harmony of morality and nature, moral consciousness is no longer primary, so that the starting point of Kant's "Moral World-View" is denied or transposed. What is postulated "in itself" as beyond human thinking should rather be affirmed of morality itself, if the latter is to be absolute.

Morality thus gives up its contradictory world-view to declare itself *"pure conscience"* (340.13), a conscience "without . . . those mental images" (340.15) Kant postulates. The self now "is *within itself* simple spirit certain of itself, which [in an] immediate [way] acts conscientiously, and in this immediacy has its truth" (340.14–16). Hegel undoubtedly refers here to Fichte, who succeeded Kant as the outstanding philosopher of German idealism. Hegel's allusion to conscience that acts in an immediate way resembles one of Fichte's theories, according to which conscience is " 'the immediate consciousness of our determinate duty.' "[39]

CONSCIENCE (340–62)[40]

Since *"pure conscience* . . . disdains such a moral world-image" (340.13–14) as one meets in Kant's postulates, one finds no discussion of a beyond in the pages Hegel devotes to conscience. In fact, there is hardly any mention of religious themes at all. However, the same kind of universal thinking that gave rise to Kant's postulates is also present in Fichte's theory of conscience, which therefore has the potential for some religious development. Thus, it is not a complete surprise to read at the very end of Hegel's analysis of conscience, in the section on "Evil and Its Pardon," the following statement: "the reconciling YES . . . is[41] the appearing God among those who know themselves as pure knowing" (362.25, 28–29) or universal thinking. This mention of "the appearing God" is examined later on; at present, it is sufficient to point out that it involves a synthesis of universal thinking with individual subjectivity. Somehow, the two poles of Kant's practical reason—the pure universal and the sensory individual—are brought together in such a way that God is said to appear in human being.

Immediately after that mention of "the appearing God," Hegel begins *PhG* VII ("Die Religion"), which analyzes religion as "absolute essence *in and for itself*, . . . the self-consciousness of spirit" (363.7–8). These phrases refer to the appearance of God in human subjectivity; *PhG* VII discusses incarnational religion. This new point of view derives from the conclusion of "Conscience" (*PhG* VI–C–c), where God appears in human being. The transition to Hegel's chapter on self-conscious religion (*PhG* VII) is clearly supplied by conscience in its final phase of "Evil and Its Pardon."[42]

Even before its final phase, conscience makes human subjectivity the center of its reflection. Hegel's own brief review of religion in the introduction to *PhG* VII indicates the shift from Kant's postulated beyond to the self-centeredness of conscience, where spirit "subjects to itself not only its objective world but also its [mental] image [of a beyond] and its determinate concepts, and is now self-consciousness at home with itself [bey sich seyendes]" (364.21–23). This development occurs inasmuch as Kant's "contradictory movement" (364.14–15) gives way to "the self conscious of itself as the fate of [divine] *essentiality* and [nature's] *actuality*" (364.14–15). In other words, everything hitherto placed outside the self is now centered around the self and its conscience.

There is nothing in Hegel's review (at the beginning of *PhG* VII) to indicate that conscience has a religion of its own. But his fuller analysis of conscience in *PhG* VI–C–c does contain two instances of something like religion. The first one is a cult of conscience worshippers (perhaps intellectuals) who appear midway through Hegel's discussion. The second is "the appearing God among those who know themselves as pure knowing" (362.28–29) at the very end of the chapter, when evil is pardoned. My study examines both of these instances of religion. But since anything is understood better when situated in its context, an overview of the whole development of conscience is the best way to begin.

Summary of Conscience

A helpful guide to its phases is provided by Hegel's title: "[VI–C–]c. Conscience, the Beautiful Soul, Evil and Its Pardon" (340.26–29). From the title alone, one might think that conscience is only the first member of a series continued by different shapes of spirit, namely the beautiful soul and then evil and its pardon. However, the last three shapes all derive from conscience and are to be understood as variant forms of it rather than as distinct shapes in their own right, as the following analysis shows.

For conscience, "pure duty . . . as *pure knowing* [is] nothing other than the *self* of consciousness, and the self of consciousness [is] *being* and *actuality*" (341.8–10); thus, the self "knows its immediate individuality as pure knowing and doing, as the true actuality and harmony" (341.15–16) that Kant postulates beyond the self. This identification of rational duty with immediate being is Fichte's theory of conscience, in which "duty . . . is immediately *actual* [consciousness and] no longer merely abstract pure consciousness" (344.28–29) as it is for Kant.[43] The link between abstract universal duty and determinate individual duty is made internally by individual conviction (347.19–20; 351.33),[44] whose linking of the two is somewhat arbitrary.[45]

One's internal conviction is then externalized by being pronounced before other selves (351.32–37), who are thereby assured that a peculiar act is nevertheless being performed as a universal duty (352.8–10) that they too can identify with. Speaking about one's convictions is, therefore, essential for the individual conscience that expects to live in community with others.[46] They recognize not the determinate individual deed but only the universal duty that motivates it (351.35–27), "for they are just this pure self-knowing and willing" (352.25) of duty, and can recognize themselves only in words expressing this "*necessary universality of the self*" (352.22) rather than in a singular deed peculiar to the individual performing it.

Conscience therefore has two sides, individual action and universal duty, joined arbitrarily by individual conviction and by words expressing this conviction. Since the two sides are not connected by any rational necessity, they soon slip apart into two distinct shapes of consciousness, both of them aware of the distance between universal duty and determinate action by an individual. The first shape is the "beautiful soul" that remains universal by avoiding action, while the second is "evil" that acts for selfish aims while continuing to speak about its universal duty. The reconciliation of the beautiful soul with evil comes about in "pardon," which ends Hegel's discussion of morality and furnishes the transition to self-conscious religion.

But are the beautiful soul and evil variant forms of conscience or something else? The *"beautiful soul"* (355.5) preserves its universality by refusing to act: it "lives in the anxiety of staining the lordship of its inner [thought] by action and existence, and in order to preserve the purity of its heart it flees contact with reality" (354.32–34). Its only "objectivity . . . is its *speech*" (354.24–25) about its moral convictions that, in form at least, are universal. When the beautiful soul is further described as a "lost" (355.3) one that "dies away in itself and disappears like a shapeless vapor" (355.5), Hegel is probably alluding to the poet Novalis who died of tuberculosis in 1801. Nevertheless, this type of soul evidently has no activity other than that of conscience as speaking, and Hegel's text implies that the *"beautiful soul"* (355.5) expresses one "meaning . . . of conscience" (355.8), since the "other meaning" (355.8) is "conscience as acting" (355.9–10) or as evil. I conclude that the beautiful soul is a pure type of the conscience that speaks; it is a variant form of conscience.[47]

"Evil" is a form of conscience also. It is "conscience as *acting*" (355.34; 355.9–10) for a *"selfish* aim" (357.35) that in general derives not from rational and universal duty but from "natural individuality" (355.28).[48] When conscience is interested in the individual, material side of moral action, pure duty judges it as "*evil*, because it is the inequality of its [individual] *being within itself* with the universal; and inasmuch as this [evil consciousness] at the same time pronounces its doing as equality with itself as [universal] duty and conscientiousness, [it is judged] as *hypocrisy*" (356.8–10). What is now called evil and hypocrisy[49] is conscience as individual action, which is now denounced by the beautiful soul (359.30; 360.17). That active type of conscience is considered evil not simply because it acts but because its action is inconsistent with universal duty. Likewise, it is hypocritical because its action is inconsistent with its words about duty.

My brief summary has established that evil and the beautiful soul are shapes of conscience itself. Consequently, their reconciliation in pardon (to be examined later) also belongs to the movement of conscience. And so when Hegel refers to "conscience" at the beginning of his chapter on self-conscious religion (364.21–32), he probably has in mind its whole development, especially evil and its pardon. This conclusion will turn out to be quite important for interpreting Hegel's transition from morality to religion.

That transition also depends of course on "evil and its pardon," which needs to be examined carefully. However, one small matter must first be discussed: Hegel's references to a religion of conscience, which are the only overtly religious passages in the whole analysis of conscience, apart from "the appearing God" (362.28–29) mentioned at the end of the chapter when evil is pardoned.

The Religion of Conscience (352.35–353.35)

Hegel describes this religion in a sardonic way:

> . . . thus conscience, in the majesty of its elevation above determinate law and every content of duty, lays whatever content it likes into its knowing and willing; it is moral genius which knows the inner voice of its immediate knowing as [a] divine voice; and inasmuch as in this knowing it also knows existence immediately, it is divine creative power alive in its concept. (352.35–353.1)

The "inner . . . divine voice" (352.37–38) that Hegel refers to must be the voice of pure duty, or practical reason, that morality considers to be the voice of God; since conscience immediately identifies its determinate sensory existence with pure duty, it "lays whatever content it likes into its [pure] knowing and willing" (352.36).[50] Thus, Hegel calls it "divine creative power alive in its concept" (352.29–353.1), where pure reason is joined to determinate existence.

Furthermore, since reason and existence are joined in conscience because the "inner . . . divine voice" (352.37–38) of duty calls for a determinate moral act, conscience can look upon its behavior as divinely willed. Thus, Hegel describes "the moral genius" (352.37)[51] of conscience as "divine service within itself; for its acting is the viewing of this its own divinity" (353.1–2). This result is to be expected because conscience considers its determinate act to be the immediate expression of its duty, which is pure and divine; the act itself translates this inner viewing of divinity into an external one. For conscience, moral action is equivalent to the liturgy of a church.

Like such a liturgy, "this solitary divine service is at the same time essentially the divine service of a *community*" (353.3–4)[52] whose group spirit consists of "the mutual assurance of their conscientiousness [and] good intentions, the rejoicing over this reciprocal purity and the refreshing [of themselves] at the lordship of knowing and pronouncing [their convictions], of cherishing and cultivating such excellence" (353.13–15). The group admires the divinely inspired behavior of its members who act according to their duty as they see it.

There is more than a little mockery in Hegel's description of this community, as well as in his portrayal of individual conscience as "moral genius" (352.37) aware of its "inner . . . divine voice" (352.37–38). Nevertheless, it is true that this religion of conscience resolves the major difficulty all the religions of consciousness face, namely the difference between an objective "*abstract consciousness*" of "God" (353.16–17, 18) and a subjective "*self-consciousness*" (353.17) or "actual consciousness" (353.19–20). The difference disappears because "in the completion of conscience the distinction between its abstract and its self-consciousness surmounts itself" (353.22–23); conscience "knows that *abstract* consciousness is precisely *this self*" (353.24–25), namely the actual empirical self.

So far the argument links abstract and empirical consciousness through the unity of the self, which as pure thinking and sensory experience is both kinds of consciousness at once. But the argument also links abstract consciousness with divine essence: "God . . . is . . . present" (353.18, 19) for abstract consciousness, which knows "the immediacy of the present essence" (353.21). By means of this abstract consciousness, God is immediately linked to the empirical self. Thus, conscience knows "that in the *immediacy* of the *relation* of the self to the in-itself, which [when] placed outside the self is abstract essence [or God] . . . , the *difference* [between them] is *surmounted*" (353.24–27). In other words, the difference between God and the actual self is obliterated for conscience, which is "the *immediate* relation" (353.29) or "unity" (353.20) of the two. Conscience, therefore, "knows the immediacy of the presence of essence in it as [the] unity of essence and its self, its self therefore as the living [God or essence] in-itself, and this its knowing as religion" (353.31–34). That is why conscience knows its "inner voice" as a "divine voice" (352.37, 38). Pure reason has duty or God for its object; and this thought has an immediate relation with the empirical self.

However, this kind of immediate relation is suspect, precisely because it is immediate. Although Hegel does not directly argue against it here, his apparently scornful description of self-worshipping conscience (352.35–353.2; 353.13–16) does make one think that he is not in complete sympathy with it. This interpretation is confirmed by what Hegel writes next. The fascination conscience has with itself makes it the "poorest shape" (354.8) of consciousness and the "absolute *untruth*" (354.11) because there is nothing for the self to be related to except itself. For conscience, "[absolute] essence is . . . no [essence] *in-itself* but [merely] itself" (354.28). Soon, the self becomes aware of its "emptiness" (355.1) and then it is none other than the "unhappy so-called *beautiful soul*" (355.4–5) already mentioned.

Even though divine essence and the actual self are brought close to one another by conscience, the synthesis is not successful because objective essence disappears in human being. Hegel's reservations about conscience lead one to believe that a proper integration respects the difference between God and the self. In *PhG* VII, "the absolute essence *in and for itself* . . . the self-consciousness of spirit" (363.7–8) will not simply be human self-consciousness, but will also retain the meaning of a universal substance on which human being depends.

Because conscience does not yet provide this point of view, further development is necessary. Hegel provides it in the section called "Evil and Its Pardon," which ends with "God appearing among those who know themselves as pure knowing" (362.28–29).

Evil and Its Pardon (355–62)[53]

"Evil and Its Pardon" describes the reconciliation of two opposing types of conscience. One is "conscience as acting" (355.9–10) for a "selfish aim" (357.35) while claiming to act from "duty and conscientiousness" (356.10); this type of conscience, then, is a singular person acting for individual aims while verbally respecting the universal law of duty. Consequently, it is judged as *"evil"* (356.8) and *"hypocrisy"* (356.10)—not by itself of course, but by its opposite. And this opposite is the second type of conscience, the beautiful soul (359.30; 360.22) that refuses to act because acting would infect its universal thought with material individuality (357.18–24). According to the beautiful soul, action on behalf of universal values is not possible; since action occurs in the realm of natural being, it is presumed to be individual and selfish. As a result, it judges acting conscience as evil for contradicting universal duty, and as hypocritical for pretending to respect it.

According to Hegel, however, "concrete action ... has [both] the universal side ... [of] duty ... [and] the particular [side] which constitutes ... the interest of the individual" (358.6–9), because "duty ... this pure aim ... has its actuality in the deed of individuality" (358.30–31). Therefore, the beautiful soul does not judge human action correctly by condemning the selfish side of it, for the selfish side is intrinsic to every individual action.

By condemning the active type of conscience "this judging consciousness is itself *base*, because it divides action [into universal duty and selfish individuality] and [so] produces its [i.e., action's] inequality with itself and holds fast" (359.3–4) to it. Such a separation of action's two components is the original reason why the beautiful soul considers the active consciousness evil (356.7–9), and now the beautiful soul commits the same fault. And because it does not acknowledge its fault—namely, the evil of its judgment—but instead considers its criticism to be the best kind of human activity (359.5–9), the judging consciousness (or beautiful soul) is no less guilty of *"hypocrisy"* (359.5) than the active one. In other words, the beautiful soul condemns others yet thinks of itself as virtuous; in fact, it is nothing but cynicism, incapable of finding virtue in any kind of purposive behavior.

Both types of conscience, then, separate universal duty from its individual actualization. Each kind of conscience—whether acting or speaking—is, therefore, evil and hypocritical, and mutual hatred is a possible result. However, something quite different occurs: active conscience initiates a movement that includes confession and pardon and terminates in a mention of "the appearing God" (362.28–29). As such, this movement is a very important one that needs to be carefully studied, especially because its conclusion leads into the chapter on incarnational religion.

What then are the significant moments of evil's confession and pardon, and why do they lead to an "appearing God" and a new viewpoint for religion? Answers to these questions are not easy to obtain.[54] The following explanation may, however, come close to Hegel's meaning.

When active conscience discovers the similarity between itself and its critic (359.10–11), it makes a confession (359.14, 24) whose content is hard to discover in Hegel's text.[55] Normally, one confesses a sin or some other kind of wrongdoing, and so one expects active conscience to admit its own evil—an expectation that seems to be met by the formula "*Ich bins*," "*it is I*" (359.24). Although the "*it*" probably refers to individual guilt, this confession of evil has a universal side as well. Recognizing that the beautiful soul is as evil as itself, the evil active conscience confesses something it has in common with its antagonist. In this confession, active conscience is, therefore, "*pronouncing* . . . its equality*" (359.13, 14) with the beautiful soul. It "views itself . . . in the other" (359.34–35) and declares aloud its own share in the similar evil of both.

It follows that by its confession, active conscience has "renounced [its] *isolated being-for-itself* and posited itself as [a] surmounted particularity and hereby as continuity with the other, as universal" (360.2–4; 361.13–14). It reveals itself as a universal thinking, and more precisely as one that sees the universal in real individual existence, because it has discovered the similarity between itself and the beautiful soul. And what it seeks through its confession is the mutually "recognizing existence" (359.16) of "community" (359.26) with the beautiful soul, who is expected to reciprocate with a similar confession (359.14–17, 24–25), so that human social existence may correspond to its universal thought.[56]

And although the beautiful soul at first refuses to accept as an equal the active conscience that confesses (359.24–360.16), eventually it does so[57] because the confessing conscience "which throws away its actuality and makes itself into a *surmounted this*[58] thereby portrays itself in fact as universal; . . . the universal consciousness thus knows itself therein" (361.13–16). When the evil, individual, active conscience portrays itself as universal, it is accepted by the beautiful soul which all along has tried to remain a consciousness of the universal.[59]

The problem then is to explain how it is possible to maintain one's individuality and yet be universal, too. Some help is obtained from the following passage: "this [active evil conscience] which throws away its actuality and makes itself into a *surmounted this* thereby portrays itself in fact as universal; it turns back from its external actuality into itself as essence; the universal consciousness thus knows itself therein" (361.13–16). The active conscience knows itself as resembling the beautiful soul and, therefore, as universal; if it knows universality, then it must be a universal thinking.

For its part, the beautiful soul, hearing its own universal thinking echoed in the confession of active conscience, pardons its antagonist (361.16) and "recognizes as good" what it formerly called "evil" (361.19). In fact, what has come to be is the identity of both because the individual consciousness also knows the universal, while the universal consciousness also knows the individual (or "evil") side of human action. That is why the individual and the universal conscience, "different" (362.2) as they are, can nevertheless see themselves in one another. Thus, in confession and pardon there is "a mutual recognizing" (361.25) of the other.[60] Each consciousness previously acknowledged only one side of the other, but now they both obtain a more total view.

Hegel attaches great importance to this "mutual recognizing"; he calls it "*absolute spirit*" (361.25) and then "the appearing God among those who know themselves as pure knowing" (362.28–29).[61] Therefore, one needs to understand as accurately as possible the "reconciliation" (361.22) that has taken place.

Two human beings, each one having a different self-understanding, not only accept one another, but also know their own selves in the other person (359.10–11; 361.15–16, 23–25). Nevertheless, they remain "different" (362.2) types of consciousness (and conscience): one is individual and active, while the other is universal and contemplative.[62]

The first consciousness "knows itself to be essence[63] as absolute *individuality* of self" (361.29–30); it is "absolute discreteness which ... knows ... itself absolute in its pure oneness" (361.32–33; 362.9). When it makes its confession, it still "has ... its aim in its *being-within-*

itself" (361.36–37), a phrase that refers first of all to individual subjectivity as opposed to the knowing of universal (362.22–24) duty
(361.35), and second to individual subjectivity as itself "universal . . .
because of the purity of its" (362.24, 25) thought. Without this universal thinking, the evil consciousness could never discover its likeness to
the beautiful soul.

The second consciousness is the beautiful soul, knowing itself as
"duty" (361.28, 35) or "universal" (361.30; 362.8) thinking, which at
first knows the individual consciousness as evil (361.30–31). But then
this universal thinking discovers that individual subjectivity is itself
"universal" (362.25) "because of the purity of its" (362.24) universal
thinking; the beautiful soul then becomes "universal *self*-knowing in
its *absolute opposite*" (362.22–23), recognizing itself in the so-called
evil or individual consciousness. Its knowing of self in its opposite
corresponds to the way individual consciousness knows itself in its
other too, namely in that same beautiful soul that recognizes only the
universal.

Both know themselves in the other only because "they know themselves as pure knowing" (362.29), which is the pure thinking of universality. Even though both kinds of consciousness are "different"
(362.2)—so different in fact that Hegel calls their opposition "absolute" (361.28) and their knowing of one another a "*consciousness*"
(362.15) of something other than oneself—"the movement of this
opposition" (362.16–17) nevertheless turns this consciousness of the
other into "*self-consciousness*" (362.16) or a knowing of one's *self* in
the other, "for this opposition is itself rather the *indiscrete continuity*
and *equality* of I=I"[64] (362.17–18). When a self "still resists its
equality with the other" (362.19–20), its thinking universality contradicts itself (362.29) because each self is "universal" (362.25) knowing.
And so "each [one] *for itself*" (362.18) resolves its contradiction and
"surmounts itself in itself" (362.20–21) through confession and pardon. Each one then recognizes itself in the other, so that the spatial
duality of self and other "returns . . . into the unity of the *self*"
(362.21–22), which is "the *actual I*, universal *self*-knowing in its
absolute opposite, in the knowing [that] is *within itself*" (362.22–24)
or individual. In simpler terms, each person recognizes its likeness to
the other; as a result, individual self-knowing is also universal.

One then observes two spatially separated selves not only expressing their sameness through language but also knowing their own subjectivity in the other subject; their "reconciling YES . . . is the *existence* of the I extended [out] to duality, [yet] which remains equal to itself therein, and in its complete renunciation and opposite has the certainty of itself" (362.25–28). Expressing itself through each individual subject is the same universal common to both.

But what exactly is this universal? It is more than a universal human form or essence because the latter by itself is not the ultimate essence of universal being. According to Hegel's *Logik*, divine essence is the underlying dialectical agent that produces human essence and existence. Thus, the essence that appears to human subjectivity is ultimately divine; this is the essence that *pure* knowing knows. Therefore, the "reconciling YES" (362.25) of confession and pardon is "the appearing God among those who know themselves as pure knowing" (362.28–29).

"The Appearing God" (362.28–29)

Hegel's discussion of "Morality" (*PhG* VI–C) concludes with a theophany that supplies the transition to his chapter on "Religion" (*PhG* VII). Even if the individual consciousness is not thinking of God at all,[65] the beautiful soul undoubtedly is, and recognizes the God it knows in the universal thinking of individual consciousness. Indeed, the beautiful soul probably views that universal thinking *as* the human appearance of God in human form; the universal does appear as human thinking, which is universal in form but individual in its material existence. Thus, the universal object of consciousness is now identified with a singular subjectivity that thinks universally and portrays itself as universal (361.13–15). Through individual thinking, universal divine essence appears in individual human existence. The object of the beautiful soul[66] then is no longer the pure God of its universal thinking, but rather God now present as the individual active conscience. As Hegel later states in his analysis of the incarnation, the *"universal itself"* (406.2) is the hidden God, while through the incarnation *"this pure universal* is however revealed as *self"* (406.3). Hegel prepares for this later incarnation in *PhG* VII–C by the present reconciliation of the beautiful soul and active conscience (at the end of *PhG* VI–C). Here, the beautiful soul's consciousness of universality identifies itself with

the individual subjectivity of human action because the latter's "confession" shows it to be a universal thinking, too.

One can interpret this reconciliation as a kind of incarnational insight not only because Hegel mentions here "the appearing God"
(362.28–29), but also because he later (in *PhG* VII–C) likens the
appearance of God in "Evil and Its Pardon" to the presence of the Holy
Spirit in the Christian church (419.38–420.8). The dialectical identity
of God and human being is already established by the reconciliation of
universal consciousness and individual consciousness, because this
reconciliation identifies a universal thinking whose object is God with
a self-centered thinking whose object is individual human existence.

As "pure knowing" (362.29), the two types of thinking are the same.
Their identity constitutes a new phenomenological object: in its pure
universal knowing, individual subjectivity is "the appearing God"
(362.28–29) or "*absolute spirit*" (361.25), since this universal knowing is "the pure knowing of self as *universal* essence" (361.23). Hegel's
argument turns upon this equation of objective essence with subjective
knowing in the beautiful soul.[67] If universal knowing is also objective
divine essence, the latter can be identified with individual subjectivity
in the "mutual recognition" (361.25) described here. Thus God appears as human subjectivity, and a new chapter begins.

NOTES

1. Since the opposition of morality and sensuality occurs in Fichte (Solomon, p. 571) and in Kant, Solomon (pp. 564–75) thinks that Fichte is also
in view whenever Hegel criticizes Kant (*PhG* 324–40). This may well be
true. However, a neater sequence is obtained if one assumes that Fichte
first appears on the phenomenological stage as conscience (*PhG* 340–62),
which certainly does allude to him (as even Solomon, p. 575, admits).

2. Although Hegel stresses knowing in his introduction to "Morality," his
reference to a "knowing will" (324.24) indicates that morality also intends action.

3. For some references to faith in Kant's own writings on moral philosophy,
see *Kant's Werke*, vol. 4: *Grundlegung zur Metaphysik der Sitten* (Berlin:
Georg Reimer, 1911), 462.33; vol. 5: *Kritik der praktischen Vernunft*
(Berlin: Georg Reimer, 1913), 126.10–11; 142.2; 146.5–6. These four
references may be found in the English translations of Lewis White Beck,

collected in a single volume, *Critique of Practical Reason and Other Writings in Moral Philosophy* (Chicago: University of Chicago Press, 1949), pp. 116, 229, 245, 247.

4. In Hegel's German, there is a verbal similarity between *"Gewissen"* (*"conscience"*) and *"gewisse"* (*"certain"*). Conscience feels certain of its truth. But certainty or "Gewißheit" is not yet "Wahrheit" or truth. In Hegel, "certainty" seems to be a subjective confidence that needs objective confirmation in order to become "truth." Even the unhappy consciousness had "certainty" (131.30–31) without truth. Indeed, the whole *PhG* moves from sensory certainty to absolute knowing only through an objectively necessary development of consciousness.

5. See Hyppolite, pp. 453–74; Kainz, 2: 92–107; Kojève, pp. 148–49 (very sketchy); Lauer, pp. 213–21; Solomon, pp. 564–75.

6. My study observes the following system to refer to parts of *PhG*: chapter, division, subdivision, section, and subsection. Thus *PhG* VI is a chapter, VI–C is a division of it, while VI–C–a & VI–C–b are subdivisions, and so on.

7. Although Hegel does not name Kant as the object of this chapter, he uses a famous "Kantian expression" in 332.27–28. One could also identify Kant in this chapter of *PhG* from Hegel's remarks on Kant in his *Vorlesungen über die Geschichte der Philosophie*. But he does not follow Kant literally; he reinterprets his famous predecessor (Kainz, 2: 95–96 and n. 180) so thoroughly that his allusions are not always clear (Kainz, 2: 92).

8. For the connection of absolute essence and pure consciousness, see *Kant's Werke*, 4: 408.37–409.3. Beck translates Kant as follows: "But when do we have the concept of God as the highest good? Solely from the idea of moral perfection which reason formulates *a priori* and which it inseparably connects with the concept of a free will" (p. 68).

9. For being as contained in thought, see also 326.19–25; 331.5–7; 364.30–32.

10. In *PhG* VI–C, "part" is used to designate one of the postulates: a divine consciousness that is "the last part of the moral world-view" (330.19). Another passage refers to the "parts" (330.30) of Kant's content; see also 331.7.

11. G. W. F. Hegel, *Werke*, TWA, 20: 367.

12. See Lauer, p. 214: morality is authentic freedom because moral obligation is self-obligation. See also Hyppolite, p. 475.

13. Nature is said to be *"without significance,"* *"bedeutungslose,"* because it is immoral and irrational.

14. The same opposition between thinking and existence is found in Kant's *Kritik der reinen Vernunft*. Thus, Hyppolite can say that Hegel's criticism of Kant on this point is aimed not only at his moral philosophy, but also at his whole system (Hyppolite, pp. 466, 468). Hyppolite also points out that for Kant, the relation of pure thinking to being or existence is "dialectic" and the source of confusion and error (pp. 467–68). For Hegel, pure thinking truly knows being. See also his discussion of Kant and Anselm in *Vorlesungen*, vol. 5: *VPR* Teil 3, *Die vollendete Religion*, ed. Jaeschke pp. 5–12, 108–19.

15. My translation slightly alters Hegel's words in order to emphasize what I understand to be his point.

16. The following remark by Hyppolite (p. 469) is illuminating: "Before acting, I can *believe* in this harmony; but when I act, I actualize it." Thus, Kant's faith in a future harmony corresponds to a thinking that has not yet acted rather than to a thinking that has been active in the world. For Kant, holiness lies in the will rather than in its deeds (Kainz, 2: 103).

17. Transposing it into a beyond does not eliminate the contradiction, however.

18. Kant uses the phrase "kingdom of God" in his *Kritik der praktischen Vernunft*. See *Kant's Werke*, 5: 128.1, 22; 5: 137.1–2. See also Beck's translation, pp. 231, 239.

19. As rational thought, these aims are universal. When applied to real existence, though, they also become individual or singular. But universal aims are not limited by their individual realizations, which actualize pure duty (334.9–11) or the universal good in a specific situation.

20. The term "immortality" is not found in Hegel's discussion of Kant in *PhG*, but it does appear in his lectures on Kant. See *Werke*, TWA, 20: 369–70. In *PhG*, Hegel says only that Kant's argument forces "consciousness . . . to always make progress in morality" (327.33–34). For Kant's own argument, see *Kant's Werke*, 5: 122–24, especially 122.17–21; Beck, pp. 225–27.

21. Hegel refers to this argument of Kant in *PhG* 329.22–24, but only as accomplishing the final aim of the world envisioned by the first postulate. God cannot bring about the harmony in the self as envisioned by the second postulate since such a harmony would nullify Kant's argument for the soul's immortality (327.23–328.15); the soul must live forever precisely because it must always strive for this unattainable harmony of its morality with its sensual existence.

22. According to Emanuel Hirsch, "Die Beisetzung der Romantiker in Hegels Phänomenologie: Ein Kommentar zu dem Abschnitte über die Moralität," *Deutsche Vierteljahrschrift für Literaturwissenschaft und*

Geistesgeschichte, 2 (1924): 512, Hegel misrepresents Kant on this point, which corresponds more to Fichte.

23. If nature is opposed to morality, a harmony between them should be impossible even in the future. What Kant says about the self's infinite progress toward its own harmony of morality and nature should also apply to the world itself.

24. By "absolute concept," Hegel must mean a concept that synthesizes abstract thought and the actual world. In such a concept, being or existence would be completely thinkable or transparent to reason, at least in principle. Hegel may not mean that everything about nature needs to be understood by the "absolute concept"; however, he does seem to mean that in such a concept the connection of thought and being would be clear.

25. This "last part" must be the postulate of a divine moral consciousness, which is the third and final postulate of Kant's moral world-view.

26. Hegel's use of the term "Vorstellung" must allude to Kant's use of it, as 331.8–10 clearly suggests. Kant probably uses it to denote a thought or idea, but in Hegel the term is pejorative because it denotes a failure of conceptual synthesis.

27. And yet what is postulated is a divine consciousness! Hegel's terminology here is compelling evidence for the interpretation that the idea of a divine consciousness (as in Kant and Christian theology) is for him no consciousness at all, but only the idea of it. For Hegel, divine consciousness must then be found in human consciousness alone, as the differentiation (and existence) of divine essence.

28. The immutable God of the unhappy consciousness is abstract and therefore opposed to the world of sensual existence.

29. Hegel points out that the unhappy consciousness is itself immutable (by its capacity to comprehend its immutable God?) but does not realize this truth and so considers itself the opposite of its abstract immutable God (122.20–23).

30. In Campe's dictionary, which is contemporary with Hegel, the first meaning (1) of "verstellen" is "anders stellen" or "transpose" (or "displace"). "Dissimulate," also in (1), is said to be an "uneigentliche Bedeutung" and is used only reflexively. Still another meaning relevant to Hegel's use of the term is (3), "falsch stellen" or "misplace." See Joachim Heinrich Campe, *Wörterbuch der Deutschen Sprache*, Fünfter und letzter Theil (Braunschweig: in der Schulbuchhandlung, 1811), s.v., "Verstellung."

31. The "moments" are probably (from Hegel's later reference) "the moments of the *self* and the [object] *in itself*" (340.4).

32. Cf. the similar contrast between "aufgestellt" and "negirt" (364.14) at the beginning of *PhG* VII.

33. Hegel also uses more pejorative terms for the movement of Kant's argument: "sich herumtreibt" (336.37) and "fortwälzt" (330.32; other verbal forms appear in 334.38 and 335.10).
34. Hyppolite (p. 467) translates "Verstellung" as "déplacement"; Lauer (p. 218), as "Dissimulation"; Kainz (2: 101), as "Dissemblance or Duplicity." Each of them, of course, recognizes the multiple meanings of this German word.
35. Probably the various postulates of practical reason, which soon lead consciousness to a world beyond this one.
36. As Kainz points out, Kant's grounding of God in morality is "ambivalent" because morality later has to be grounded in God (2: 100–101).
37. According to Hyppolite, the "fundamental contradiction . . . of the whole Kantian system . . . , according to Hegel" (p. 468), is that the rational self is supposed to be autonomous and free (p. 454) and yet it postulates its truth beyond itself (p. 468).
38. Although Kant seems to have two different views of nature, they might be combined into the single idea of a nature that is gradually subdued by moral reason. Yet even if this idea could be justified, there would still remain the contradiction that morality is supposed to subdue a nature that must always resist it. For this contradiction, see 328.2–11.
39. Quoted by Copleston, 7: 65.
40. See Hyppolite, pp. 475–510; Kainz, 2: 107–24; Kojève, pp. 149–54, 157, 195; Lauer, pp. 221–29; Solomon, pp. 575–79, 622–25. Hirsch's article (see above, n. 22) is a masterly study of Hegel's allusions to German Romanticism in this part of *PhG*. A brief summary of Hirsch's identifications may be found in Ernst Behler, "Friedrich Schlegel und Hegel," *Hegel-Studien* 2 (1963): 205. For an earlier version of my discussion of "Conscience," see Daniel P. Jamros, " 'The Appearing God' in Hegel's *Phenomenology of Spirit*," *CLIO* 19 (1990): 353–65.
41. The precise appearance of God consists of what the principal characters have "among" (362.29) themselves, namely the "reconciling YES" (362.25) of mutual acceptance.
42. Like all the religions that have preceded, conscience derives from universal thinking. But unlike them, conscience identifies its universal thought (divine essence) with individual human existence.
43. Yet it is not only Fichte whom Hegel has in mind here. According to Hyppolite (p. 488) and *GW* 9: 517 (note to 344.17–18), the paragraph just quoted from also contains a clear allusion to Jacobi.
44. A theme found in Goethe (Kainz, 2: 111 n. 211) and Fichte (Kainz, 2: 113 n. 216), among others.

45. Hegel's analysis clearly suggests that conscience raises individual bias into a universal norm and, therefore, deludes itself about its moral worth. Lauer's explanation (pp. 222–25) of Hegel's critique is especially clear, as is Solomon's (pp. 566–67).

46. Fichte grounds the church on the sharing of common convictions (Kainz, 2: 114 n. 220; 2: 115 n. 223).

47. Although the beautiful soul was a standard literary figure around 1800, giving rise to a "literature of the self" (Hyppolite, p. 495), it is difficult to link precise texts from this literature to precise passages in Hegel. According to Hyppolite, important figures like Schiller, Jacobi, Schleiermacher, Goethe, and Novalis all contributed to the literary theme of the beautiful soul (pp. 496–97). But the only precise allusion he identifies in Hegel's text is to Novalis's writings (p. 499). Hegel himself in his *Aesthetik* refers to the beautiful soul in Jacobi's *Woldemar*, but in a way that offers no help to the reader of *PhG*; see *Hegel's Aesthetics*, trans. T. M. Knox, 1: 241–42. Hirsch (p. 520) points out that Hegel in his *Vorlesungen über die Geschichte der Philosophie* (S. W. 15, 644) refers to Novalis as a "beautiful soul" (TWA, 20: 418).

48. This evil conscience is Friedrich Schlegel, according to Hirsch (p. 522), who points out that Hegel's *Vorlesungen über die Geschichte der Philosophie* (S. W. 15, 642) attributes evil's hypocrisy (*GW* 9: 356.10) to Schlegel; TWA 20: 416. Behler seems to support this identification (p. 208); he also thinks that Hegel's interpretation has little support in Schlegel's own texts.

49. Behler suggests Schleiermacher's *Vertraute Briefe über Lucinde* for the hypocrisy Hegel had in mind (p. 207). But this identification is unconvincing. Since Behler (p. 201) follows Hirsch (p. 523) in identifying evil's confession as Schlegel's *Lucinde*, Schleiermacher's "hypocritical" defense of it would have to follow the confession. In Hegel's text, however, hypocrisy (*GW* 9: 356–57) precedes confession (*GW* 9: 359). Hirsch (p. 522) links evil's hypocrisy to Schlegel himself and finds no allusion to Schleiermacher (pp. 524–25) in Hegel's discussion of conscience.

50. Cf. the last paragraph of Goethe's *Bekenntnisse einer schönen Seele* (Book VI of *Wilhelm Meisters Lehrjahre*): "I hardly recall a commandment; nothing appears to me in the shape of a law. There is an instinct which guides me and always leads me right. I follow my opinions with freedom and know as little of constraint as of remorse." The German passage is quoted in Prof. Dr. Franz Schulz, *Klassik und Romantik der Deutschen*, II. Teil, *Wesen und Form der Klassisch-Romantischen Literatur* (Stuttgart: J. B. Metzlersche Verlagsbuchhandlung, 1959 [earlier eds. 1952, 1940]), p. 278. For an English translation, see J. W. von Goethe,

Wilhelm Meister's Apprenticeship, trans. Thomas Carlyle (1824); reprint ed., Harvard Classics (New York: P. F. Collier & Son, 1917), p. 421.

51. An allusion to Jacobi's *Woldemar*, according to Hirsch, p. 517.

52. Fichte wrote about community and recognition; see Copleston, 7: 69, 71, 74. But perhaps Hegel is referring to some literary group or fictional situation that one cannot identify precisely today. Although Hirsch establishes a number of connections between early German Romanticism and Hegel's treatment of "Conscience," many questions of identification still remain.

53. See Hyppolite, pp. 500–10; Kojève, pp. 147, 152–54, 157, 195; Lauer, pp. 228–29; Solomon, pp. 577–79, 622–25; Hirsch, pp. 520–25.

54. One of the reasons for this difficulty is people's ignorance of the precise historical or fictional situation Hegel had in mind. Hyppolite writes of "the ambiguity of this Hegelian dialectic of the remission of sins"— ambiguous because of the multiple interpretations possible for its concrete reference (pp. 501, 506). Kojève however has no such hesitation, linking "Evil and Its Pardon" to Napoleon (see below, "*The Appearing God*"); but such a reference is far from certain.

55. For Hirsch, who identifies the evil conscience as Friedrich Schlegel, there is no such problem; the confession is with "no doubt" (Hirsch, p. 522) Schlegel's *Lucinde*, published in 1799. Based on Schlegel's affair with Dorothea Veit, this autobiographical novel (or confession) rejects the chaste love portrayed by the beautiful soul of Jacobi's *Woldemar*; see *Friedrich Schlegel's Lucinde and the Fragments*, trans. with an introduction by Peter Firchow (Minneapolis: University of Minnesota Press, 1971), pp. 21, 24. In his *Aesthetics* (trans. T. M. Knox, 1: 508), Hegel refers to *Lucinde*'s "depravity."

56. Although the beautiful soul never seems to make this confession, it does give itself up (361.17–22) when it pardons evil (361.16). Perhaps a confession by the beautiful soul is lacking because such an act would simply acknowledge another evil. In pardon one gets instead a recognition of the good universal in individual existence.

57. Since the beautiful soul that refuses to accept the confession goes mad and apparently dies of consumption (360.28–30), the acceptance must be made by another beautiful soul. The one who dies may well be the same one whom Hegel alludes to earlier (355.5) and whom both Hirsch (p. 520) and Hyppolite (*Structure*, p. 499) identify as Novalis. But then Hegel's reference to madness (360.28) is puzzling since the poet who verged on insanity was Hölderlin and not Novalis. Perhaps Hegel is referring to both of them as two instances of a single type. His *Vorlesungen über die*

Geschichte der Philosophie (TWA 20: 418) makes the same slight distinction between Novalis's "yearning" and someone else's "madness." Hirsch (p. 524) considers Hölderlin more likely than Novalis for a hardhearted refusal of community. Chronologically, both fit: Novalis died of tuberculosis in 1801, and Hölderlin's madness began in 1802.

58. I.e., its individuality is surmounted (360.2–4). Similar terminology is used to refer to the risen Jesus in *PhG* VII–C: his "immediate existence" is "surmounted" (415.8–9, 10) by "the constituting of a community" (415.13–14).

59. Kainz notes a certain parallel to Goethe's *Bekenntnisse einer schönen Seele*, in which the "beautiful soul" recognizes her own potential for sin after hearing the confession of an older friend named Philo (Kainz 2: 122 n. 237). But the parallel is incomplete: Philo's confession (p. 395 in the English edition; see above, n. 50) is not made because he considers the beautiful soul a partner in his evil; Goethe's "beautiful soul" does not see her friend as an instance of universal thinking, which for Hegel is the main point.

60. Hirsch (p. 525) identifies the forgiving consciousness as Hegel himself, whose "highest philosophical thought unifies the Romantic consciousness [that has been] torn apart within itself." This may be correct; as far as I know, no other contemporary figure has been proposed. But one should be cautious about identifying Hegel with pardon at this point in *PhG*. Evil's confession and its pardon occur through a "pure knowing" (362.29) that will be surmounted by incarnational religion in *PhG* VII, which in turn will be surpassed by the "Absolute Knowing" of Hegel's philosophy in *PhG* VIII. The reconciliation found in this pardon is, therefore, a limited figure of consciousness; it is not the "highest philosophical thought" of Hegelian dialectic at the time of *PhG*.

A second reason for caution is Hegel's later comment on *Lucinde* (according to Hirsch, the real historical phenomenon corresponding to evil's confession) in his *Aesthetics*, in which he hardly sounds like someone who has forgiven Schlegel's confession. In reference to another work, Hegel says that in it "moral depravity was not made into something sacred and of the highest excellence as it was at the time of Friedrich von Schlegel's *Lucinde*" (trans. Knox, 1: 508). While this remark identifies Schlegel's *Lucinde* as evil, it hardly portrays Hegel as the forgiving, beautiful soul. But Hegel might well be the one who interprets that forgiveness (by someone else) as "the appearing God" needed for *PhG* VII.

61. Solomon (pp. 578, 622–25) suggests that the beautiful soul who forgives

evil is Jesus himself. But forgiveness is expected from any follower of Jesus; there is no difficulty in supposing that a beautiful soul inspired by Fichte's theory of conscience would also be a forgiving Christian. Furthermore, "Evil and Its Pardon" has God appearing only in pure knowing (362.28–29), which is precisely the deficiency (364.21–26) remedied by the incarnation in *PhG* VII. Thus Jesus, who is God in the flesh rather than in pure thinking alone, appears in *PhG* VII but not in *PhG* VI. Hirsch (pp. 527–29) observes that although Hegel's early essays consider the beautiful soul as the highest consciousness and identify Jesus with it, *PhG* VI views the beautiful soul as a limited consciousness and does not at all identify Jesus with it.

62. Kojève thinks the active conscience is Napoleon, while the forgiving conscience is Hegel himself, the philosopher who understands the universal significance of Napoleon (pp. 95, 147, 152–53, 157, 195). Kojève writes: "C'est la *réalité* de Napoleon *révélée* par Hegel qui est le *erscheinender Gott*" (p. 157). Yet the only demonstrable connection between Napoleon and Hegel's discussion of conscience is the French saying, "No man is a hero to his valet" (*PhG* 358.32–359.2; see also the corresponding note, *GW* 9: 518), which Napoleon may have made famous (Hyppolite, p. 504, calls it a "parole de Napoléon," but according to Bartlett it was known a century earlier). There seems to be no more concrete evidence for identifying Hegel's analysis of the active conscience with Napoleon. And did the Emperor ever confess his likeness to the beautiful soul's wicked side?

63. Here, the term "essence" may simply refer to a value rather than to a universal form. On the other hand, the individual consciousness may possibly be affirming the universal (and essential) reality of singular individuality.

64. The formula "I=I" is attributed to Fichte in Hegel's *Vorlesungen über die Geschichte der Philosophie*. See *Werke*, TWA, 20: 394–95.

65. The precise universal it thinks may only be its own likeness to other humans.

66. In "Absolute Knowing," the beautiful soul is recalled as the type of consciousness that identifies objective universal essence with an individual's pure universal knowing (426.11–14), and thus as the thinking through which divine essence views itself (426.1–3). The beautiful soul (425.37) thereby provides the subjective thinking of spirit's absolute knowing (425.29, 33); religion provides the objective content (425.23–26). See Brito, pp. 169–71.

67. When Hegel in "Absolute Knowing" reviews earlier shapes of conscious-

ness, he calls the beautiful soul's pure knowing (425.37–426.2) "not only the [human] viewing of the divine, but the [divine] self-viewing of that same [divine essence]" (426.2–3). Unlike the initial shape of conscience, which identifies its immediate individual existence with universal essence, the beautiful soul finds essence in its pure individual knowing.

CHAPTER IV

RELIGION

AFTER "MORALITY" COMES "Religion." This chapter uses the concept
of spirit developed by morality's final phase, "Evil and Its Pardon"
(419.39–420.1), which identifies universal essence with human subjectivity. Religion itself has appeared earlier, but not in this new shape of
spirit. True to his principle of establishing a new object of consciousness from the development of subjective knowing (60.5–7), Hegel now
has in view a complex object: spirit understood as divine essence
incarnate in individual thinking. The object is developed by conscience, where pure knowing is both universal divine essence and
individual human subjectivity. This identification provides a new object for consciousness, namely God as human subjectivity; it also
defines a new[1] type of consciousness, religion as incarnational. Since
human subjectivity now belongs within its divine object, spirit acquires
a new meaning, too. It is not simply the social world of human community (as in *PhG* VI), but more fundamentally divine essence itself,
which knows itself in human subjectivity and which seeks an external
shape adequate to its knowing. When *PhG* VII begins, divine essence
has already appeared as human thinking. This meaning of "spirit" is
presupposed throughout "Die Religion." The chapter moves forward
by developing the external objects in which spirit (divine essence as
human inwardness) recognizes itself.

The following careful examination of Hegel's text, which is very
dense and detailed, verifies these general remarks.

128

HEGEL'S INTRODUCTION TO "DIE RELIGION" (362-68)

Hegel begins *PhG* VII[2] by announcing that it treats religion from a new standpoint:

> In the former shapes which in general differentiate themselves as *consciousness, self-consciousness, reason* and *spirit, religion* has of course also come forth on the whole as consciousness of *absolute essence*; but only from the *standpoint of consciousness* which is conscious of absolute essence; in those forms however [there] has not appeared absolute essence *in and for itself*; [there has] not [appeared] the self-consciousness of spirit. (363.3–8)

Two broad types of religion are thus distinguished: one is a "consciousness of *absolute essence*"; the other is a "self-consciousness of spirit" or "absolute essence *in and for itself.*" Both types are described in terminology that needs to be explained.

By the "consciousness of *absolute essence*," Hegel refers to religious recognition of a transcendent God who is beyond the real world and human being. Evidence for this interpretation is found in Hegel's analysis of the unhappy consciousness, which does not know "the immutable *in and for itself*"[3] but only as an "immutability of consciousness, which [immutability] consequently . . . is still afflicted with an opposite" (123.34, 32–33), namely, the mutable human consciousness opposed to divine immutability. A similar statement is also found in Hegel's analysis of Christian faith in heaven, which is "*religion . . .* not yet . . . *in and for itself*" (287.7, 8–9), but only "pure consciousness" of "*substance*" or "*essence*" (287.35, 36, 37); this faith "still has the determinacy of [being an] opposite to actuality as *this* [worldly kind] in general and to that [actuality] of [human] self-consciousness in particular" (287.38–288.1).[4] Both the unhappy consciousness and faith in heaven are examples of religion "from the *standpoint of consciousness*" (363.6) because they are conscious of an "*absolute essence*" (363.5) opposed to human consciousness. In this type of religion, consciousness has its precise meaning: awareness of an object opposed to conscious knowing or subjectivity (59.31–32; 369.6).

Therefore, the second type of religion must be the kind that overcomes this opposition between divine essence and human being. "Absolute essence" is known "*in and for itself*" (363.7) when it is no longer "afflicted with an opposite" (123.33), or when actually existing human being understands itself as a differentiation of divine objectivity (as in the absolute idea of Hegel's *Logik*). Then divine essence "in itself" is known as containing human subjectivity, whose being "for itself" is the way in which deity is "for itself." More precisely, human subjectivity's universal thinking is what enables divine essence to be "for itself" in human being, as the end of "Evil and its Pardon" makes clear: when individual human being thinks universally, it is the appearance of universal divine essence—"the appearing God" (362.28–29) of conscience. Divine essence is "for itself" in this universal thinking, which it determines and in which it appears.

This development has important consequences for Hegel's argument. It indicates that the fundamental theme of *PhG* VII consists of the different stages of divine incarnation[5] in the history of religion. This new object (God incarnate) appears as human subjectivity. However, the object also appears as a subject in its own right since human subjectivity is the appearance of divine essence. When Hegel calls absolute essence "in and for itself," he means that such an essence has its own logic "in itself" and still remains "for itself" when appearing as human being. Absolute essence possesses itself in the latter's thinking, and so is truly "for itself" in its human manifestation. God is the hidden agent who controls human history and who appears (in the incarnation) as the true subject of human subjectivity.

Such a religion can also be called "the self-consciousness of spirit" (363.7–8): "self-consciousness"[6] because divine essence knows itself through human thinking; only then is it "spirit," which Hegel defines as "*essence* . . . which *essentially* assumes human shape" (387.26–27) or as "essence which essentially is *self-consciousness*" (405.25).[7] Substance acquires this consciousness of itself when it appears as human consciousness. And then it no longer appears as a divine object facing human consciousness but as an object that knows itself through human consciousness. The precise meaning of consciousness as an *opposition* between human subject and divine object no longer applies when the object appropriates human subjectivity; thus, the second type of religion is no longer "from the *standpoint of consciousness*" (363.6), but from the standpoint of *self*-consciousness. This kind of self-consciousness in religion is possible only when substance attains the level of absolute spirit[8] because only then does it appear as human self-consciousness.

And this knowing of spirit is not merely a subjective one. When Hegel calls it "absolute essence *in and for itself*" (363.7), he places everything, including human subjectivity, within absolute essence. This development of the object vanquishes the independence of human subjectivity. Human consciousness views its incorporation[9] into God, who then has no opposite; as Hegel writes later on about the alleged fall of human being, "the absolute essence would only have this empty name [of absolute] if in truth there were an *other* than it, if there were a *falling away* from it" (415.23–24).[10] Clearly, Hegel's view is that *everything* must belong to divine essence.

Initially, however, religion does not have an objective divine essence that includes everything. Because the concept of spirit is constituted by "pure knowing" (362.9, 10, 24, 29) in conscience, the divine objectivity has only an intellectual relation to human subjectivity, and so excludes empirical human existence.

As the immediate successor of conscience in its concluding shape of evil and its pardon, incarnational religion begins its development as a pure intellectual knowing. Hegel acknowledges this deficiency. In conscience, spirit "has . . . for itself, as *object imagined*, the significance of being universal spirit which contains within itself all essence and all actuality . . . enclosed in it . . . just in the way as when we say *all actuality*; it is universal actuality [as] *thought*" (364.23–25, 30, 31–32). Spirit is therefore (as conscience) the thinking of all reality, "but it is not in the form of free actuality or of independently appearing nature" (364.25–26)—a phrase that means that spirit's abstract thought does not yet include its empirical being.

What Hegel writes about conscience is also true of incarnational religion at the beginning of its development: "in religion" spirit "does not have the form of free *other-being*" (364.33, 34) in empirical existence; "in religion spirit knowing itself is immediately[11] its own pure *self-consciousness*" (364.17–18), a pure thinking abstracted from spirit's empirical being. In religion, spirit's real "*existence*" is therefore "distinguished from its *self-consciousness*,[12] and its own actuality falls outside of religion" (364.34–36). In other words, because God is humanity's universal thinking but not its real existence, "religion" and spirit's "life in its actual world" (364.37, 38) are different (365.18–19). Hegel is obviously referring to the familiar separation of religion from the real world, and he attributes the separation to the abstract thinking by which absolute spirit begins its development.

This deficiency can be remedied by the further development of incarnational religion. Because "spirit in its world and spirit conscious of itself as spirit, or spirit in religion, are the same, the completion of religion thus consists in both becoming equal to one another" (364.39–365.2). This means that spirit's real existence and its abstract thinking (the divine presence) are to be identified.[13] This result requires "not only that its actuality is grasped by religion, but conversely that [spirit] as conscious of itself become actual to itself and *object* of its [empirical] consciousness" (365.2–5). If actuality were simply "grasped by religion," one would have something like the pure universal knowing of conscience. Spirit must go further and become actually empirical, so that its divine essence includes its own empirical being.

Spirit will then be truly actual; it will not only have an "actuality included" (365.6) in thought, but will have real actuality as the "independent free existence" (365.8–9) of empirical human being. Spirit will then know itself not simply in thought (as God appearing in abstract universal thinking) but will be "spirit conscious of itself" (365.11) in both its aspects as "spirit in its world and . . . [as] spirit in religion" (364.39–365.1), or as universal divine essence, which also includes the empirical existence of human being. This expectation anticipates the Christian doctrines of an incarnate divine Son and an indwelling divine Spirit.[14]

So far, then, Hegel has indicated a starting point for *PhG* VII and a goal to be reached. Spirit begins with a pure universal thinking of all reality, wherein universal divine essence appears as human self-consciousness. This pure thought recognizes divine essence as incarnate—but incarnate only in thinking, not in the material world. This partly human, abstractly incarnate God is filled out gradually. Thus one finds a progressive incarnation of God, the various stages of which constitute the history of religion.

Like everything else in *PhG*, this history causes Hegel's reader many difficulties of interpretation. One that arises in the opening pages of *PhG* VII concerns the very beginning of incarnational religion, the pure universal thought in which spirit "contains within itself all essence and all actuality . . . universal actuality [that is] *thought*" (364.25, 32). But if pure thinking is the starting point of religion, why do the first religions view God in nature?

The answer is found in the same pure thinking that contains all being in a general way. Here, self-consciousness "has for itself, as *object imagined*, the significance of being universal spirit" (364.24–25). And as a simple object for its own consciousness, it has the "*shape* or form of being" (364.27), the most elementary form of pure objectivity. Consequently spirit knows itself in the form of being, within its thought (364.29–32). This consciousness (the result of conscience) then begins its development in incarnational religion (367.31–35) in the shape of immediate being, the simplest type of objectivity and thus the most immediate: "at first knowing itself *immediately* spirit is thus [for] itself spirit in the *form* of *immediacy*, and the determinacy of the shape in which it appears to itself is that of *being*" (367.35–37) or nature. Spirit as incarnational has for its "first actuality . . . *immediate* and thus *natural religion*; in it spirit knows itself as its object in [a] natural or immediate shape" (368.19–21). The transition between "the appearing God" (362.28–29) of conscience and spirit as natural religion is, therefore, quite rigorous. Spirit (universal being or divine essence as individual subjectivity) knows itself immediately in the pure thought of conscience and then knows itself as immediate being in natural religion.[15]

Spirit worships a natural shape, such as a plant or animal, not because it is a natural thing but because "this being is . . . *filled* . . . with spirit and is known by itself as all truth and actuality" (367.37; 368.2–3). When spirit (or deity thinking itself) views itself in a thing of nature, there is still a great difference between spirit and the natural shape that it fills: the "*filling* is . . . not equal . . . to its *shape*" (368.3–4) because spirit is more than nature. Spirit cannot really know itself in a shape that does not express thinking. Natural religion must therefore progress and eventually become Christianity, in which the shape of essence thinking itself is that of human or spiritual being. The original concept of religion—that it provide an object wherein spirit can view itself—can be fulfilled only in a fully human incarnation. In this fulfillment, spirit finds an external shape or objective truth adequate for its inner certainty (368.5–6) of being the self-knowing of essence; only then is it "actual as absolute spirit" (368.4–5).

However, religion does not pass directly from its natural phase into its Christian fulfillment. In between the two is the *"artistic religion"* (368.23) of ancient Greece, in which "the shape [of spirit] elevates itself to the form of the *self* through the *producing* of consciousness, whereby this [latter] views in its object its doing, or the self" (368.23–26). Through art, spirit puts human shape into natural materials and so transforms the gods of natural religion into anthropomorphic deities. This intermediate stage is necessary: art shapes material from nature, where spirit saw itself earlier; this divine presence in nature is then altered (373.27–28) by spirit, which views itself in its work (368.23–26) and so begins to grasp its own freedom from nature. However, in Greek religion the self of the god is only an imagined one, and this *"imagined* [divine] self is not the *actual* [human] self" (369.29). Appearing only in art, Zeus is not a real self.

In Christianity, the third phase of religion, spirit appears as an actual human self—a shape that surpasses the merely "thought or imagined" (405.10) self attributed to God by Greek and other religions. Furthermore, the Christian shape of spirit unites the divergent shapes of natural and Greek religion. Whereas the former gives spirit a shape taken from nature's immediate existence and the latter gives it an imagined self, in the divine shape of Christianity nature and subjectivity are united when "the *self* is just as much an *immediate* [empirical being] as [empirical] *immediacy* is [the] self" (368.26–28). As a real self, Christ also contains the moment of natural existence.

Thus, in Christianity, actual spirit knows *itself* as the shape of God. Hegel calls Christianity "the *manifest religion*" (368.31) because in it "spirit" (368.28) "is imagined as it is in and for itself" (368.31)— ultimate essence "in itself" also conscious "for itself" in empirical human being. These two aspects of an objective "in itself" and a subjective "for itself" combine the "form of consciousness" and of "self-consciousness" (368.28, 29) found in earlier religions. In the "form of consciousness," spirit views itself in an immediate object different from the self, as in the various natural religions; in the form of "self-consciousness," God appears in human shape, as in Greek religion. In Christianity both aspects are synthesized, so that essence knows itself through human being in its fullness.

In short, religion develops when spirit adds more and more of its actual existence to its pure knowing. In conscience, a definite concept of absolute spirit emerges: divine essence knowing itself as individual subjectivity. The latter contains all actuality in its pure universal knowing and so has an inward certainty of being divine essence. This obscure *"certainty of itself"* then acquires objective *"truth"* (368.5–6) when it finds its proper empirical shape, namely God incarnate in the flesh. Since human subjectivity is more than pure knowing, absolute spirit must come to know itself in the rest of human life as well. Then "the *shape* in which it appears for its consciousness fully equals its essence, and it views itself as it is" (366.22–24), namely as God in fully existent form. "The difference . . . between *actual* spirit and [spirit] which knows itself [inwardly] as spirit . . . is . . . surmounted" (367.27–29) when spirit (God as existent thinking) is also present empirically. As a result, outer shape matches inner certainty. Spirit's "consciousness [of objectivity] and its [inner] self-consciousness are equalized" (367.30) when its inner self-knowledge corresponds to the empirically incarnate God.[16]

Religion's necessary use of actual spirit gives religion a certain superiority, which Hegel indicates by various formulations. Synthesizing[17] the four earlier moments known as consciousness, self-consciousness, reason, and immediate spirit (365.21–23), religion is their *"simple* totality or . . . absolute self" (365.27–28), "their *ground"* (366.11), "their substance" (367.3–4), and "their true actuality" (367.10–11); it is their "subject" and they are its "predicates" (367.22). Incarnational religion underlies these other forms of knowing because religion begins with pure subjectivity, proceeds to make it empirical, and views this whole development as an appearance of divine substance. The "self-knowing spirit" (364.17) of incarnational religion is nothing other than human reason understanding itself as "the appearing God" (362.28–29). In the traditional sense of worshipping a divine essence external to human being, Christianity is a supernatural religion that brings to human nature something beyond it. But Hegel bases incarnational religion (including Christianity) on reason,[18] which knows that universal divine essence appears as human subjectivity. When reason discovers this truth, it can begin to know itself as a differentiation of divine essence, and so becomes absolute spirit. Since God appears through human intellect (the self-thinking of God), the incarnation begins in reason and spreads from there to the rest of human life.

Incarnational religion is then a gradual development, resembling (366.20–21) earlier parts of *PhG*. Knowing itself as divine appearance, intellect (absolute spirit) must also find this meaning in its empirical existence. The determinate stages of this movement make up the history of incarnational religion.

NATURAL RELIGION (369–75)

In "Natural Religion," spirit knows itself as immediate being or nature. Three specific religions are examined: Persian ("Light"), Indian ("Plant and Animal"), and Egyptian ("The Artisan"). Their titles immediately indicate a great deal about Hegel's analysis. The progression from inanimate nature ("Light"), to living organisms ("Plant and Animal"), and then to human activity ("The Artisan") corresponds to spirit's growing awareness of its own essence; it also points to the discovery of its humanity in the artistic religion of ancient Greece.

Hegel's Introduction to Natural Religion (369–70)

Before analyzing specific natural religions, Hegel makes some general remarks[19] that clarify his approach to all kinds of religion. One comment[20] concerns the general nature of religion as the self-knowing of spirit, which divides itself into consciousness of an object and the self-consciousness of its own subjectivity:

> . . . spirit knowing itself is consciousness of itself, and is to itself in the form of [something] objective, it *is*;[21] and is at the same time [subjective] *being-for-itself*. It *is for itself*, it is the side of *self*-consciousness, and [this] of course against the side of its consciousness, or of relating itself to itself as *object*. (369.3–6)

This text alludes to earlier discussions. In religion, spirit is conscious of itself in two forms: "for itself" when conscious of divine essence as its own human subjectivity, and in an "objective" way when conscious of this meaning in an external human or subhuman shape. When this divine shape is imagined as an object different from the worshipping human subject, the shape is known as a separate divine essence standing over against human subjectivity.

However, the empirical human subject is the real (though still hidden) reference of its imagined objective god. Therefore, a second remark of Hegel's concerns the inevitable overcoming of their difference. The "movement [of religion] has the goal of surmounting this chief difference [between divine object and human subject] and of giving to the shape which is object of consciousness the form of self-consciousness" (369.24–26). This means that the divine shapes or objects of religion are ultimately given clear and explicit human form.

A third comment concerns the way this goal is reached. According to Hegel, a divine essence does not take on real human form when "the god is *imagined as self consciousness*" because then "the *imagined* self [of a god] is not the *actual* [self of human being]" (369.28–29).[22] The imagined god has actual human form only when the latter "is put into" (369.31) the former, a move that is accomplished when the imagined self is "comprehended" (369.32) as "*its own*" (369.35) by the actual self. Only then has the actual self "completely appropriated to itself" (370.8–9) the god's imagined selfhood, and "consequently views itself in it" (369.35).[23] Hegel apparently means that any divine self (whether it is Zeus's or Yahweh's) is properly understood only as the actual human self. Thus, an independent divine subjectivity is only a projection of human subjectivity, which imagines its deity to have a self resembling its own. The truth, however, is that divine essence has already differentiated itself into human subjectivity, which knows itself in every incarnation of God.

A fourth remark explains how religions differ: "one religion differentiates itself from another according to the *determinacy* of this shape, in which spirit knows itself" (369.14–15). Hegel does not exactly mean that religions differ by the kinds of gods they know, for in fact "the images that appear to distinguish one actual religion from another occur in each one" (369.20–21). Rather, he means that although there are many images of gods in every religion, empirical spirit corresponds to only one of them, and so this one determinate image is the "shape in which spirit knows itself" (369.14–15). For example, "the incarnation of God, which occurs in oriental religions, has no truth [in them] because their actual spirit is without this reconciliation" (370.12–14); in other words, the oriental spirit does not consider its actual self to be divine, and so its actual self does not know itself in the figure of an incarnate God. Thus, one religion differs from another by the self-knowledge of empirical spirit from which the universal divine essence (known in thought) gets its determinate shape.

In a fifth comment, Hegel deals with religion's use of images:

> . . . spirit knowing itself is consciousness of itself. . . . In its consciousness is . . . the *determinacy* of the shape in which it appears to itself and knows [itself]. We are concerned only with this [determinate shape] in this consideration of religion, for its unshaped essence or its pure concept has already arisen. (369.3, 6–10)

The "pure concept" referred to is "the concept of spirit [that] came to be for us as we entered into religion" (419.39), namely, at the end of *PhG* VI–C where evil was pardoned; this concept identifies universal essence with individual subjectivity. In the form of imagination, its content occurs even in ancient religion as the "imagined shape" of the gods. Religion, then, differs from the pure concept just because it uses an image or shape, which Hegel defines as "existence held in thought, as well as a thought which exists [for] itself [in thought]" (369.13–14). He does not pursue this point any further in his introduction to natural religion. However, he has already indicated (in his earlier introduction to the chapter) that when religion completes its development, spirit is not yet complete because "the *shape* itself and the *image* is still the unconquered side from which it [namely, spirit] must pass over into the *concept*,[24] in order to wholly dissolve the form of objectivity" (368.32–34) standing over against the subject.

Even though religion (when compared to absolute knowing) is incomplete, one should not regard its contribution to the argument of *PhG* lightly. Because religion finally brings real empirical human existence into the concept of spirit, it enables Hegel to surmount "Morality" with "Absolute Knowing." "Morality" identifies individual human being with universal divine essence only in an intellectual way, so that spirit is "not in the form of [a] free actuality or of independently appearing nature" (364.25–26) but only in the form of "pure knowing" (362.29). The transition from this "pure knowing" of "Morality" to Hegel's "Absolute Knowing" (in which universal divine essence appears as human reason) is made by incarnational religion in *PhG* VII. This chapter describes how spirit first comes to know itself through divine shapes before it attains "Absolute Knowing." Historically, such images of God are the first expressions of the concept of spirit. They reveal the gradual incarnations through which divine essence appears in more and more human form.

The Religion of Light[25] (370–72)

Here, Hegel turns to specific religions, the first of which is the Persian[26] religion of light. As discussed in the introduction to *PhG* VII, self-conscious religion begins with "spirit knowing itself . . . as [an] *object imagined* . . . the universal spirit . . . which contains all essence and all actuality within itself . . . [as] universal actuality [that is] *thought*" (364.17, 24, 25, 32). This object is spirit's own universal thought of all reality, "the pure ego which . . . has within itself as *universal object* the certainty of itself; or this object is for it the penetration of all thinking and all actuality" (370.32–371.3).

Since this is only the beginning of a dialectical movement, the object appears in a simple and immediate way. Spirit appears as light, a crude form of elemental being. And through this divine shape, spirit "views itself in the form of *being*" (371.6–7); at this point, spirit resembles something found in the natural world. On the other hand, since this object incarnates the ultimate and universal *essence* that exists as human thinking, it is not simply elementary being but "being filled with spirit" (371.9). Divine light may therefore be understood as a kind of energetic spiritual matter.

Again, at the beginning of its dialectical movement, this divine object is far from its complete incarnation. Instead of a friendly anthropomorphic deity, one finds an overpowering force that subdues empirical human being. The shape of God in this religion also has (in addition to the form of being) "the form of *master*[27] [over] against the [human] self-consciousness shrinking back from [this] its [divine] object" (371.10–11). The Persian religion of light reflects the famous relation of master and slave that Hegel describes in *PhG* IV–A. All creatures are as nothing before their omnipotent divine master.[28]

But because this master is found in a religion of *spirit*, its essence must show some tendency toward a human incarnation. To be sure, this tendency expresses itself only in the most rudimentary way; this divine "*being* filled with the concept of spirit is thus the *shape* of the *simple* relation of spirit to itself, or the shape of shapelessness" (371.12–13). Its incarnations have no definite shape. God is "the pure *essence* [of] *light* containing and filling everything . . . [and] which preserves itself in its formless substantiality" (371.14–15). In this pure intellectual light, human being has no individual existence.[29] Indeed the religion of light does not yet know any individual as subsistent for although divine light "shapes itself to the forms of nature" (371.21), these forms are still "outpourings of light" (371.18) "which do not progress to [individual] independence but remain only names of the many-named One" (371.28–29). Everything is light because everything is still contained in the one simple determinate shape of light.

Such a religion is far from dull, however; its divine light is a "giddy life" (371.33) manifesting itself in "disappearing shapes" (371.34), the "creations" (371.17) of light that remains light in all its "streams of fire" (371.19–20). Since light has no determinate shape other than itself, its religion considers everything to be an immediate manifestation of deity, which is pure essence in the shape of light. But such manifestations occur precisely because religion is now expressing spirit, "the [divine] *essence* which is [human] *self-consciousness*" (370.24). Spirit views itself (as object) in these individual shapes of light.

Spirit then develops itself into a higher form of divine incarnation: because "this giddy life . . . must determine itself to *being-for-itself*, and give subsistence to its disappearing shapes" (371.33–34), light is replaced by a religion of "Plant and Animal." And there is a good reason for this development. Divine light is universal essence objectifying itself into individual shapes, all of which are characterized by the same immediate being that light has. However, "the *immediate being* [of divine light] . . . is itself the *negative* power which dissolves its differences.[30] It is thus in truth the *self*; spirit, therefore, passes over into knowing itself in the form of the self" (371.34–37). For this reason spirit has to become a human incarnation of God—but not all at once. The next step is simply that "pure light throws apart its simplicity . . . and sacrifices itself to being-for-itself, [so][31] that the individual takes to itself subsistence in its [divine] substance" (371.37–372.3). Then spirit knows itself as a living individual and so gives itself the shape of a plant or animal.

Plant and Animal (372–73)[32]

When spirit "throws apart its simplicity" (372.1) of universal thought in favor of individual subsistence, "self-conscious spirit . . . has gone out of its shapeless essence into itself, or elevated its immediacy to the self in general" (372.6–7). Since there are many selves, human spirit is now conscious of itself "as a manifold of being-for-itself" (372.8), as "atoms of spirit" (372.11) that have no overall cohesion.[33] The result is a chaotic group of "weaker and stronger, richer and poorer spirits" (372.10) that constitute a "pantheism" (372.10) of "plant shapes" (372.20) and then "animal shapes" (372.23) in ancient India.[34]

In the religious of *PhG* VII, spirit objectifies itself by giving universal essence a shape resembling human individuality. In *"flower-religion"* (372.12), the shape is only a flower, "the merely selfless image of the self" (372.12–13)—"selfless" because it hardly resembles a human self, yet still an "image of the self" because it has (in contrast with emanations of light) a fixed individuality. Since flowers exist side by side without any visible activity and interaction, they express "innocence . . . the repose and impotence of individuality viewing" (372.12, 14) itself in a divine flower.

When spirit knows itself in animal shapes, a new religion emerges. No longer viewing itself as merely individual (as in flower-religion) but as *acting* on behalf of its individuality, spirit gives itself a corresponding objective shape. Thus, its "pantheism" (372.10) now expresses itself as animal life, as *"hostile* movement . . . the seriousness of struggling life . . . destructive being-for-itself" (372.11, 13, 14–15). Spirit then passes from "the innocence of *flower-religion* . . . into the guilt of *animal-religion*" (372.12, 13–14). Hegel even gives a phenomenological reason for this transition: individual things (the basis of flower-religion) are individual and different from one another "through determinacy and negativity" (372.17–18). As such, they come to oppose one another in animal-religion, in which "the hate of their being-for-itself consumes them" (372.20–21).

Socially,[35] these individuals (or individual groups) are "a crowd of individualized unsociable tribal spirits which in their hate fight one another to the death" (372.22–23). In terms of religion, they "are conscious of determinate animal shapes as their essence" (372.23–24) and, therefore, worship animal gods. The individuals' social behavior and religion are derived from a consciousness of their animal selves: "they are nothing other than animal spirits, animal lives separating themselves [and] conscious without universality" (372.24–25).[36] And since animal religion expresses individuality as hostile and destructive, "the determinacy of purely negative being-for-itself destroys itself, and spirit . . . steps into another shape" (372.26–28): "The Artisan" (373.10–11) of Egyptian religion.

The step is a logical one when the animal is viewed as a "purely negative" (372.26) or purely destructive force whose fight "to the death" (372.23) will destroy rather than preserve its life. The animal's destructive inclinations can then be understood as directed not only against other individuals but also against itself, and so animalistic self-destruction can become the artisan's work, which is "the self . . . destroying itself, i.e., becoming a thing" (372.29–30). The self destroys itself insofar as it puts itself into a thing. But this thing is nevertheless an image of spirit, which "produces its image [as] being-for-itself put out into the form of an object" (373.6–7). The self is now a maker of objects that contain itself.[37]

The Artisan (373–75)[38]

Hegel's view of ancient Egypt[39] is that in it "spirit . . . produces itself as object" (373.12, 13) in what it makes. When he adds that spirit "has not grasped the thought of itself" (373.13–14) and that "its doing . . . is an instinctual working, as bees build their cells" (373.12, 14), he clarifies his meaning: in Egyptian religion, spirit does not yet know itself as human or as thinking spirit, but only as manual labor. Although human being discovers itself through its labor, the mere fact of laboring seems to designate a subhuman state of existence.[40] Its works, therefore, give divine essence a subhuman shape; only at the very end of its development does ancient Egypt reach human self-awareness.

Spirit's first productions in Egyptian religion are "pyramids and obelisks" (373.17) that symbolize itself. Here, Persia's divine light or *"being in itself* becomes the material which it [namely, spirit] works on" (373.27–28) and makes into a sacred object. Not yet an image of the living worker, this type of work also reflects its distance from the artisan (373.27–30) inasmuch as "the work is not yet . . . filled by spirit" (373.16). The pyramid receives only "an alien departed spirit" (373.22), not a living one, into its lifeless interior (373.21–24); the obelisk receives the rays of the sun externally and thus in an unspiritual way (373.24–26).

Such works indicate a divine presence in a sacred object made by humans and, therefore, a divine incarnation in something human. But because the object is only a material product of human labor and not yet living spirit, the incarnation of God is not yet a human one. Yet as the works begin to approach human form, the divine incarnation (located in the work) becomes more and more human. This goal underlies the entire discussion of Egyptian religion. On the surface, Hegel's analysis appears to concern only the relation between human labor and its works. But the deeper concept of divine incarnation, which those works embody, is also implicit in this analysis.

Next, Hegel shows (through an intricate examination) how spirit expresses itself in the works of an artisan. Earlier works of Egyptian art objectify the separation of universal essence "in itself" and human existence "for itself" (373.27–30) by creating a massive and quasi-universal material object (such as a pyramid or an obelisk) connected externally to a sign of human individuality (such as a deceased king or a ray of light, respectively). When these two aspects of the work "are brought closer to one another" (373.22), the work becomes more spiritual and combines divine essence with human existence. As the work becomes more human, it also "steps closer to the [artisan's] working self-consciousness and this [consciousness thereby] arrives at a knowing of itself[41] . . . in the work" (374.3–5). In this way, the objectification of spirit in art approaches the existing humanity of the artisan.

For examples of this more spiritual work, Hegel turns to statue and temple,[42] representing "imagined spirit and its surrounding shell" (373.33–374.1)—a double object symbolizing the "individuality" of the artisan and the "universality" of divine essence (374.2). The temple is shaped beyond the linear shape (373.17) of pyramid and obelisk and given a "more animated form" when the artisan uses "plant-life" (374.12–13) as a model[43] for a "more animated rounding" (374.22). This is an allusion to the use of round columns[44] in temple architecture. The temple then becomes more lifelike. And the statue gives to its crude image of human subjectivity the material solidity of obelisk, pyramid, and temple; therefore, it "brings closer to actuality the spirit previously departed from existence [and] interior[45] to the [massive universal object] or external[46] [to it], and thereby makes the work more equal to the actual self-consciousness [of the artisan]" (374.26–28). Insofar as the pyramid, obelisk, or temple represent larger masses, they stand for the universal divine essence. When the mass takes on human form, it corresponds to the humanization of divine essence. Thus, the two sides of the work have come to approach each other. Furthermore, since their earlier distance from each other symbolizes the separation of artisan and object (373.27–30), their nearness now symbolizes the growing presence of the artisan within the humanized objective work (374.2–4). As the work itself becomes more human in shape, it obviously approaches the real humanity of the artisan.

But what kind of human image does the artisan put into this material? The statue slowly develops into a reflection of its maker, first as an "animal shape" (374.29), then as animal "mixed with the shape of thought, with human [shape]" (374.34–35),[47] and finally as a fully human shape (375.1–2) that makes a noise when struck by "the ray of the rising sun" (375.3).[48] But the statue that is made to utter sound in this way is obviously not a real self. Because it "lacks . . . language" (374.37), "the work lacks the shape and existence in which the self exists as self" (374.35–36). Language is the true sign of the human self. The sound "made by light . . . is only noise and not language, [and] shows only an outer self, not the inner" (375.4–5).

Yet the inner self is signified by something else already produced: the temple, "which is the *cover of the inner*; and this inner is at first still the simple darkness, the unmoved, the black formless stone" (375.9–11)[49] that is "soundless" (375.17). As such, the temple represents an outer covering with a hidden inner meaning, while the surrounding statue portrays an outer human shape that makes noise. In slightly different ways, both of them "contain *inwardness* and *existence*—the two moments of spirit" (375.12–13). Neither one, however, is equal to the artisan. Through temple and statue, the artisan is known only as an "*activity*" (374.5–6) that makes them and that "knows its content not yet in itself, but in its work, which is a thing" (374.6–7). These works, therefore, still signify spirit insofar as it "has not yet grasped the thought of itself" (373.13–14) as a human self.

In a final attempt at self-discovery, the artisan produces a shape indicating the moment when spirit emerges from nature as consciousness of self. This shape is the sphinx,[50] a "mixing of natural and self-conscious shape" (375.20). Hegel describes the many varieties[51] of the sphinx as if they represent the painful birth of human thought and speech: "these ambiguous essences puzzling to themselves—the conscious wrestling with the unconscious, the simple inner [wrestling] with the many-shaped outer, the obscurity of thought coupling with the clarity of expression—[these] break out into the language of deep wisdom hard to understand" (375.20–24). And with language,[52] the work becomes a "self conscious, self-pronouncing inner" (375.27–28), fully human and resembling the artisan. The works of Egyptian religion, then, rid themselves of their "mixings with the unconscious mode of immediate natural shape" (375.31–32). The works also portray conscious human being, which knows itself to be spirit and which expresses its inner spiritual character on its bodily exterior: "these monstrosities in shape, word, and deed dissolve themselves into a spiritual shaping—into an outer gone into itself, into an inner which makes itself outer from [within] itself and on itself" (375.32–35). The inner consciousness of self expresses itself outwardly in a bodily way.

Hegel thus describes the evolution of Egyptian religious art as a depiction of spirit's gradual grasping of itself. In the beginning of that evolution, spirit produces only an "unconscious work" (375.26) indicating the deficient self-knowledge of its maker. At this stage, spirit's work is "instinctual" (375.25) or half-animal, and the worker is only an "artisan" (375.27). However, when spirit makes itself the "object of its consciousness" (375.31) by portraying itself as its object, it becomes an "*artist*" (375.36) that knows how to make a work spiritual. The transition is a gradual one, with the decisive and final move occurring when the sphinx begins to speak. At this moment, a nearly human shape is made to express itself in a human—that is, in a thoughtful and spiritual—way. Spirit then begins a new phase of its history in the Greek religion of art, which portrays divine essence in human shape.

THE GREEK RELIGION OF ART (376–99)

Greek religion[53] begins where Egyptian religion ends, namely with the production of a work of art portraying deity in human form, "the form of consciousness itself" (376.3–4). Sculpture provides a clear example: in the Greek statues of anthropomorphic deities, "human shape strips off the animal [shape] it was mixed with" (379.1) in Egyptian religion,[54] in which animal and human features are often combined. This anthropomorphic development applies to other arts as well. In general, it makes the Greek artist a "spiritual worker" (376.7) portraying spirit according to its proper definition: spirit is divine *"essence . . . which essentially* assumes human shape" (387.26, 27). Spirit, therefore, must express itself in human form, and it does this in the Greek religion of art, where spirit comes to "know itself in the shape of . . . the *self"* (368.22, 23). And since the self is individual, Hegel also designates Greek religion as the portrayal of "absolute substance . . . in the form of individuality" (402.37–403.1). In Greek religion, then, deity is imagined as an individual human self.

On the other hand, this anthropomorphic religion is only a limited portrayal of spirit. What Hegel writes about one of its cults reveals the limits of the whole religion: it emphasizes *"the essence . . .* which *is immediately united* with *the self"* (385.29–30), but it also "dispenses with that abstract *simplicity*[55] of essence, and therefore [with] its *depth"* (385.28–29). In contrast to the Persian religion of light (385.21–23), Greek religion emphasizes deity's human shape rather than its divine independence, the simplicity and depth from which everything else derives. Thus Greek religion does not know God as spirit, as essence "that *essentially* assumes human shape" (387.27) from within its own logical depth.

Greek religion also shows only "the renunciations of absolute substance . . . in[to] the form of [human] individuality" (402.37–403.1) but not the inverse renunciation of human individuality before universal essence. In Christianity, however, the incarnation of God into human individuality is accompanied by a corresponding human self-renunciation, whereby human *"self-consciousness* renounces itself and makes [itself] into thinghood or the universal self" (403.19–20). The self-sacrifice shows that "self-consciousness . . . *in itself* is the univer-

sal essence" (403.25–26). Thus, Christianity surmounts Greek anthropomorphism; the self sacrifices its individual selfish side and shows its
unity with universal divine essence.

Such a comparison helps one to appreciate the exact contribution of
the Greek religion of art, where spirit comes to know itself as free
individuality. A similar discovery was already present in the Greek
religion of the underworld and is described in an earlier chapter (VI–A)
of *PhG*. There the underworld is a haven for the individual person as
such, who is respected as individual only when dead; in actual life, the
person belongs to a people and participates in its ethical system or
"Sittlichkeit." But gradually the ethical system is overpowered by the
increasing force of individualism, whose victory is the end of Greek
"Sittlichkeit" and the beginning of legal personality in Rome. This
long development from "Sittlichkeit" to individual freedom is also
portrayed in the series of works that make up "The Religion of Art."

Greek Society and Its Artists (376–78)

Hegel begins his analysis of the religion of art with a brief description
of Greek society (376–78), which knows itself in its religion. Dominat-
ing his description is the theme of a universal social order giving way
to individual subjectivity—the same theme found in the Greek religion
of the underworld (*PhG* VI–A).[56] One cannot comprehend the religion
of art without first understanding the emergence of individuality in the
"Sittlichkeit" or social order[57] of ancient Greece.

Ethical spirit or "Sittlichkeit" describes the Greek city-state, a society in which individuals freely participate in the life of the community.
Here, spirit finds a real existence as the universal common life shared
by many individual subjects. Natural religion, on the other hand, fails
to acknowledge free individuality. Neither in religion nor in society
does the ancient Orient value subjectivity. Thus, in Persian religion
"the being-for-self of self-consciousness is contained only negatively,
only [to] pass away" (376.14–15), and in the Hindu castes of India "the
universal freedom of individuals is missing" (376.18) altogether. In
contrast to that of Oriental religion and society, the spirit of Greek life
"is not only the universal substance of all individual [persons]"
(376.10), as in the natural religions, but also "has individuality"

(376.12) and is known by those individuals "as their own essence and work" (376.12–13). In the ancient city-state, individuals discuss public policy and contribute to public life in a thoughtful, self-conscious way. The ethical spirit of Greece, therefore, portrays its deities as human individuals.

Hegel's argument suggests that natural religion is not fully human because it has not discovered free subjectivity. In the religion of light, everything participates in light, which rules over all. Individual subjectivity views itself as a natural thing that simply illustrates this one universal essence (376.13–15; 381.21–27). And so the absence of individual freedom belongs to natural religion, where human beings view themselves as nature, which is not free.

In Egyptian religion, this lack of freedom appears in the kind of labor performed by artisans, "an instinctual working, as bees build their cells" (373.14). One can well imagine a large crowd of such artisans laboring over huge pyramids with little awareness of their own spiritual character (for this is now struggling to emerge into their consciousness) and with no sense of freedom. Theirs is an "instinctual working . . . sunk into [material] existence" (377.22–23) and so their products are "the *mixing* of strange forms of thought and [what is] natural" (376.5–6). As a result, Egyptians give spirit an animal shape.

In contrast to this half-animal kind of religion is the Greek spirit with its "free spiritual activity" (377.25) of a self that has "its substance in free ethicality" (377.24) or that knows itself to be a free citizen. Individuals participate in the making of laws, which they accept and obey. Thus, Hegel describes the Greeks as "the free people in which the [universal] ethic makes up the substance of all, the actuality and existence of which [substance] each and every individual [person] knows as its will and deed" (376.18–20). Here, there is no conflict between individual aims and universal thought, and yet the potential for division exists simply because individuals are free.

That early period of harmony between individual and society modifies Oriental totalitarianism, where human freedom has not yet emerged from nature. Greeks grow beyond nature and feel their freedom. But the memory of totalitarianism gives them a wholesome respect for the community they belong to. Thus in its first developments, individual consciousness "has not yet gone out of its reposeful [universal] ethic . . . into itself" (376.28, 29) as individual; given the group's differentiation into particular social roles (376.29–31), "the individual [person] is content with the limitation of its existence and has not yet grasped the limitless thought of its free self" (376.32–33). Here, spirit is universal and also personal, but it has not yet discovered the full extent of its freedom as individual.

Hegel's reference to "limitless thought" suggests that spirit grows in freedom as it discovers more and more the universal scope of individual thought. This process must occur within Greek ethical society because Hegel attributes the rise of "pure self-consciousness" (377.31–32) to the way in which "the individual [citizen] . . . has in ethical obedience and service worked itself free [from] all unconscious existence and firm determinacy" (377.34–35). In this way the individual subject frees itself not only from nature, but also from the ethical norms imposed on it by its natural gender. As a result, freedom comes into being through the individual use of mind in service to the community.

This ancient form of democracy dooms itself, however, because free community life requires the consent of thoughtful individuals who more and more come to know themselves as independent. Eventually, one's "trusting in the [collective universal] substance returns into trusting in *oneself* and into the *certainty of self*" (376.34–377.1), so that "the self . . . knows itself as free individuality" (377.14–15) and "spirit . . . has now stepped out into the extreme of self-consciousness grasping itself as essence" (377.18, 19–20). This development toward personal individuality is "the perishing of ethicality" (377.12) because "individuality gone into itself" (377.6–7) no longer finds its full satisfaction in universal community life.

Because this individualism cannot be expressed in the ethical world of the political community, it asserts itself in religious art. According to Hegel, "ethical spirit's religion is . . . its elevation above its [political and social] actuality, the return *out of its* [empirical social] *truth* into the pure *knowing of self*" (376.21–23). Religion, then, results from individual thinking rather than from public life. What appears however is not simply more individualism because spirit is universal essence as individual subjectivity. Thus, divine shapes are generated by individual creativity: "the spirit certain within itself . . . now produces out of the purity of the self its essence elevated above actuality" (377.19–21). Pure thinking is the medium through which the gods appear. Hegel's reference to "the *substance* born out of the self" (377.26–27) clearly indicates that universal divine essence appears through creative human thinking.

But in the religion of art, universal substance becomes "pure form" (377.33–34) or "fluid essence" (377.36) shaped by individual intellectual "*activity*" (377.32–33); universal essence has advanced from the determinism of nature (found in the earlier Greek religion of the underworld) into thinking subjectivity (377.34–35). The gods now take on forms developed by artistic interpretation. Hegel describes this process as "the night in which [divine] substance was betrayed[58] and made itself into [a knowing human] subject" (377.36–37).

If substance "made itself" into such a subject, then the individual artist (375.36) is clearly being moved by a larger force, namely by divine substance itself. Universal essence now expresses itself through individual thought. Hegel continues: "out of this night of pure [individual] self-certainty . . . ethical spirit rises as the shape freed from nature and its immediate [empirical] existence" (377.37–39). The work of art derives not only from its individual creator, but also from the ethical world's universal substance, which appears through the universal thinking of individual artists.

Hegel's description of artistic labor in ancient Greece is worth examining for its fusion of universal and individual factors. When substance passes into thinking subjectivity, "ethical spirit" (377.38) has "fled from its [collective] body" (378.1) and feels the pain of its loss.[59] It then "selects an individual . . . as the vessel of its pain" (378.2)—an individual who will give a new shape to the still "unshaped essence" (378.7) of spirit. The "universal" (378.9) takes possession of this individual mind, which thereby "suffers violence" (378.3) and "loses freedom" (378.4) before this universal force present in thought. But soon enough "that positive might of universality is vanquished by the pure self of the individual, . . . the negative might" (378.5–6) of individual thought in the artist whose "pure activity . . . wrestles with the unshaped essence" and becomes "master over it" (378.7). The result of this mastery is the artistic "work . . . the universal spirit individualized and imaged" (378.9) in the statue (382.23) of a god. This work of art, therefore, expresses the universal as a free divine individual.[60]

Since the god's free individuality has been produced by an artist, who typifies the real freedom acquired in Greece by pure individual thinking, the god is an image of the artist's own individual humanity. The image also contains universal substance: universal essence knows itself through the artist, who portrays this divine subjectivity as a god. And because the religious image of deity is actually a portrayal of the artist, the main direction of Greek art is now fixed. Its further development will consist of attempts to solve this one major problem: how to adequately depict the artist in the work of art,[61] whose very existence portrays the god as separate from the artist. In such a separation, spirit (divine essence as human existence) is represented only by art's anthropomorphic gods, not by real human being. This problem the artist faces is also the general problem of all religion in Hegel's *PhG*, namely how to bring actual human being into a divine object of consciousness.

Summary of the Religion of Art

Hegel's analysis of the religion of art is too long to be examined in detail here. Having discussed already its general significance, I attempt only a summary and briefly treat a few selected points.

Anticipating the plan of his *Enzyklopädie*, whose three major parts are Logic, Nature, and Spirit, Hegel in his *PhG* divides "The Religion of Art" (376–99) into three subdivisions: "The Abstract Work of Art" (378–85), "The Living Work of Art" (385–88), and "The Spiritual Work of Art" (388–99).[62] As these titles indicate, Greek art (in Hegel's analysis) follows an orderly development corresponding to the different stages[63] according to which spirit grasps itself as divine essence in human form.

In "The Abstract Work of Art," Hegel analyzes the statue and its temple (378.12–380.23); the hymn (380.24–381.4; 382.20–27); the oracle (381.5–382.19); and various cultic activities (382.28–385.15), including sacrifices and sacred meals (383.13–384.30). In "The Living Work of Art,"[64] he writes about the mysteries of Ceres and Bacchus (385.18–387.19) and athletic celebrations (387.20–388.2). And finally in "The Spiritual Work of Art," Hegel displays his knowledge of Greek literature by studying its three major types: epic (388.30–392.12), tragedy (392.13–397.27), and comedy (397.28–399.35).

Orientation

In Hegel's survey of the history of Greek art, the analyses of particular
themes are so interesting in their detail that one can lose sight of their
significance in relation to the larger development they contribute to.
Thus, it is helpful at this point to recall the fundamental goal of Greek
religion, namely to portray "absolute substance . . . in the form of
individuality" (402.37–403.1). One should also note that "individuality" can refer either to a divine self proper to deity or to the human
self in which the god appears. Hegel himself notes this difference in his
introduction to natural religion: "the god is *imagined* as [a divine] *self-
consciousness*. The *imagined* [divine] self is [however] not the actual
[human self]" (369.28–29). In this passage, Hegel makes it clear that a
divine self is only an imagined but not a real self. Such a divine self
exists only in human imagination; the real God is an idea that differentiates itself into *human* selfhood. In cult, both selves appear when the
divine self comes to join a human one.

However, the underlying significance of this movement is that the
imagined divine self points to its real self in human existence, and not
that both kinds of self are brought together. Since the divine self is not
actual, it must be an image of the actual human self, which knows itself
in a preliminary way through the divine shape it has created. Universal
essence thus expresses itself through human self-consciousness, but
not yet as actually being this consciousness.

The Abstract Work of Art (378–85)[65]

Hegel's use of the term "abstract" for the statue (382.22–23; 384.38)
of a god (378.33–34) is unusual because nothing seems less abstract
than the human appearance of Greek gods in statues. The word means
that the statue[66] is an abstract rendition or visual idea of spirit, not the
living reality itself. Hegel compares "the immediate and objective
mode" (378.13) of the statue as a "*thing*" (378.19) with an "animated
work of art" (378.16) or with "artistic spirit's . . . active consciousness" (378.17–18). Thus, the statue is abstract not because it is material
but because a material thing can portray spirit in only an abstract (or
lifeless) way.[67] As an image of spirit, the statue "is, as the immediate

[work of art], the abstract and individual [work of art]" (378.12)—
abstract because lifeless, and individual with its own singular existence.[68] In both respects, it stands apart from the artist who made it.

In his introduction to Greek art, Hegel characterizes its works as
"the universal spirit [of an ethical people] individualized and imagined" (378.9). His description of the gods portrayed in the statues
further develops this formulation. Each god is an *"essence"* (379.7)
uniting nature and spirit (379.8), an essence that is "an individual folk-
spirit" (379.11; 388.18–19) distinct from the people (379.9) it is the
essence of. Such an essence is portrayed as "a *single* shape" (379.10)
because it "grasps together into restful individuality" (379.28) "the
unrest of infinite individuation" (379.23) found in nature and human
society. Thus, the statue is essence or "substance . . . in the form of
individuality, as a thing" (402.37–403.1). This thing also has divine
significance as a god or *"essence* over against the [human] *self-
consciousness* which . . . [is its] birthplace" (379.29–30).[69] The statue
of a god portrays an anthropomorphic divine individuality and so
cannot be identified with any empirical individual.

Attempts to surmount the separation between deity and human being
soon appear. In the oracle, the god has the more human existence of
speech. But since the oracular god speaks through "an *alien* self-
consciousness" (381.12), an inspired seer who is *"individual"* (381.15)
and "separated from the self-consciousness of the community"
(381.15), the difference between divine and human being is still maintained. Thus, the oracle is an example of abstract art that imitates
human speech but is still different from human being.

The communal hymn, however, unifies the god with human self-
consciousness, whose language is the "element" (380.32) of the
"shape" (380.32) assumed by the god. Hegel even seems to identify
god and hymn when he writes that "the god . . . is the work of art
animated in itself" (380.32–33) and that the hymn is the "becoming-
objective" of divine "essence" (380.35). Yet since the hymn is the
product of *"pure thinking* or devotion" (380.36), which is obviously
separated from actual life (383.32), it too must be abstract in relation to
empirical consciousness, even though for *abstract* consciousness (or
pure thinking) there is no separation at all between itself and its god.
Nor can there be a separation because "this devotion is the immediate

pure satisfaction of the self through and within itself" (382.37–383.1); its universal god is really present as its own universal thought.[70] Yet just because abstract consciousness leaves out the empirical side of spirit, its divine objectification is "too much enclosed within the self [and as interior] comes too little to [a definite] shaping" (382.25–26). More actuality is needed for the god to join the self's determinate empirical existence.

When the hymn's abstract consciousness of unity with divine essence is expanded into an "*abstract cult*" (383.5) carried on by "the purified soul which . . . is one with [divine] essence" (383.1–2), the self's empirical side is still ignored. A pure soul works hard (383.8–12) at being the "*abode prepared*" (383.4) for its god. But the unity it achieves with its god is necessarily "*a secret*, i.e., a merely imagined, unactual accomplishment" (383.13–14) existing only in its thought. Aware of this limitation and probably grasping that "an unactual action [unwirkliche Handlung] contradicts itself" (383.14–15), the abstract soul must move on to "*actual* [or bodily] action [*wirkliche* Handlung]" (383.14) in the "actual cult" (383.17) of sacrifice and sacred meal (383.36–384.30). By such a procedure, spirit attempts to bring the god into its actual empirical self. This movement prefigures the incarnation of God in Christ.

Through the sacred meal (consuming what is not sacrificed), human being knows in a sensible and corporeal way its union with deity. The earlier condition for this consciousness is that deity be present in the food ingested: divine "essence must *in itself* already have sacrificed itself . . . [by having] given itself *existence* and made itself into the *individual animal* and into *fruit*" (384.11–13; 384.5–7). Then during the meal this divine food passes into human being, so that this "*objective* existence of essence [is] changed into [the worshipper's] *self-conscious* [existence], and the self has the consciousness of its unity with essence" (384.28–30).

Yet such a consciousness does not last because eating is a transient act that "robs itself of its existence" (383.33–34) almost immediately. The permanent significance of the act may well remain in the mind, but this durable "meaning lies . . . only in devotion" (384.31–32), which is abstract rather than corporeal or material. A permanent external unity between deity and human being has not been reached by the "actual cult" (383.17) of sacrifice and meal.

This deficiency is remedied by giving to "devotion an *objective subsistence* [*gegenständliches Bestehen*]" (384.35) by labor for "the god's dwelling and ornament" (384.36–37). Through their gifts, all the folk can view themselves as the god's own people (384.38–385.2), which affirms itself too; for when the folk honors the god with jewelry and festivals (385.8–10), it then has as "the proofs of his favor . . . the enjoyment of its own wealth and adornment" (385.12, 14–15) in the immediate present.[71]

The general conclusion Hegel draws from this cult is that it not only makes individuals know "they are the people of their god" (385.25) who is their universal substance, but affirms them as individuals in their own right because the god also typifies their own individuality. Persian religion, in contrast, worships "the essence [of] light which [is] without a self [and] does not contain within itself the certainty of individuals, but is rather only their universal essence and the lordly power in which they disappear . . . they are the people of their god . . . but their actual self . . . is rejected" (385.21–27). In Greek religion, however, "essence . . . has in itself the self" (385.32); "*essence . . . is immediately united* with *the self*" (385.29–30) in the cult (385.33) and also insofar as divine essence is imagined as a self (385.32) resembling humans. Therefore, "its appearance is friendly to consciousness" (385.32–33) or to "the people whose *self* is recognized in its substance" (386.2–3) or deity.

The Living Work of Art (385–88)[72]

In his next subdivision, "The Living Work of Art," Hegel describes how Greek religion moves closer to its goal of depicting deity as existing human individuality. Two different kinds of cult are portrayed here: the mysteries of Ceres and Bacchus (386.12–387.19), who are also mentioned in the previous subdivision as part of the actual cult of sacrifice and sacred meal (384.6–7); and athletic festivals[73] (387.20–388.2, 17–27), which honor "the beautiful wrestler"[74] (388.19) whose body is "an animated living work of art" (387.35–36). While the former cult actually brings about a mystical union of deity and human being (386.25–37), the latter has no such result (387.24–26); it simply honors the athlete instead of a god's image (387.31). Both cults are connected by the living human body, which is nourished by food and drink in the mysteries and which is the center of attention in athletic competition.

In the mysteries, deity is first of all in the form of nature, but only to be consumed by the higher and more spiritual existence of human being (386.13–23). As a result, "the self knows itself one with essence, and thus the latter is revealed" (386.26–27); it is revealed because it "has been put . . . in[to] the immediate certainty of self" (386.29, 28) where knowledge[75] occurs. *What* is revealed, or the content of this revelation, is of course divine essence,[76] which here is "the spirit of nature" (387.14) giving itself to human being as "bread and wine" (387.15). Consequently, deity joins human selfhood only in a deficient way. As bread, divine essence is (like Ceres who appears and disappears) "the movement of partly . . . stepping into consciousness . . . [and] of partly again . . . losing itself in the self" (387.2–5). As wine, this divine essence acquires a drunken human actuality (387.6–11) in which "the self is beside itself in bacchic inspiration" (388.5).

Thus, "the spirit of nature" (387.14) has a "self-conscious life" (387.14) in human being, but "Ceres and Bacchus" (387.15) are not gods "whose individuality includes within itself [human] self-consciousness as [an] essential moment" (387.16–17). Deity is not completely human as Ceres and Bacchus; they belong merely to the "objective force of nature" (386.14) that enters human being as food and drink. If in these gods "the earth-spirit in its metamorphosis" (386.21) offers itself to human being, this spirit still "has not offered itself to it . . . as *self-conscious* [human] spirit, and [so] the mystery of bread and wine is not yet [the] mystery of flesh and blood" (387.17–19), as in the sacrament where Christians partake of God's *human* incarnation.

But human being is at the center of the other cult described in this subdivision, the cult of "the beautiful wrestler" (388.19) as "an animated living work of art" (387.35–36). Human being "puts itself in the place of the statue" (387.31) when an athlete "instead of a stone god receives among his people the honor of being the highest bodily portrayal of their essence" (387.37–388.2).

Although this athlete portrays essence and specifically "the living *corporeity* of essence" (387.29–30), he is not viewed as an incarnation of deity because human being "does not yet place into such a [cult] the significance of absolute essence" (387.25–26). For Greek religion, only "*essence* is . . . manifest, not yet spirit; not as such [an essence] which *essentially* assumes human shape" (387.26–27) to appear as a complete human being. The athlete is no such divine incarnation. His ideal corporeity is only an "*abstract* moment . . . of essence" (387.29–30), a partial feature of spirit but not spirit itself. Even his beautiful corporeity cannot represent the national spirit of his people, which contains far more than a body can portray (388.20–26). The athlete's corporeity instead represents the universal humanity (388.26–27) cultivated in the Olympic games and thus reflects the decline of national deities (388.17–19).[77] Greek spirit then expresses itself in the universal content of Homeric epic.

The Spiritual Work of Art: Epic (388–92)

Hegel's third and final subdivision pertaining to the religion of art analyzes epic (388–92), tragedy (392–97), and comedy (397–99).[78] They are examples of "the spiritual work of art" (388.29), which is evidently linguistic. This new kind of art emerges by combining the outwardness of the athlete's body with the inwardness of bacchic enthusiasm (388.5–10). Language is the result because in language the body's outer existence is penetrated by inward mind (388.15–16). Thus, an intelligible transition is made from the "living" to the "spiritual" work of art.

But language alone does not make art spiritual; it also appears in the "abstract" work of art as hymn and oracle (380.24–382.27). The new factors in epic are the clarity of thoughtful speech (388.13–16) and a universal content; the latter derives from the universal character of the athlete's body, whose corporeity prescinds from tribal particularity (388.16–27). These new factors advance epic beyond the narrow individual content of hymn and oracle (388.10–12) and away from the unclarity of "bacchic frenzy" (388.12). They also give literature a universal perspective retained by tragedy and comedy.[79] Greek literature, therefore, is spiritual because it deals thoughtfully with the real world common to all the Greek peoples, and so has a relatively universal and clear point of view.

In epic,[80] this universal content appears in the "one pantheon" (388.32) of all the Greek gods, whose empirical counterpart is the "common undertaking" (389.4–5) of all the Greek peoples against

Troy.[81] Spirit's "pure viewing of itself as *universal humanity* . . . shapes for this work a total people and thereby a total heaven" (389.1, 4–5) of gods and heroes. When the Greeks express their newly discovered universality through a confederation of heroes from particular tribes under Agamemnon's leadership, their individual tribal gods become members of a pantheon headed by Zeus (389.12–20). Thus, the universal[82] religious content corresponds to an empirical and political universality because the gods are the personified essences of various tribes, "the particular beautiful folk-spirits [which now] unite themselves into one pantheon" (388.31–32).

In Hegel's words, spirit's "pure viewing of itself as *universal humanity* . . . shapes a total heaven" (389.1, 5). Here, one again finds universal essence molding itself through human imagination. Hegel calls language the "element and lodging" (388.32) of Homer's pantheon; appearing as thoughts (or mental images) the gods pass into language, "the [outward] existence of this [inner] image" (389.32). The gods are now being shaped by a master of language in a *spiritual* work of art.

Although gods and heroes are imagined in poetic language, the poet has no place among them. He remains outside[83] his fictional world of gods and heroes as "the organ disappearing in its content; not his own self counts, but his muse, his universal song" (390.2–3). But the real self gradually enters the work of art. In epic, the poet still has no role in the story (392.4–8); in tragedy, however, "*actual* human beings . . . put on the masks [Personen] of heroes" (392.27–28). And in comedy, the actors no longer portray legendary heroes but "the self . . . as actual . . . in its own bareness and ordinariness" (398.2, 4–5). In this way, the concept of spirit appears more clearly since art's gradual inclusion of real human being brings divine essence and human subjectivity closer together.

To be sure, epic narrative *form* excludes the real self of the artist; therefore, the gods of epic have no unity with an empirical self. But within the narrative *content*, human beings do appear. These are the heroes, who like the gods are imagined in art (390.6–8) and who do enjoy "a friendly external relation" (398.27) with their gods. In order to understand this "relation of divine to human" (390.10) *within* the artist's imagination, one must examine the nature of imagination itself, which affects the whole epic world (390.20–23). What Hegel writes about "Vorstellung" in reference to the Greek gods is especially important because the term reappears in his analysis of Christianity.

According to Hegel, "*imagination*" is "the synthetic linking of self-conscious [thought] and external existence" (389.31–32) or "the *synthetic* linking of universal [thought] and individual" (390.21) being. As a result, universal thoughts are imagined as existing entities. Thus, the gods are depicted as real beings who act like free individuals (390.25–27). As universal thoughts, however, they are also "the universal powers . . . of acting [human] individuality" (390.25–30), "the universal substances of what *self-conscious* [human] essence *in itself* is and does" (389.21). Since they have an essential connection with humanity, their concern with human affairs is not accidental (389.22–26). But because imagination makes the gods into separate beings,[84] this "essential unity initially hides under the form of a friendly external relation of both worlds" (389.26–27).

Epic poetry then has two parallel causes of human action: self-conscious human beings and their universal divine forces. Human action is attributed both to human and divine persons in an inconsistent way (390.23–25) because "both gods and humans have done . . . one and the same thing" (390.28–29). Imagination gives them a personal existence of their own, so these universal essences act like heavenly persons who duplicate the earthly work of humans. Even their intervention in human affairs "is a laughable superfluity, since they in fact [already] are the [essential] force of acting [human] individuality" (390.29–30). Their intrinsic relation to earth makes them depend on humans for honor and nourishment and even for something to do (390.32–36; 391.1–2), all of which conflicts with their also being "the [independent] universal which escapes this connection" (391.3) and the creative origin of nature and human being (390.36–37). Such inconsistencies are the result of imagination, which personifies essence; the gods, then, behave not like essences but like people interacting with other people.

Homer's gods also interact among themselves since they are many rather than one. This polytheism originates in the grouping of different tribal gods (388.31–32)[85] under the loose command of Zeus (389.14–17, 19–20). Homer's many gods are "*determinate* elements, *particular* gods, who thus are related to [each] other" (391.11–12). They oppose one another and enter into conflict (391.13)—which is not only "a comic self-forgetting of their eternal nature" (391.13–14), but which also ensures that some divine actions will not succeed (391.17–21). Limited by their abstractness and determinacy, none of them is the one universal God found in Persian religion and then in Judaism and Christianity. Instead, universal essence appears in epic as "the *incomprehensible [begrifflose] emptiness* of *necessity*" (391.30), "the *pure force* of the *negative* . . . about which they [the gods] can do nothing" (391.25–26), "for these *determinate* natures do not find themselves in this purity" (391.31–32). This pure negative is "the [necessary] *unity of the concept*" (391.33) personified as fate or "*necessity*" (391.30); Hegel also calls it "the *universal self*" (391.28), thereby distinguishing it from the empirical "*individual self* of mortals" (391.27). The one universal power overshadows the many gods, each of which represents only part of the actual world; their "contradictory substantiality . . . is subjected" (391.33–34) to necessity. Lacking positive content, it is nevertheless a divine figure that indicates the unity of essence or substance. The many gods cannot themselves be necessity, which would require their synthesis in "the *unity of the concept*" (391.33).

But what of necessity's relation to the poet? Both are excluded from the imagined world of gods and heroes (392.1, 6–8), and so their connection must be significant. According to Hegel, "*actual individuality* . . . splits into its moments, which [have] not yet found each other and united. The one individual, the *abstract* unactual [one], is necessity . . . the other [is] the singer [or bard], the *actual* individual" (392.4–8). In this text, necessity is a moment of real human personality. But why does Hegel make this connection? Probably because in his concept of spirit, necessity (along with substance)[86] belongs in human subjectivity: "self-consciousness . . . is in fact the negative power, the unity of . . . *substantial* essence and of *abstract* necessity; it is the spiritual unity into which everything returns" (397.11–14). Spirit is the appearance of deity as human being, in which substance and logical necessity find a real existence in thinking. At present, the work of art does not yet equal spirit. It includes only scattered images of substance, but not their necessary unity; nor does it contain the self as real. For spirit to know itself in the work, both necessity and the self "must draw closer to the content [of the work] . . . necessity has to fill itself with the content [and] the other, the speech of the bard, must [likewise] have a share in [the content]" (392.9–11). This need leads to tragedy, where logical necessity and real speech enter the work of art.

Although epic excludes a true empirical subjectivity and a single divine essence, it has of course contributed to the self-knowing of spirit. The world of gods and heroes imagines the convergence of universal essence and human subjectivity in a number of ways. The Olympian deities take on features of human selfhood and act like human beings. They also symbolize the essential forces behind human activity. And their involvement in human affairs indicates the "essential unity" (389.26) of divine and human being. In Homeric epic, spirit continues to move toward its concept of divine "*essence* . . . which *essentially* assumes human shape" (387.26–27).

The Spiritual Work of Art: Tragedy (392–97)

Although in tragedy[87] divine essence and human reality still do not fuse together completely, spirit comes closer to this goal in two ways. First, real human actors play the roles of the heroes who deal with divine powers. And second, divine substance itself is more unified by logical necessity, resulting in fewer powers that have a greater correspondence to individual human being.

The first way is obvious. In tragedy, "*actual* humans . . . put on the personas of the heroes, and portray them not [by] narrating but by an actual speaking of their own" (392.27–29). Tragedy abandons the narrative style of epic; the "hero is himself the speaker" (392.18). This development brings the work of art closer "to the immediate actuality of . . . existence" (393.29–30). The divine world portrayed in the work thus comes closer to empirical human life.

Hegel gives much more attention to the second way because it concerns the tragic action and its content. His complex analysis contains a number of related points: conceptual division and unification, the simpler divine world found in tragedy, the lesser number of human characters, and the approach of divine essence to human subjectivity. The last point depends on the others and is the most important one, since it concerns the shape of spirit. But Hegel's underlying aim— understanding the concept of spirit—is not always in clear view; he does not often mention spirit in his analysis of tragedy. However, he provides readers with enough indications to remind them of the major theme of *PhG* VII: the "self-consciousness of spirit" (363.8). It reappears here when Hegel reminds his reader of tragedy's meaning: "spirit . . . attains in its religion . . . [a] consciousness about itself" (393.33, 35). To discover this consciousness, one needs to examine deity's relation to human being in tragedy, for spirit is deity as human subjectivity, "*essence* . . . which *essentially* assumes human shape" (387.26–27).

Both gods and humans now appear in simpler form. Logical necessity, or "the *unity of the concept*" (391.33), gives the content of tragedy (392.9–10) a tighter unity, reducing the many gods and heroes of epic to an essential minimum. In this way, spirit "portrays itself to its consciousness in its purer form and simpler shaping" (393.35–36). The simplification applies to both gods (394.5–6) and human characters (394.11–12).

This conceptual simplicity also determines the plot's conflict because in tragedy, "spirit steps forth [on the stage] . . . in the simple division of the concept" (393.23–24). Since a concept unifies its parts, it contains internal division as well as unity. The concept Hegel has in mind also appears earlier in his analysis of tragedy in the Greek religion of the underworld.[88] Hegel reminds his readers of that previous treatment (393.33–34) in these terms:

> . . . ethical substance divided itself through its concept, according to its *content*, into the two powers that were determined as *divine* and *human*, or underearthly and upper[earthly] right—the former [right being] the *family*, the latter the *state's power*—and the first of which was the *female*, the other the *male character*. (394.1–5)

In other words, the one substance of Greek society divides itself into family and state. Their conflict is personified in the struggle between women and men,[89] who respectively uphold (what Hegel does not identify here, namely) individual family members and universal community interests. Each gender or character represents one side of the concept, so that neither character promotes the whole. Each gender knowingly pursues its own goal, and so is consciously the agent of one fundamental force, while unwittingly offending the other.

This division also points to a division within each character, which knows its own aim and ignores its opposite. The difference between knowing and unknowing (394.13–395.13) thus provides another important theme for Hegel's analysis. One must then consider two kinds of opposition. The social form is complex: the family's divine law of the underworld, upheld by women, and the state's human law, promoted by men. This division supplies the two main characters for the conflict. Since the second opposition results from the first one (each character acknowledges only the role of its gender), the underlying subject[90] of the second opposition is again substance itself: "essence [also] divides itself . . . according to *knowing*" (394.13).[91]

Tragedy thus contains two sets of oppositions within one substance, thereby limiting the number of possible gods. Personifying the underlying unity of Greek society is Zeus, "the *shape* of *substance*" (395.29–30). Human characters individualize family and state, but both institutions have the same god (395.17–19) because each one is the highest substance (395.17) for its character. Therefore, Zeus alone is the god of both institutions (395.15–17) and of each character, who "knows and acknowledges . . . only one highest power, and this Zeus as only the power of the state or of the hearth" (396.33–35). The social conflict has no god but Zeus alone since each human character considers its own law the sole expression of Zeus. The first division, therefore, does not multiply deities. It needs only three figures: the two human characters and Zeus.

The second division occurs within each human character (395.20–21). According to this division, Apollo (396.23) is the "revealing god" (395.28) of knowing, while "the Fury keeping itself hidden" (395.28–29) is the quasi-divine figure for ignorance of an essential power that later takes its revenge.[92] The second opposition adds two more figures to the tragedy, bringing the total to five: Zeus, the two human characters, and now Apollo and the Fury. For convenience, one may consider the two latter shapes divine, though technically the Fury is not a god.

Zeus rules over the other two divine shapes. Knowing and ignorance have the two sides of substance for their content, and so "the *shape* of *substance*, Zeus, is the necessity of the *relation* to one another of both" (395.29–30) Apollo and the Fury, of knowing and unknowing. Zeus, therefore, is not only "the power of the state or of the hearth" (396.34–35), but also the father of Apollo and the power of the ignored Fury (394.25; 396.35–37), "who sits with *Zeus* on the throne and enjoys equal prestige with . . . [Apollo] the knowing god" (395.11–13).

The relation of these two shapes to Zeus also indicates his connection to the acting human characters. At the beginning of a tragedy, each character personifies one side of the whole substance (395.6–7), thereby provoking the wrath of the side that it does not know (395.9–11, 35–39). Corresponding only to what each character knows, Apollo's revelations (394.25–28) are deceitful (396.4, 36) because both sides equally belong to substance (395.9–10); in the end, then, they cancel one another out and return into the whole (396.17–24)[93] or "into simple Zeus" (396.24). If the existence of two human characters indicates an external division of substance, their "mutual perishing" (396.12) indicates their unity in the one substance of Zeus. Moreover, this unity occurs not simply in substance, but also *within* each character through "the difference of knowing and unknowing [that] falls within *each* one of the *actual self-consciousnesses*" (395.20–21) in the plot. Hegel's analysis brings the opposition of substance (the first division) into individual human being (the second division). The analysis thus implies a shape of spirit that needs to be examined carefully.

How does tragedy promote the appearance of divine substance as human being? One could say that Apollo and the Fury incarnate themselves in each character's knowing and unknowing. Such a statement, however, is misleading since Apollo and the Fury are "two individual shapes . . . only in abstraction . . . in *imagination*" (395.21, 20, 27).[94] In reality, such gods do not exist, and comedy rightly scoffs at them. On the other hand, Apollo and the Fury are more than images of human functions. They indicate that *substance* appears in human knowing and unknowing: the conceptual division of substance reproduces itself in the individual characters. Because each character incarnates the conflict of Greek society, it also incarnates divine substance as divided. But precisely because the substance is divided and only one side of it is known to each character, substance as a whole does not appear in any character's knowing. Thus, no character is a full incarnation of substance. Greek tragedy is not Christianity, but it does come closer to the Christian shape of spirit.

Hegel suggests this clearly enough by linking spirit, substance, and the characters: "spirit steps forth . . . in the simple division of the concept . . . substance . . . in its two . . . forces. The elemental *universal* essences are at the same time self-conscious *individualities*—heroes" (393.23–26) who individualize the two forces of substance and who therefore constitute the object in which spirit views itself. Hegel attributes this development to the simplicity of the concept, through which "the previously multiform . . . circle of gods reduces itself to these [two] powers, which . . . are brought closer to proper individuality" (394.5–7) as found in the heroes, the "universal individuation" (393.29) used by tragedy.

A simpler substance does not necessarily come closer to human being, as the religion of light proves. Tragedy however follows epic, which views the gods as universal forces of human action. But epic's "earlier scattering of the whole into multiple and abstract forces, which appear substantized, is the *dissolution* of the [human] *subject* which comprehends them only as *moments* in its self" (394.7–9) rather than as its essence. A character's essence must be single. When tragedy unifies those moments into only two fundamental powers and individuates each one in a human self-consciousness, it creates the "essential . . . individuality . . . [of] absolute characters" (396.32),[95] "heroes who put their consciousness into one of these powers" (393.26–27). Devoting themselves to the divine essence they know, these characters "constitute its operation and actuality" (393.28); they are the fictional individuals in whom the essence now exists. And thus they portray "spirit . . . in its purer form and simpler shaping" (393.33–36).

Spirit, however, is not fully portrayed in tragedy. For one thing, the division of substance means that Zeus himself lacks total integration. He is, therefore, distinguished from the dissolving unity of necessity or fate (397.12–13, 20). The characters who identify with only one side of Zeus "do not know themselves but rather perish" (397.9–10) in that higher unity. Since they do not know themselves in it, they cannot be the conscious appearance of necessity or fate.

More important, the empirical self is not the stage character who incarnates an elemental power of substance. For Hegel, spirit means that divine essence appears as real human being, which "in fact is the unity of Zeus, of *substantial* essence and *abstract* necessity, . . . the spiritual unity into which everything returns" (397.14). But in tragedy, "actual self-consciousness is still distinguished from substance and fate" (397.14–15). Separated from these higher powers, actual individuality is found in two places. One is the "chorus or rather the onlooking crowd whom this movement of divine life as an *alien* [power] fills with fear" (397.16–17), yet neither the chorus nor the crowd appears in the plot of the tragedy. The other site of actual individuality is behind the hero's mask: the actor's real self, which does not appear in the plot because the character "divides into its mask and into the [real] actor, [or] into the persona and the actual self" (397.22–23). Thus in tragedy, the actual self is still separated from the work of art. A different kind of work appears when drama begins to portray the actual self as the result or fate of tragedy's mythical world (394.24–27). Tragedy then becomes comedy.

The Spiritual Work of Art: Comedy (397–99)

Hegel persuasively concludes his discussion of the religion of art with an analysis of comedy,[96] which continues tragedy's "depopulation of heaven" (396.25). Tragedy reduces the chorus's Homeric pantheon to Zeus, Apollo and the Fury because the heroes need no other deities (395.14–15). But whereas tragic heroes passionately promote one side of Zeus, comic characters affirm their actual individual selves and mock every universal essence.

Homer's gods are an easy target since "these elemental essences as *universal* moments are no self and not actual" (397.29–30). These gods "are indeed fitted out with the form of individuality, but this [form] is only fancied [into] them" (397.30–31), a "superficial individuality which imagination loaned to the divine essentialities" (399.1–2). In comedy, human being shows itself superior: it speaks ironically about the gods even while wearing the mask of one (397.33–36), and even drops the mask to show the ordinary human playing the role of the god (398.1–5). Thus, "actual self-consciousness portrays itself as the fate of the gods" (397.28–29), and the empirical self enters the work of art.

Like the universal gods of epic, "divine substance" in its "meaning of natural and ethical essentiality" (398.9–10) also fares badly. This meaning is also found in cult and tragedy. In the cult of Ceres and Bacchus (387.15), "the mystery of bread and wine" (398.14–15), human being appropriates to itself the "meaning of the inner essence" (398.15) of nature. There the gods turn into human being. In comedy, the self "is conscious of the irony of this meaning in general" (398.16–17), leaving nature with no divine significance in "the nudity of its immediate existence" (399.3). The meaning of "ethical essentiality"

(398.17) refers to tragedy, which portrays "the folk in its two sides of the state . . . and family individuality" (398.18). But now individuals take over the social order (398.25) in order to pursue their own ends (398.29–30),[97] and so comedy can show "the laughable contrast" (398.23) between "the universal as a theory and what is to be done in practice" (398.28–29) by individual action.[98]

"Ethical essentiality" (398.17) also refers to philosophy, "self-conscious pure knowing, or the rational thinking of the universal" (398.19–20), which "lifts divine essence away from its contingent shape" (398.31) of "various ethical maxims" (398.32–33) and "lifts it up into the simple ideas of the *beautiful* and *good*" (398.34–35). But these ideas "are filled with any content" by "the force of dialectical knowing" (399.6–7),[99] so that "the pure thoughts of the beautiful and good show the comic spectacle . . . of becoming empty, and precisely by that [they become] the game of [individual] opinion and of the arbitrariness of contingent individuality" (399.10–11, 13–14). Thus, the individual self usurps not only nature but also the ethical social order and ethical thinking, all of which used to have a universal meaning or divine significance.

Everything universal now vanishes into the self, which is its destiny. As a result, subjectivity assumes the role of necessity or fate because in comedy the self extinguishes every universal. In epic and tragedy, fate is "the *universal self*" (391.28) imagined as an alien power separated from the human self (399.15–17); in comedy, they converge. By its impudence, "the *individual self* is the negative force through and in which the gods, as well as their moments—existing nature and the thoughts of its determinacies—disappear" (399.17–19). But whereas fate is only "the emptiness of disappearing" (399.19), the self is a determinate reality that, in fact, is "the sole actuality" (399.20–21) of all the universals previously revered by Greek religion.

Evidently, Greek religion must end when it turns into a self-centered humanism (399.21–22). There are no longer any gods or universal forces distinct from the self. Because "individual consciousness in the certainty of itself is what portrays itself as this absolute power, this [absolute power] has lost the form of an *imagined* [being] *separated* in general from *consciousness* and alien to it" (399.22–25). Everything universal or essential is dissolved in the living and thinking self (399.30–33). And this self that is now the focus of drama is the real self. It is not a legendary hero larger than life, but the ordinary self of the actor and spectator (399.28–30); similarly, it is not pure thought in its abstract side, but the whole self "in its thinking, existence, and doing" (399.31–32). Greek religion thus concludes with "a well-being . . . of consciousness" (399.34–35) happy with itself.

In comedy's enjoyment of the self, "the religion of art . . . has completely returned into itself" (399.21–22). True to its principle of portraying "absolute substance . . . in the form of individuality" (402.37–403.1), the religion of art now makes real human individuality the absolute substance. Greek religion ends here, but not religion itself. Comedy's "irreligious" (400.19) claim that "the self is the absolute essence" (400.13) expresses a "frivolity" (400.13)[100] that human thoughtfulness reverses.

As divine essence in human shape (387.26–27), spirit cannot know itself truly in comedy's one-sided humanism, in which universal essence disappears. The concept of spirit found in *PhG* VII has human subjectivity knowing itself as universal divine essence. Incarnational religion differentiates this concept into a series of specific religions that vary according to the human shape they give to God. In the natural religions, divine essence appears in subhuman shapes taken from nature, while in the religion of art it has a variety of human shapes. Not until comedy does the real self appear at the center of religion, and this development is necessary for the "self-consciousness of spirit" (363.8). But in comedy, the real self is too impudent and practical to consider itself as the appearance of a deeper essence.

Thus, religion has not yet given morality's concept of spirit its full reality. The real self affirmed by Greek comedy is not "the completely universal" (362.24–25) ego of morality. This real self must now descend into its thought and grasp itself as the existence of universal essence. This development constitutes Christianity,[101] which affirms the incarnation of God in a real human being.

NOTES

1. New for *PhG* but not for religion itself, as Hegel interprets it. According to him, conscience has rediscovered a principle with a long tradition that supplies material for "Die Religion." This rediscovery permits Hegel to

go back in time, as he often does when beginning a new chapter, but *within* each chapter he follows historical sequence. Thus, *PhG* VI provides a history of European spirit as the dialectic of social world and individual subjectivity. The chapter analyzes Greek and Christian religion and ends with German idealism. *PhG* VII deals with absolute spirit as divine incarnation and from this new point of view offers another analysis of Greek and Christian religion.

2. For discussions of Hegel's introduction to *PhG* VII, see Hyppolite, pp. 511–25; Kainz, 2: 128–31; Kojève, pp. 196–224 (a thorough but Marxist examination of Hegel's text); Lauer, pp. 230–34.

3. In 366.16–17, "an und für sich" is equivalent to "Ganzes," which has nothing opposite to itself; any opposition would be within the whole and would be surmounted by the whole.

4. Faith opposes to actuality its own "pure consciousness." For the unhappy consciousness, the opposite of actuality is divine immutability. The latter conscious emphasizes objectivity; the former, subjectivity.

5. Walter Jaeschke, *Reason in Religion: the Foundations of Hegel's Philosophy of Religion*, trans. J. Michael Stewart and Peter C. Hodgson (Berkeley and Los Angeles: University of California Press, 1990), p. 204: "the religiohistorical conception of the *Phenomenology* is that of an incarnation of God in human form." The German edition appeared in 1986.

6. However, God is not a *knowing* subject before human being. By "subject," Hegel means a "self-moving" (20.20) agent that causes its "own doing" (29.37), a "self-producing, [self-]advancing process returning into itself" (45.21–22). These passages (all taken from Hegel's Preface to *PhG*) indicate that subjectivity has a more general meaning than consciousness does. Obviously, Hegel's description can refer to human thinking and often does; the "knowing [human] subject" (17.5) is, of course, a constant part of *PhG*. But Hegel (referring to Aristotle) also applies the term "subject" to nature as purposeful (20.14–16), in which conscious intellectual purpose plays no apparent role. Indeed, Hegel himself in his *Enzyklopädie* uses the term "*subject*" for the "*animal* organism" (§ 337; TWA 9.337), and such a usage corresponds to its general meaning in the Preface to *PhG*. But when applied to divine substance, the term seems to refer to the logical or metaphysical unfolding of divine essence. When Hegel claims that "everything . . . depends . . . on grasping and expressing the true [absolute essence] not as *substance* but also as *subject*" (18.3–5), he means that "substance is . . . *subject* . . . insofar as it is the movement of positing itself, or the self-mediation of its becoming other" (18.18–21). In this otherness, it becomes both human knowing and objec-

tive being (18.6–8). Thus deity includes nature and human subjectivity, but its own subjectivity consists in its being the agent of its development into those determinate forms of existence.

7. Both of these passages say "essentially" because the shaping takes place from the side of essence.

8. One of the earlier moments of religion is also called "spirit" (363.4); it is the moment that produced the Greek religion of the underworld, Christian faith in heaven, and philosophical morality. But this kind of spirit is not what Hegel has in mind for *PhG* VII. The earlier type is called "immediate spirit, which is not yet consciousness of spirit" (365.23–24); it is not yet the self-conscious spirit of *PhG* VII. "Immediate" spirit is not conscious of itself as spirit because human being does not yet appear as the differentiation of divine essence. In *PhG* VII, however, spirit is the "*absolute spirit*" (361.25) that emerges as "the appearing God" (363.28–29) of "Evil and Its Pardon."

9. This point figures prominently in the examination of *PhG* VII by Brito (who appeals to Heinrichs; see Brito, p. 143 n. 196). When divine essence reveals itself as the human self (p. 166), human being becomes an appearance or manifestation of absolute essence (pp. 107–8, 120, 143 n. 196, 181–82). He further points out that such an idea has no parallel in the *Jenenser Logik und Metaphysik*; thus, *PhG* VII "rests . . . on a logic of *appearance* [*Erscheinung*] which Hegel develops . . . for the first time" (p. 143 n. 196).

10. Another way of stating Hegel's position is to say that the absolutely universal would not be absolutely universal if it excluded singular existence from itself.

11. I.e., at the beginning of its development.

12. The term "self-consciousness" is itself ambiguous because it can refer to abstract thinking (as in 364.17–36) or to the actual sensual self (as in 369.23–29). However, the full meaning of "self-consciousness" obviously incorporates both sides, and this synthesis is the aim of *PhG* VII (364.36–365.5).

13. Because the two spirits are the same, they develop in parallel ways and influence one another even before they converge. See below, nn. 15, 17.

14. It also indicates their limitation: they do not fully integrate the empirical world into divine presence. The Son and the Spirit remain in "the form of objectivity" (368.34) opposed to the knowing subject. As objects of consciousness, they have a "*shape*" in "*imagination*" (368.32, 33), which keeps the object distinct from the knowing subject. The incarnate Son and indwelling Spirit are not yet the "*concept*" (368.34) that completely unifies inward thought and empirical human existence by compre-

hending deity as an essence that differentiates itself into rational human being. Only when this takes place will spirit be fully conscious of itself and "dissolve . . . the form of objectivity" (368.34–35) found in religious imagination. Its knowing will then be absolute, or complete. When human reason comprehends reality as pure thought, it identifies itself with universal essence and dissolves every form of objectivity. Thus, philosophy achieves the goal of religion.

15. This knowledge refers to divine essence appearing as pure knowing. But spirit also has its life in the world, and initially its religion does not include this life. How does its empirical self-awareness compare to its religion? Hegel's long discussion (365.18–367.26) of the correlation between religion and empirical spirit indicates that a determinate religion corresponds to a determinate actual spirit (366.25–26). Its empirical self-awareness must then correspond to its absolute self-awareness in religion. When primitive spirit sees itself as a thing of nature in its daily life, it also places its internal awareness of deity into a thing of nature, and so appears as natural religion. This religion occurs as long as spirit views itself as a thing of nature: first as light, then as plant and animal, and finally as half-animal and half-human. In the Greek religion of art, spirit finally views itself as individual human personality.

In all these religions, spirit gives its universal essence a specific individual form corresponding to the human self-awareness of a given culture. Hyppolite (pp. 518–21) explains how empirical spirit supplies determinate symbols for religion, so that a given religion reflects the culture of which it is the religion. See also *PhG* 370.9–14.

16. Hegel remarks that this development also respects the status of real existence. Since the pure knowing of conscience knows all actuality only in its thought (364.30–32), it does not give actuality "its full right, namely . . . of being . . . independent free existence" (365.8–9). When spirit recognizes itself in God incarnate, it must also respect the separate existence of Jesus as a distinctive (human) person.

17. Religion binds together similar aspects from each moment (367.10–17). For example, natural religion in its immediate stage as the religion of light binds together the sensory immediacy of consciousness and the lordship of immediate self-consciousness (371.4–11). Religions differ by the particular aspects they synthesize.

18. Hyppolite points out that natural, artistic, and revealed religion respectively correspond to consciousness, self-consciousness, and reason (p. 525), the three main divisions of *PhG* according to Hegel's table of contents, which must have been drawn up after the writing of the text because the latter does not observe this organization in its chapter titles.

See *Werke*, TWA 3: 497. One of the consequences of this three-fold division is that most of *PhG*, including religion, then becomes a form of reason. See Hoffmeister's remarks in his edition of Hegel's *PhG*, pp. 575–76.

19. For commentary, see Kojève, pp. 225–39; Lauer, pp. 235–36; Kainz, 2: 132–34, who correctly notes (2: 134 n. 9) that Hegel's introduction to natural religion applies to all kinds of religion, whether "natural" or not.

20. For greater clarity, I have transposed the order of Hegel's remarks.

21. In natural religion, spirit knows itself as objective *being* in subhuman shape.

22. Therefore God does not have a superhuman, divine self-consciousness; divine self-consciousness is human. Lauer's interpretation of this passage is that divine Spirit must be present *in* human self-consciousness (p. 236). This view implies that God is still a distinct self-consciousness revealing itself to human self-consciousness. Divine and human self-consciousness then cooperate in the way maintained by traditional treatises on indwelling grace. But divine self-consciousness is imagined as *distinct* from human self-consciousness. In Lauer's view, God still has an imagined self distinct from the actual human self.

23. Kojève refers to the whole passage (369.21–35) because it "confirms my global interpretation of Chapter VII . . . man must realize that *he* has created God" (p. 235). But Hegel's argument is that God finds real expression as human being and not that God is invented by the human mind.

24. I.e., absolute knowing, which differs from the "pure concept" (369.9) by including real existence: reality is itself rational.

25. In German, "Das Lichtwesen," which is hard to translate exactly. For brief commentary, see Hyppolite, p. 526; Kainz, 2: 134–35; Kojève, pp. 239–40; Lauer, p. 236; Solomon, pp. 599–600, 601, 603, 604.

26. In this religion divine essence is light and creatures are its emanations. All the "forms of nature" (371.21), the "manifold forces of existence and the shapes of actuality" (371.20), are "pourings of light" (371.18), which is their essence. This type of religion corresponds very well to Zoroastrianism as Hegel describes it in his *Aesthetics* (trans. T. M. Knox, 1: 325–32). Thus, it makes good sense to identify *PhG*'s "Lichtwesen" with Persian Zoroastrianism. Jaeschke (pp. 199–204), however, claims that *PhG*'s religion of light is really Judaism. Evidence for his view is well supplied by some close verbal parallels between *PhG*'s description of the religion of light and Hegel's portrayal of Judaism in his lectures of 1821 and 1824. However, working counter to Jaeschke's proposal is the idea behind *PhG*'s "Lichtwesen," in which deity is identified with light; in Judaism,

light is only the garment of God (Psalm 104:2, quoted by Jaeschke, p. 202) but not the divine essence itself. But *PhG*'s argument in "Lichtwesen" is that divine essence *exists* as light. For this reason, I prefer to identify "Lichtwesen" with Persian religion. In Judaism, "light" is hardly a central image, nor is it viewed as a rudimentary incarnation of God. Solomon accepts the usual identification of the religion of light with Zoroastrianism (pp. 600, 601, 603) but wonders whether Judaism (pp. 600, 601, 604) was also in Hegel's mind. Kainz provides the relevant evidence concisely but clearly (2: 134–35 nn. 10–11).

27. As being, light resembles the immediately given object of sensory certainty, the first form of *consciousness* (371.5–6); as master, it recalls the master-slave dialectic that is the first object of *self-consciousness* (371.9–10).

28. Hyppolite points out that the empirical and political counterpart of this religion is oriental despotism, which parallels the slavery of human beings before their divine master (*Structure*, p. 526).

29. Thus, in the religion of light, divine substance does not include spirit's real existence (385.21–27).

30. In *PhG* immediate being, the object of sensory certainty, develops into self-conscious thinking.

31. Here, "daß" appears to mean "so that." See Campe, vol. 3 (1807), s.v., "Daß." Its third meaning is "damit," "so that."

32. For brief commentary, see Hyppolite, pp. 526–27; Kainz, 2: 135–36; Kojève, p. 240; Lauer, pp. 236–37; Solomon, pp. 600–01.

33. As suggested by "*Wahrnehmung*" (372.9), which grasps a variety of attributes but is not yet the synthetic unity of the concept. Hegel correlates the three types of natural religion with the three forms of consciousness (*PhG* I, II, III): the religion of light with sensory certainty, plant-and-animal religion with perception, and Egyptian religion with understanding (373.15).

34. Identified by a reference to castes later on: the "unsociable folk-spirits" (377.22) of animal religion arrange themselves "into castes" through "the subjugation of . . . peoples hating one another" (376.16). Elsewhere, Hegel points out that fertility religions were found all over the East, though especially in India (*Aesthetics*, trans. T. M. Knox, 2: 641; see also 1: 445, 447, 453). Furthermore, in his *Philosophy of History*, Hegel specifically mentions beasts and flowers as divine objects for India (trans. J. Sibree, p. 141)—a remark that echoes *PhG*'s mention of "*flower-religion*" (372.12) in "Plant and Animal." Hyppolite refers "Plant and Animal" to "the early religions of India." See G. W. F. Hegel, *La Phénoménologie de l'esprit*, trans. Jean Hyppolite, 2 vols. (Paris: Aubier,

Editions Montaigne, 1941), 2: 216 n. 12. (Referred to in subsequent notes as Hyppolite's translation; his commentary *Genèse et Structure* is referred to simply as Hyppolite.)

35. The "*actual* self-consciousness" (372.21) that parallels the religious one.

36. Universality is missing from the relations *among* individual tribes, but it must be present *within* each tribe simply to establish the group as an entity containing many members. Tribal identity then expresses its universal essence in a divine shape. Without such universal thinking, there would be no religion and no tribe.

37. On the other hand, the worker's "doing is not only negative, but also in repose and positive" (372.31–32), because the thing produced is not destroyed, and so the artisan combines the destructiveness of animal-religion with the repose of plant-religion (372.11, 14). In addition to these two aspects, Egyptian religion also transposes something from the religion of light, whose universal and holy "immediate *being-in-itself*" (373.1) is transformed into the profane "common existence" (373.5) of material shaped by the artisan. What human being handles cannot be considered holy.

38. Hegel's German word "Werkmeister" suggests that human being is now "master" over its "work." Gradually it comes to be aware of this fact; the stages of its awareness make up the history of Egyptian religion.

39. For commentary, see Hyppolite, *Structure*, pp. 527–28; Kainz, 2: 136–38; Kojève, pp. 240–41; Lauer, pp. 237–38; Solomon, pp. 601–04.

40. According to Hegel, Egyptian antiquities reveal "this endless impulse to work, to describe or represent outwardly what is as yet only inward, contained in idea, and for this reason has not become clear to mind." This passage is found in Hegel's *Lectures on the Philosophy of Religion*, trans. Rev. E. B. Speirs and J. Burdon Sanderson, 3 vols. (1895; reprint ed., New York: The Humanities Press, 1962), 2: 109. For Hegel's German text, see *VPR*, ed. Jaeschke, 4a: 525.

41. More precisely, "as it is in and for itself" (374.4); i.e., as universal essence "in itself" and conscious "for itself."

42. See Hyppolite's translation, 2: 219 n. 19.

43. When plant life is subdued by human thought (374.16–19), it is no longer holy but merely useful (374.13–16).

44. Hyppolite's translation, 2: 220 n. 20. Egyptian columns also used leaf-like decorations at the base—a fact noted in Hegel's lectures on art—but he does not seem to be referring to this point here.

45. An allusion to the departed spirit inside a material pyramid.

46. An allusion to the ray of light striking an obelisk.

47. Human bodies with animal heads.

48. An allusion to the statue of Memnon; see Hyppolite's translation, 2: 220 n. 23. Hegel also refers to this statue in his *Aesthetics*, trans. T. M. Knox, 1: 358, and in his *Philosophy of History*, trans. J. Sibree, p. 199.

49. Although "black formless stone" seems to be an allusion to Mecca, and is so understood by a note in Hyppolite's translation (2: 221 n. 24), a more coherent sense is obtained if one takes Hegel to be referring to a dark temple interior. In his analysis of Greek sculpture, Hegel refers to the "black stone" (378.34) from which is shaped a human form of deity. The hidden inner meaning of Egyptian religion then becomes clear.

50. The "riddling sphinx" (394.29) is mentioned in Hegel's analysis of Greek tragedy and in his *Philosophy of History*, trans. J. Sibree, pp. 213, 220.

51. See Hegel's *Aesthetics*, trans. T. M. Knox, 1: 360–61.

52. According to Greek myth, the sphinx asked Oedipus a riddle (Appolodorus III.v.8, as cited by Knox; see previous note). The answer to the riddle is human being, and the answer is given by a Greek; both of these aspects point to the Greek religion of art, which portrays human being clearly. Hegel is probably alluding to this answer here since the next stage of religion in *PhG* is the Greek religion of art. But his argument requires only that the question be posed, for the question is what converts Egyptian work into human language.

53. For commentary, see Hyppolite, pp. 528–37; Kainz, 2: 138–54; Kojève, pp. 241–55; Lauer, pp. 238–44; Solomon, pp. 604–14.

54. Also in earlier Greek religion (378.33–379.22).

55. A reference to "simple substance" (385.26).

56. Belonging to "immediate spirit" (365.23), the religion of the underworld believes in personal immortality and in this way elevates individuality above the state. As "absolute spirit," the religion of art gives individual human shape to divine essence by creating works of art.

57. Kojève draws attention to the existence of slavery in ancient Greece, where art creates a fictional world (p. 243) for masters who become artists (p. 242) because manual labor is done by slaves (pp. 241–42). Hegel's description of Greek religion, however, makes no allusions to slavery and has a much more positive attitude toward art.

58. An allusion to I Cor. 11:23. The resurrection of Jesus parallels creative art. Just as Greek substance (or culture) lives through the artist, God incarnate (after the death of Jesus) lives as the Christian church.

59. See also 377.19–20: "spirit certain within itself . . . grieves over the loss of its world. . . ." Lauer thinks this passage refers to Greek tragedy (p. 238), but the context suggests Greek art in general, or only its beginning; tragedy comes later.

60. According to Hegel, this combination is needed for "absolute art"

(377.22), where absolute essence differentiates itself into shapes resembling free human being. Natural religion expresses the absolute in art, but not as free human being (377.22–25), while Christianity (377.25–30) goes beyond art by recognizing "its concept" (377.29) of God and self in "*this* [real] *self*" (377.28) rather than in an imaginary self produced by art. Only in Greece does absolute spirit portray itself as art.

61. See, for example, 380: 12–13: "the artist thus experiences in his work [here, the statue of a god] that he [has] produced *no* essence *equal to himself.*" See also 392.7–8: "the *actual* individual, the bard, . . . sinks [away to disappear] in [the world of] his imagination."

62. This progression from abstract to living art, and then to spiritual art, resembles the sequence of natural religions in which thinking first sees itself as abstract essence in the religion of light, then as living and akin to plant and animal, and finally as quasi-spiritual in the instinctive and half-human labor of the Egyptian artisan. A similar sequence is observable in "Manifest Religion," which first describes an abstract divine Trinity apart from creation, then a living human Son who delivers human being from slavery to its life in nature, and finally a divine Spirit in the Christian church.

63. Hyppolite explains the three stages as follows (*Structure*, p. 530): in the abstract work of art, the gods are separated from human being; in the living work of art, human being itself is the shape of deity; and in the spiritual work of art, divine substance merges into human self-certitude.

64. Obviously, Hegel uses the term "art" in a broad sense here. The same point applies to some of the cults described in the abstract work of art.

65. For commentary, see Hyppolite, pp. 530–32; Kainz, 2: 140–45; Kojève, pp. 244–47; Lauer, pp. 239–41.

66. Continuing a topic developed in his treatment of the Egyptian "Artisan," Hegel analyzes in the Greek "Abstract Work of Art" not only the statue, but also the temple (*PhG*, 378.19–32; Hyppolite's translation, 2: 227 nn. 15–16). To simplify my own discussion, I have left out of it Hegel's analysis of the Greek temple.

67. Kainz defines it well: "abstract" means "isolated from living thought" (2: 142 n. 24).

68. In contrast to the hymn, which expresses the universal self-consciousness of a community.

69. Hyppolite compares the separation of statue from artist with the separation of idea from subjectivity in Greek philosophy (pp. 530–31).

70. Like the unhappy consciousness (125.31–33), the devout soul experiences its universal thinking as the appearance of universal essence.

71. When Hegel adds "not in hope and in a late[r] actuality" (385.13), he contrasts Greek religion with Judeo-Christian eschatology.

72. For commentary, see Kojève, pp. 248–50; Hyppolite, *Structure*, pp. 532–33; Lauer, p. 241; Kainz, 2: 145–47.

73. Probably the Olympic games, because the athletic cult overcomes tribal particularity in favor of universal humanity (388.17–27).

74. According to modern dictionaries, Hegel's term "Fechter" means "fencer" or "gladiator." Neither meaning matches the usual practice of ancient Greek festivals.

75. More specifically, essence in the form of *nature* is known by empirical consciousness (386.30–35), while *essence* in the form of nature is known by intellectual consciousness (386.36–37). Kojève claims that the emphasis on empirical consciousness in this passage (386.33–35) "refutes the alleged 'panlogism' of Hegel" (p. 249). But Hegel seems to be insisting upon the need for both kinds of consciousness because empirical consciousness alone is "gedankenlose" (386.36), i.e., "thoughtless" in the sense of "unthinking."

76. The "Lichtwesen" (386.24), since different religions reveal the same universal essence in different ways.

77. Hyppolite (p. 532) considers the cult of corporeity an example of immediate unity between deity and human being. This is a puzzling remark because Hegel gives this cult no positive religious significance.

78. All three genres are named explicitly (389.33; 392.13; 397.28).

79. In tragedy, the individual follows a universal law; in comedy, the universal is dissolved in individual selfhood.

80. For brief commentary, see Hyppolite, p. 534; Kainz, 2: 147–49; Kojève, pp. 250–51; Lauer, pp. 242–43.

81. A good example of how religion parallels empirical spirit. See also 389.18–19 and n. 15 above.

82. Although the basic meaning of "universal" does not change, it has different levels of application. Initially, each god is the universal essence of a single people or tribe. Those particular gods now work together in a more universal group corresponding to the confederation of heroes from various Greek peoples. The political confederation is not a single people, and the religious pantheon is not a single divine essence. The collection of heroes remains affected by individualism, and so is not yet the one universal government (389.5–8) of abstract universal thought (389.14–15, 34–35) later developed in Rome.

83. Hyppolite compares the epic poet's absence from his work to the separation of a sculptor from the statue (pp. 530, 533). In tragedy (the next stage

of Greek art), a living actor is used. Whereas epic resembles the abstract work of art, tragedy resembles the living work of art (p. 530).

84. In his *Aesthetics*, trans. T. M. Knox, 1: 225–26, Hegel points out the contradiction: the gods are really human being, yet they are also independent.

85. In this grouping, the tribal gods remain distinct because they symbolize different features of human individuality. The more each deity approaches a complete empirical personality, the more it acquires aspects personified by other gods. Then "their characters lose . . . the sharpness of their peculiarity and mix themselves [up] in their ambiguity" (391.16–17).

86. Necessity properly belongs to divine substance, but since thought does not unify the Homeric deities, they also seem distinct from logical necessity. In tragedy, divine substance expresses a concept (393.22–25; 394.1; 396.31) and thus expresses necessity (395.29–30) as well. But even in tragedy necessity (also called "fate") is never thoroughly integrated with substance; they remain parallel shapes of deity (393.14–16, 20–21; 397.13, 15, 20–21). If substance were completely penetrated by necessity, it would be "the *unity of the concept*" (391.33) and thus one God. It would also appear (through its internal self-differentiation) in human form, as in Hegel's own system.

87. For commentary, see Hyppolite, p. 535; Kainz, 2: 149–52; Kojève, pp. 251–54; Lauer, pp. 243–44.

88. There, Hegel draws on the story of Antigone; here, for the religion of art, on Orestes. See Hyppolite's translation, 2: 250–51 nn. 74, 76, 79.

89. Kojève's reference (p. 253) to slavery—the master is particular because he is not a woman and not a slave—indicates his own concern more than Hegel's, which here deals with men and women only.

90. One finds the same relation between divine substance (the underlying subject) and human being (self-conscious individual subjectivity) in Hegel's interpretation of Christ.

91. Hegel refers the first division to "*content*" (394.1) and the second one to "*form*" (394.13).

92. The division into knowing and unknowing complicates Hegel's analysis. His treatment would be neater if the Fury corresponded to the female character, and Apollo to the male. However, this neat correspondence cannot be adopted because 396.6–9 clearly states that either law can be unknown. Therefore, both male and female characters are subject to the revenge of the Fury.

93. See Hegel's *Aesthetics*, trans. T. M. Knox, 2: 1215: tragedy cancels conflicts as conflicts.

94. Tragedy continues to use imagination when it personifies the gods needed

for its plot, even though it has been previously (392.13–18) called conceptual rather than imaginative. And Homer's religion of unconceptual imagination (396.37–397.5) also continues to exist. In the spectators, represented by the drama's chorus (392.37–393.1; 393.30–32), one finds the older religion of epic (392.35–37) with its polytheism and fear of fate (393.12–16; 397.16–17), along with an inability to comprehend the logical necessity of the action (393.20–21). Most of the gods the chorus recognizes have no significance for the main action of the tragedy (397.1–5).

95. In contrast to the Homeric gods, whose individuality does not indicate essence consistently (396.25–29). These gods also lack true individuality. Since they personify moments of the human self, "individuality is consequently only the superficial form of those essences" (394.10). Such comparisons between gods and human characters occur because the latter replace the former.

96. For commentary, see Hyppolite, pp. 536–37; Kainz, 2: 152–54; Kojève, pp. 254–55; Lauer, p. 244.

97. A reference to Aristophanes, *The Knights*; see Hyppolite's translation, 2: 255 n. 90.

98. The same criticism of pure universality is found in Hegel's discussions of Kant and the beautiful soul. See my chapter III.

99. A reference to Aristophanes, *The Clouds*; see Hyppolite's translation, 2: 256 n. 93.

100. Solomon's reaction is quite revealing: "though Hegel seems to find a certain 'levity' in the proposition 'The Self is absolute Being' . . . , I must confess that I miss the joke" (p. 612). He misses it because of his excessively humanistic interpretation, which follows Strauss and Kojève. According to that interpretation, Hegel's own position is not much different from the outlook of comedy. Solomon, therefore, takes Hegel to mean that "Greek comedy is just as much religion as Sunday Mass" (p. 612). In general, Solomon considers Hegel an atheist (p. 582) who identifies God with humanity (p. 587) or the self (p. 593). Religion is replaced by a subjective "holistic consciousness of everything in life" (p. 593) as a unity (p. 594), and of human unity in particular (p. 597). Hegel's absolute knowing likewise becomes a knowledge not of God but of "the essential rationality and acceptability of the human world" (p. 638) known through "that holistic sense of unity he calls 'Spirit' " (p. 639). For Hegel, however, this rationality is more substantial. God is the underlying essence of all existence; divine essence defines itself as nature and then as human existence. For Hegel, therefore, the irreligious outlook of Greek comedy is frivolous because it mocks every thought of an underlying essence.

101. Solomon rightly points out that in "both the *Phenomenology* and the later lectures on the *Philosophy of Religion*, Hegel is obviously attempting to minimize the importance of Greek *Volk*-religion, *vis-à-vis* Christianity. . . . Greek religion is now viewed as a primitive anticipation of Christianity" (p. 613; see also p. 609).

CHAPTER V

MANIFEST RELIGION (400–21)[1]

HEGEL CONCLUDES HIS chapter on religion with Christianity, where "the simple content is . . . this incarnation of divine essence" (405.14–15). Through this incarnation, spirit reaches the goal of religion, which is to unify self-consciousness with consciousness of a divine object (369.23–26). When human being knows itself as the incarnation of God, human subjectivity corresponds to the divine shape that is the object of consciousness; "spirit then is just as [much a] *consciousness* of itself as its *objective* substance, as [on the other hand] simple *self-consciousness* remaining within itself" (401.2–4). In Christianity, this knowing surmounts the "pure knowing" (362.29) of "Evil and Its Pardon" by including a sensory component: God appears in the flesh, to coincide with empirical human subjectivity (406.11–15; 407.7–13). Spirit then has an object adequate to its inner knowing, where divine essence first appears as human subjectivity. This empirical knowing achieves the goal of religion, and so concludes its development. The only remaining difficulty concerns the Christian use of imagination, which puts up a slight barrier between subjective human thinking and objective divine essence (368.32–35; 408.17–25). Comprehension dissolves the barrier and fully integrates divine essence with human thinking. But such comprehension is "Absolute Knowing" (*PhG* VIII) rather than religion. Thus, only philosophy can satisfy spirit's need to know itself completely.

181

Despite this limitation, Christianity reveals[2] to the world "the true
... *content*" (408.22) of God and of speculative thinking (407.1–4).
For Hegel, this content suitably appears not in the parochial setting of
Palestinian Christianity, but in the much wider context of the Roman
empire: it is "the *faith of the world* ... that spirit *exists* as a self-
consciousness, i.e., as an actual human being, that it is [there] for
immediate [sensory] certainty, that believing consciousness *sees* and
feels and *hears*[3] this divinity" (404.34–37). Questions concerning the
historical Jesus are not important here since belief supplies the consciousness of God's incarnation in a real person.

Hegel divides his analysis into two main parts: the earthly incarnate
God and the Trinity known by theology. These themes, in turn, correspond to immediate experience and to thinking: "this first [incarnate]
being manifest is itself *immediate*" (407.16) and is followed by the
"mediation or thinking" (407.17) that converts the immediate presence
of God incarnate into spirit's ecclesial presence. The latter completes
the Trinity and gives Christian theology its content. Because imagination characterizes ecclesial spirit (407.27–30), its trinitarian theology
is developed by imagination rather than by conceptual thinking
(408.17–20).

Under "incarnation," I also examine Hegel's discussion of its preparation and its logical necessity, as well as its development into ecclesial
spirit. The following pages, therefore, divide Hegel's treatment of
"Manifest Religion" into two main sections: the incarnation (400.3–
408.29) and the Trinity (408.30–421.18). Both of them show how
thoroughly Hegel rationalizes—and demythologizes—Christian belief.

THE INCARNATION REINTERPRETED (400.3–408.29)

It is clear that Hegel's view of Christianity is not Christianity's view of
itself. When he claims that self-consciousness "through its sacrifice
produces substance as subject" (400.29–30), one even has the impression that Christian revelation somehow results from human thinking. A
more extensive examination of Hegel's text confirms this impression.
The incarnation requires no special divine intervention inviting faith,
but only the proper development of human thought. Hegel turns the

incarnation into a rational fact. As a rational fact, however, the incarnation expresses the truth about human existence.

Hegel begins his analysis of Christian belief by reviewing the Greek religion of art. This religion ends in the humanism of comedy, which affirms real human individuality while scoffing at everything universal, substantial, or divine: "all essentiality is sunk in the spirit which in the individuality of consciousness is completely certain of itself" (400.11– 12). At this time, therefore, "*the self is the absolute essence*" (400.13); "nothing in the form of essence steps over against" (400.16) it. The individual self acknowledges only itself and its empirical world.

In general, Greek religion also produces an "incarnation of divine essence" (400.7) because "through the religion of art spirit has stepped out of the form of *substance* into the [form] of the *subject*" (400.3–4). But these incarnations do not fully contain the empirical self. Not until comedy does "this [divine-human] unity . . . go over to the [one-sided] extreme of the self" (400.10–11). Greek anthropomorphism thus reaches a logical conclusion: spirit discovers its humanity, but at the cost of its divinity. This "irreligious actual spirit" (400.19) of comedy is nevertheless a "frivolity" (400.13) that needs correcting. But any such change must begin in the self, which is now (at the end of the Greek world) the real center of interest and the one acknowledged power.

According to Hegel, then, "this reversal is brought about *for* and *through self-consciousness* itself" (400.26–27). What precisely must self-consciousness do in order to effect this reversal? Since the reversal is made by a conscious "renunciation[4] [Entäußerung]" (400.28) and "sacrifice [Aufopferung]" (400.30), Hegel must have in mind some type of dying to self. And since "individuality" (400.11) dominates the self that ends the Greek world, the sacrifice that constitutes Christianity is a dying to the *individual* self and a recognition of universal substance, yet in such a way that the self does not "merely disappear in the frightful [universal] substance" (400.5–6) of "natural religion" (400.25) but is "preserved in its renunciation" (400.27–28) as free individuality.

How can such a result be achieved? One expects the "renunciation" and "sacrifice" to refer to Jesus's death. But *PhG* has already suggested a different interpretation: a previous "renunciation" (362.21,

26–27) occurs in "Evil and Its Pardon," which identifies individual subjectivity with its universal knowing and which sees in this combination "the appearing God" (362.28–29). Later on, Hegel calls this pure universal knowing "not only the [human] viewing of the divine but the self-viewing of the same [divine substance]" (426.2–3). Therefore, universal knowing is for Hegel the divine appearance that also preserves individual human subjectivity. This knowing also elucidates the meaning of spirit as essence "that *essentially* assumes human shape" (387.27): universal divine essence appears as human being when the latter acknowledges its individual subjectivity as also universal.

Faith in the incarnation likewise emerges when "the renunciation of self-consciousness . . . [expresses] this, that *for it* is [the idea] that [divine] substance is [human] self-consciousness and [is] thereby spirit" (403.25, 27–28). Here, the "Entäußerung" is clearly a matter of knowing. Its precise details are examined later; at this point, its general nature as a *knowing* (about self-consciousness and substance) is noted. Hegel explains God's ecclesial presence in the same way, as the "pure *inwardness* of *knowing*" (420.20). Of course, "the devout consciousness" (420.22) fails to see "that this depth of the pure self is the power through which *abstract essence* [or God] is pulled down from its abstraction and elevated to the self through the might of this pure devotion" (420.26–28). For the Christian church, God's presence in human being is a gracious gift and has a quality different from human thinking. But for Hegel, "the pure becoming-inward of knowing is *in itself* absolute simplicity or [divine] substance" (420.23–24), which appears as human thinking.[5]

Historically, the recovery of universal thinking is the work of Rome, which inherits comedy's individualism. Roman culture makes "the individual person" (401.15) into "*absolute essence*" (401.7) by the "pure thinking" (401.14) and "abstract universality of law" (401.10). The abstract universal thought of Rome also robs individuals of participating in the political life of a people (389.8–12, 15–17), and effectively renders insignificant the older gods personifying a national substance. Thus, Rome also is "the unhappy consciousness" (401.28)[6] "*that God is dead*" (401.35) because it is "the loss of all *essentiality* in this certainty of self" (401.32) or in pure individual thinking.[7] Rome took the ancient pagan world inward into thought; the empire was the "*remembering internalization [Er-Innerung]* of the spirit still *exter-*

nalized in the . . . art-works" (402.29, 30–31) of Greek religion. Yet this turning inward into thought makes possible Christian faith.[8] Rome is the "spirit of the tragic fate which gathers all those individual gods and attributes of [divine] substance into one pantheon, into spirit self-conscious of itself as spirit" (402.31–33). Then God's appearance in the flesh brings to this unhappy consciousness a "joy . . . [that] grips the whole world" (407.9–10) finding itself in God again.

Self-Renunciation

The rediscovery of God occurs when consciousness reverses comedy's "proposition . . . [that] *the self is the absolute essence*" (400.12–13). This "reversal . . . lowers the self to the predicate and raises the substance to the subject" (400.21–22) of a contrary proposition.[9] However, since the new proposition occurs "*for* and *through self-consciousness*" (400.26), the latter is "preserved in its renunciation and remains the subject of substance" (400.28). It seems contradictory to affirm that self-consciousness remains the subject when by its own doing substance becomes the subject, yet such is Hegel's contention. When human self-consciousness "through its sacrifice *produces* substance as subject, this [subject] remains its own self" (400.29–31). Though the sacrifice remains unexplained, its importance is clear: it constitutes the full incarnation of God, or "the unification and penetration of both natures [divine and human], in which both [natures] are with equal worth . . . *essential* [and] also only *moments*" (400.34–401.2) of their unity. (See below, note 28, for an explanation.)

Once comedy becomes unhappy Roman consciousness, "spirit self-conscious of itself as spirit" (402.33) is ready to appear; "all conditions of its emergence are at hand" (402.34). The unhappy consciousness is the "midpoint and collective birth pangs of its emergence—the simplicity of the pure concept" (403.15–16) of "spirit becoming self-consciousness" (403.13). Rome inherits comedy's frivolous thesis that "*the self is the absolute essence*" (400.13) and makes it into the legal proposition that "*the self as such*, the *abstract person is absolute essence*" (401.6–7). The empire's law expresses "the pantheon of abstract universality, of pure thought" (401.13–14) in which the life of Greek political existence and its corresponding religion disappear (401.10–12); the individual self has lost its cultural content and leads only the abstract life of thinking (401.16–20), which makes it an unhappy consciousness (401.22–23). Knowing the loss of its immediate (political) existence and its personified gods (402.1–2), this pure *"certainty of self"* (401.32) is the negation of actual existence and also "the pain . . . *that God is dead"* (401.34–35).

This "irreligious actual spirit . . . will . . . contain the reversal of the same" (400.19–21) spirit, for the pure thinking of the unhappy consciousness turns into its opposite. The empty thinking of unhappy consciousness, the *"simple* self-conscious negativity" (405.8) or irreligious "actual spirit" (405.7), becomes the *"simple* positive self" (405.6–7) of Christian "religious spirit" (405.6) when its emptiness acquires a positive content. And this content is a simple one: pure unhappy thinking "renounces itself and makes [itself] into thinghood or the universal self" (403.20), and so turns Christian.

What exactly does the renunciation refer to? If to the death of Christ, then the "thinghood" is his corpse; but a corpse cannot "make itself into the universal self."[10] Moreover, when as a result of its "renunciation" (404.34) spirit "steps into existence" (403.30, 35), Hegel alludes to the virgin birth (403.31–32) rather than to the resurrection. The renunciation then refers to the incarnation itself. But this interpretation likewise fails because the "mutual renunciation" (404.34) of divine substance and human self-consciousness requires not a human birth but an adult human being. Too many difficulties result from supposing that the self-renouncing consciousness is primarily Jesus.[11] These difficulties disappear when one realizes that the renunciation belongs to the unhappy consciousness in general, the "actual world-spirit" (404.29–30) that then becomes "the *faith of the world"* (404.34–35) in God incarnate. One can then understand Hegel's text explaining "the renunciation of self-consciousness [as] this, . . . that *for it* [the renouncing self-consciousness] is [the knowledge] that [divine] substance [as incarnate] is [human] self-consciousness and precisely because of that [is it] spirit" (403.25–28). Spirit appears as God incarnate *for* believing consciousness; it is the object of consciousness for Christian faith. In these texts, renunciation refers not to Jesus himself, but to the unhappy consciousness that turns Christian.

When the unhappy consciousness "renounces itself and makes [itself] into thinghood or the universal self" (403.20), it repeats a movement that is analyzed at the beginning of *PhG* V as the transition from unhappy consciousness to reason. There, the movement of individual consciousness "wrestled its being-for-itself out of itself and made it into being" (132.10) because reason knows the objective world as itself. This movement parallels the current one in *PhG* VII from pure self-certainty to thinghood. The earlier consciousness came to know itself as "universal" (132.11) being since "reason is the certainty of being all *reality* . . . universal . . . reality . . . the *pure essentiality* of being" (134.20–23), and the current consciousness becomes "the universal self" (403.20) that knows "being as [the] self . . . and . . . all existence as spiritual essence" (403.37–38) because of "*its own* renunciation" (403.36). In both sections, the unhappy consciousness replaces its negative relation to the world with a positive one (132.21–22; 405.6–8). Thus, the earlier transition from unhappy medieval consciousness to Renaissance reason resembles the self-renunciation through which Roman unhappy consciousness becomes Christian faith.

Belief in the incarnation emerges because "the renunciation of self-consciousness [expresses] this, that *in itself* it is the universal essence" (403.25–26) or divine. It renounces its intellectual isolation when (like reason) it knows its own thinking as identical in principle to the whole objective world. And since this objective world is "being in general or substance" (403.39), the identity of world and self also means the identity of self and divine substance. Incarnational religion in *PhG* VII has all along been spirit as that very identity of self and substance, but only Christianity gives divine substance the full form of empirical human being.

Christianity, however, requires not only a human self-renunciation, but also a corresponding one by divine substance. Otherwise, the humanity of God would not be grounded in divine essence. The incarnation must be a divine work and must be known as one. For Hegel, this also means rational necessity or divine essence "in itself," whose rationality appears in human thinking. If "the renunciation of self-consciousness [expresses] this, that *in itself* it is universal essence" (403.25–26), then "the renunciation of substance, its becoming self-consciousness, expresses . . . this, that *in itself* it is [human] self-consciousness" (403.22–25). Incarnation is an internal necessity within divine essence because spirit is divine "*essence* . . . which *essentially* assumes human shape" (387.26–27). The following section examines this objective necessity.

Conceptual Necessity and Christian Faith

Hegel speaks of a subjective renunciation that "knows being as [the] self . . . and . . . all existence as a spiritual essence" (403.37–38), and that "gives nature as well as history, the world and the mythical images of preceding religions an inner meaning other than the one they . . . immediately offer to consciousness" (404.5–7). In brief, this is a renunciation that gives existence a spiritual interpretation. But then "all existence is [a] spiritual essence only from the *standpoint of consciousness*, not in itself. Spirit is in this way only *fancied* into existence; this fancying [Einbilden] is the *visionary enthusiasm*"[12] (404.2–4) that gives existence a meaning it does not have in itself. Genuine spirit requires, however, that "being in general or substance . . . for its part *in itself* also [have] renounced itself and become self-consciousness" (403.39–404.2). Both subject and object must renounce themselves in order for spirit to appear.

Their "mutual renunciation" (404.34) is necessary because the subjective renunciation affirms the objective one. When self-consciousness "renounces itself and makes [itself] into thinghood or the universal self" (403.20), it identifies itself with being and substance: the "renunciation of self-consciousness [expresses] this, that [objectively] *in itself* it is universal essence" (403.25–26). Since the self is affirming something objective, the object must display the affirmation's truth. Otherwise, human "self-consciousness one-sidedly grasps only *its own* renunciation" (403.36) and becomes "*visionary enthusiasm*" (404.4). If A is B, then B is A; the self-conscious renunciation (that human being is universal essence) implies the objective one that universal essence is human being. Therefore, "that this meaning of the objective . . . not be mere fancy,[13] it must be *in itself*, that is, *first* spring forth to consciousness from the *concept* and emerge in its necessity" (404.12–14).

But how does the human subject come to know about the renunciation in divine substance? Hegel's own system provides the argument, as does *PhG* (though indirectly); here, "*in itself*, i.e., according to the very necessity of the concept, . . . *being* or *immediacy* . . . renounces itself and becomes 'I' for consciousness" (404.19, 20, 21–22).[14] Since divine "substance" is "being in general" (403.39), this movement from being to thinking applies to divine essence, which thus becomes known as human thinking. Objective being (divine essence) turns into human subjectivity.

Of course, Hegel's works did not exist for the Roman empire. Nevertheless, the movement analyzed in *PhG* was in some way known to the unhappy consciousness of pagan Rome, which affirmed it as the incarnation of God: "that absolute spirit *in itself* and thus also for its *consciousness* gave itself the shape of self-consciousness now so appears, that it is the *faith of the world* that spirit *exists* as a self-consciousness, i.e., as an actual human" (404.33–36). For the phenomenologist, this incarnation "means nothing other than [this], that actual spirit arrived at this knowing of itself" (404.29–30) as divine, namely as the conscious expression of "the *immediate* [being] *in itself* of spirit" (404.28) or of *"existing necessity"* (404.23–24). In other words, human being knows "being in general or substance" (404.39) as having "likewise for its part *in itself* renounced itself and become [human] self-consciousness" (404.1–2). Christianity thus knows the incarnation as a revelation accomplished by divine substance in itself. By affirming the incarnation as a work of *God*, Christianity suggests Hegel's interpretation of it as "the unconscious[15] transition of *necessity*" (403.23–24), even though Christians do not comprehend its necessity nor acknowledge its unconscious aspect. For Christianity, the incarnation instead indicates God's incomprehensible mercy, which in faith is "imagined as a voluntary doing" (414.38) by God rather than as an unconscious, conceptual necessity.

From this perspective of a self-renunciation by divine substance, the corresponding one by the unhappy consciousness may seem unnecessary. But if self-consciousness did not renounce itself, it would not identify itself with being and substance. Its identity with divine substance, then, would not enter its consciousness, and so could not be affirmed. It would not even occur in fact, for the self-conscious renunciation lets divine essence direct human subjectivity; without such control, divine essence would not have totally *become* self-consciousness. But self-consciousness does renounce itself and so experiences its identity with God.

Indeed, "believing consciousness *sees* and *feels* and *hears* this divinity" (404.36–37) as a real human self. It knows "being in general or substance" (403.39) as having "*in itself* [objectively] . . . renounced itself and become self-consciousness" (404.1–2), and so finds God in reality. Christian faith "starts with immediate existence and knows God in it" (405.3–4). This faith, in turn, depends on the subjective renunciation whereby the empty unhappy consciousness "has become [a] *simple* positive self" (405.6–7) identified with being and substance. The object of religious consciousness is then spirit in its true shape, divine essence as real human subjectivity: "the self of existing spirit consequently has the form of complete immediacy. . . . this God is viewed immediately [in a] sensory [way] as [a] self, as an actual individual human being; only so *is*[16] he [namely, God] self-consciousness" (405.8–13). God appears not as the imagined self of previous religions (405.10–12), but as a real human self.[17]

Revelation

Through "this incarnation of divine essence . . . divine essence is *revealed*" (405.18, 23). In human being, divine "substance is . . . in its accidentality nevertheless reflected into itself . . . *into itself*, i.e., insofar as it is *subject*[18] or *self*" (405.19–22). When substance renounces itself to become human, it does not lose its identity as essence because human thinking is the objective appearance of essence; human subjectivity (unlike animal subjectivity) is also objective, through intelligence. In Christianity, "divine essence is consequently *revealed*. . . . It is known, just because it is known as spirit, as essence that is essentially *self-consciousness*" (405.22–25), or human being.

Humanity is not an instrument used by God's higher power, but is the essential medium of revelation. Only as human can God be revealed to human being:

> There is something secret for *consciousness* in its object when it is an *other* or *alien* for it, and when it does not know it as *itself*. This being secret ceases when absolute essence as spirit is object of [believing] consciousness; for then it is as [a] *self* in its relation to it; i.e., this [believing consciousness] knows itself immediately therein. (405.25–30)

Because God is human, believing consciousness finds itself in this object; spirit knows itself in spirit. The difference between God's incarnate self and the believing self presents no problem because "the self [of another] is no alien but . . . the immediately universal" (405.32–33) as "Evil and Its Pardon" indicates. And since Christianity is based on self-renunciation whereby subjective thinking recognizes itself as objective, the believing consciousness knows itself in its object. The self is "the pure concept, pure thinking or [subjective] *being-for-self* which is immediately *being*" (405.33–34), the subjectivity in which universal objectivity appears.

Indeed, the universal thinking of self-renouncing selves *is* the appearance of universal essence. This essence is the subject of divine predicates like the "holy creator of heaven and earth" (405.36–37), but in these predicates "the *subject* itself [is] not yet manifest" (406.1) because these "*determinations* of the universal [essence] are not *this universal* itself" (406.1–2). As human subjectivity, however, the divine "*subject* itself . . . *this pure universal* is . . . manifest as [the] *self*" (406.2–3) because in human thinking objective essence appears. And since universal essence appears as human thinking, the latter is likewise universal; the self of God incarnate is also "the personal [self-] certainty of that [believing] self for which it is there" (406.4–5). Otherwise faith would not know itself in God incarnate.

This incarnate God is "the true shape of spirit" (406.6) or universal essence as individual subjectivity. Containing all being in principle, subjectivity as universal objectivity is "the pure concept" (405.33) revealing everything. Therefore, spirit "is known as self-consciousness and is in this [latter] immediately manifest since it is this [consciousness] itself" (406.7–8). But if God appears as human subjectivity, then "the divine nature is the same thing as human [nature], and this unity is what is viewed" (406.8–10) in God incarnate. Here, Hegel draws the logical conclusion of his position, and finds it also in Christianity.

A corollary of Hegel's position is that Christianity has a completely rational origin; there is no divine intervention into the history of human thinking. Such an intervention would be the work of a mysterious providence acting in ways one could not comprehend. There is no trace of this traditional Christian doctrine in Hegel's analysis. For him, revelation occurs when consciousness renounces itself to become rational objectivity, and recognizes itself as the appearance of universal essence and all objective being.

Such revelation brings religion to its goal: the object of consciousness—God's human appearance—resembles the consciousness to which it appears. As a result, "consciousness or the way essence is for it . . . is equal to its self-consciousness" because "this shape [of essence] is itself a self-consciousness" (406.11–13). This object resulting from the self-renunciation of substance corresponds precisely to the self-consciousness that renounces itself and identifies itself with being and universal essence. The object for consciousness is God as a human self-consciousness, a shape that is "at the same time [an] object [as] *being* and . . . [that] likewise immediately has the meaning of *pure thinking*, of absolute essence" (406.13–15). God incarnate and believing consciousness match one another perfectly.

If substance renounces itself and becomes human through its own conceptual necessity (404.13–14), then its own concept requires the incarnation. Absolute essence thus completes itself; it "seems to have *descended* from its eternal simplicity, but in fact it has thereby only reached its *highest* essence" (406.16–17). As the essence of empirical being, or "being in general or substance" (403.39), deity reaches its maximal perfection when it differentiates itself into the highest empirical being. And this obviously is rational human being. When "the concept of essence . . . has attained its simple purity, it is the absolute *abstraction* which is *pure thinking* and thereby the pure individuality of the self" (406.17–20).

How this development occurs is best left to the *Logik* and *Enzyklopädie*, which describe it in detail.[19] In *PhG*, however, one finds the general movement from being to thinking, and in "Evil and Its Pardon" a precise identification of universal essence with individual subjectivity. This identification then develops itself as incarnational religion and reaches a logical conclusion in Christianity, for the pure thinking of subjectivity is also "because of its simplicity the *immediate* or *being*" (406.20). In other words, as human subjectivity God must also be empirical, and for a very precise reason: pure thinking intends pure being; human thinking points to reality.[20] When the unhappy consciousness "renounces itself and makes [itself] into thinghood" (403.20), it subjectively acknowledges this identity between its thinking and empirical being. And the self-renunciation of divine substance means that the stuff of the universe (thought or divine essence) develops into human being, whose pure thinking is the sensory consciousness of being (406.21–22). But pure thinking also retains the character of essence. Thus, rational human being is at the same time empirical existence *and* the appearance of God: "that the highest essence is seen, heard etc. as an existing self-consciousness . . . is . . . the completion of its concept" (406.24–26).

Conversely, consciousness knows its pure thinking not only as being, but also as essence; it "renounces itself and makes [itself] into thinghood or the universal self" (403.20), namely into being and essence. Subjective thinking makes itself objective and thus identifies itself with "being in general or substance" (403.39). In its own renunciation, it grasps (though obscurely) its own thinking as universal essence. Thus it must ultimately recognize every self, including its own, as the appearance of God: such universality belongs to essence as well as to thinking. Initially, however, subjectivity knows God's human appearance empirically as another individual when it acknowledges Jesus as God incarnate. The identity of essence and human thinking is manifested first by a sensory example. But the sensory example is clear only to a self-renouncing consciousness, for only such a consciousness knows the identity of essence and human being.

This consciousness's own renunciation enables it to recognize the renunciation of substance as an objective empirical fact. Thus, for this "religious consciousness . . . immediacy has indivisibly the meaning of not only an *existing* self-consciousness but [also] of absolute *essence* purely thought" (406.29–31). It knows "this *unity* of being and essence, of *thinking* which immediately *is existence* . . . ; for this unity of being and thinking is *self-consciousness* and is itself *there*" (406.33–36) as God incarnate. This convergence of being and essence in pure thinking reveals God, who is "*manifest* as *he is*; *he is there [ist da]*[21] as he is *in himself*" (407.1). The hidden essence of God appears as human thinking that knows being and, thus, as empirical human being. And spirit is precisely this appearance of essence; God "is there as spirit" (407.1) since spirit is the human appearance of God. Divine self-revelation and incarnation are mandatory in the concept (406.5–6) of God as essence that becomes human.

There is then a correspondence between Hegelian philosophy and Christian faith: "what we are conscious of in our concept, [namely] that *being* is *essence*, religious consciousness is [also] conscious of" (406.31–32). Christian faith naively knows this identity as God's empirical incarnation, but Hegel understands it as pure thinking. And because thought or divine essence is the stuff of the universe, only thinking truly knows God. In fact, God *is* the thought that thinks itself as human being. Thus, "God is attainable in pure speculative[22] knowing alone, and is only in it and is [this knowing] itself, for he is spirit" (407.1–3) or essence that appears as thinking. Since "this speculative knowing is the knowing of the manifest religion" (407.3–4), Christianity does know God correctly. Both philosophy and Christianity know spirit as "*thinking* or pure essence, and this thinking as being and as existence, and existence as the negative of itself, thereby as self, *this*[23] [individual self] and universal[24] self; this [is] just [what] the manifest religion [also] knows" (407.4–7).

Thus the "hopes and expectations of the preceding world push forward to this [Christian] revelation alone, to view what absolute essence is and to find themselves in it; . . . for it is spirit . . . essence . . . as *immediate* [human] self-consciousness" (407.7–12). For Hegel, Christianity brings to the ancient world a divine shape in which self-consciousness can recognize itself as absolute. In Christian faith, one finds "spirit knowing itself as spirit" (407.14), essence knowing itself through humanity, and humanity knowing itself as divine.

But since "God is attainable in pure speculative knowing alone" (407.1–2) Christianity is true because it corresponds to Hegelian philosophy, rather than the reverse. Hegel's analysis even argues that Christianity came to know the incarnation by pure thinking, when the unhappy consciousness renounced itself and recognized subjective thinking as objective. Only this conversion to the *objectivity* of thinking enables consciousness to recognize divine essence in empirical human being. And if this interpretation is correct, then the incarnation is not the assumption by God of a specific human being, but a permanent possibility in the human race. Given the proper development of consciousness, any appropriate person could have been acknowledged as the incarnation of God. Indeed, any *number* of suitable persons could have been recognized as divine humans because the principle of spirit refers to everyone. Hegel does not question explicitly the uniqueness of Jesus, but his interpretation clearly contains the question. For Hegel, Jesus is not the only Son of God, but rather the occasion for human being to discover its identity. When it renounces itself, the unhappy Roman consciousness becomes Christian faith; such a self-renouncing consciousness would find itself objectified in any holy person—in any self-consciousness that renounced itself completely.

After Jesus

Now if the incarnation illustrates a universal truth about human being, divine presence cannot be restricted to Jesus alone. Hegel had this idea even before he wrote *PhG*. In his unpublished Jena manuscripts one reads: "*God* is the *depth of the spirit certain of itself*—thereby is He the self of all . . . he is a *man* . . . and *all individuals* are *this individual—divine nature is not . . . other than human* [nature]."[25] In *PhG*, several aspects of Hegel's analysis echo this idea. God's incarnation brings joy to the world which discovers it, because believing consciousness identifies itself with God incarnate. Hegel also explains the incarnation as the appearance of universal essence in universal thinking, which all humans have. And by its resemblance to speculative philosophy, Christianity has a universal truth to propose to the world: that God's incarnation refers to "*this* [self] and universal self" (407.6), or to the self as individual and as multiple. Further, Hegel's claim that "divine nature is the same thing as human [nature]" (406.8–9) is a universal statement. One can find additional arguments, too, since every part of Hegel's analysis implies that what appeared in Jesus belongs to every human being.

Christianity affirms this universality as well, in its doctrine of the church as the dwelling of the Holy Spirit. Hegel sees this doctrine as a logical development of the incarnation. In Jesus, God's manifestation is "*immediate*" (407.16) in sensory being. This feature gives the incarnation reality but also limits it to a single person: "spirit is . . . this *individual* self-consciousness opposed to *universal* [self-consciousness]; it is [an] excluding one" (407.18–20) rather than an inclusive all. Thus, believing consciousness "does not yet know spirit as its [own self], or spirit is not yet there as universal, as every self, in the way it is [the] *individual* self" (407.22–24) of Jesus.

When Hegel writes that spirit must exist in all believers, the term "spirit" does not mean a divine helper given to the human Christ (which would be a traditional Christian position); it means the incarnation itself, the divine-human unity found in Jesus, in whom *spirit* is revealed (405.14–17). Spirit is Hegel's term for God's appearance in human being, and it applies to the incarnate God as well as to the church.

After Jesus, however, spirit does not acquire directly "the form *of thinking* itself, *of the concept as concept*" (407.28), which would apply it to every self. In the form of the concept, spirit is the self as universal and also as individual, the self as universal found in *many* individuals, "the universal self . . . which in its immediate actuality is also . . . universality" (407.24–26). The concept of spirit would reveal spirit as intrinsically universal, or as occurring in "every self" (407.23–24) by virtue of deity's essential development into human personality. But such thinking lies in the future. At the time of Christianity's beginning, spirit had just been revealed in its fresh immediacy as a living human being. Nevertheless, this one instance does not fully correspond to the concept of spirit as divine essence in human form since both aspects (deity and humanity) are universal in extent and must become this for consciousness.

Believing consciousness, therefore, goes further by knowing spirit as universal. But this universality first comes into consciousness as an image rather than as a concept. For faith, spirit becomes the "universality of actuality, the allness of selves" (407.29), or spirit in the church. Through this development, spirit moves from the individual existence of Jesus to a more universal shape. The new shape results from "the elevation of existence into imagination" (407.29–30); spirit is no longer present as an empirical human being, but as a mental image of God's presence in the faithful.[26]

First comes the disappearance of the individual incarnate God, who dies like every human according to the nature of "*sensory being*. He is the *immediately* present God; thereby his *being* passes over into a *having-been*" (407.33–35). Believing consciousness no longer has its immediate object. When it loses this object, it ceases to be sensory and becomes instead spiritual: "only because it *has* seen [and] heard him does it become itself spiritual consciousness, or as he previously rose for it as [a] *sensory existence* is he now risen *in spirit*" (407.37–408.1). Here Hegel obviously alludes to the Christian belief in the resurrection of Christ and his interior presence in the church. The focus, however, is on believing consciousness rather than on Jesus himself. What might have happened to Jesus after his death is not discussed. The spirit in which Jesus rises (407.39) is the "spiritual consciousness" (407.38) of believers. (I return to this question later, in Hegel's analysis of trinitarian theology.)

In the first part of "Manifest Religion," Hegel simply explains believing in the resurrection as the overcoming of a limitation in believing consciousness itself. In its original sensory experience of the incarnate God, "it is itself only immediate consciousness, which has not surmounted the inequality of objectivity . . . it knows [only] this objective individual [Jesus] but not itself as spirit" (408.1–4). Since the goal of religion is to overcome this inequality between subject and object (369.23–26), spirit has to include the believing subject as well. Christianity's initial experience of God incarnate brings faith closer to its object but does not remove the inequality between them. Only the concept of spirit as universal "in pure thinking" (408.3) will completely eliminate this inequality since it will identify God with every human, by definition.

This conceptual universality gives to spirit an internal goal that explains the passage from the individual existence of Jesus to his universal presence for belief. As God incarnate, he embodies the concept of spirit, which (like every concept) is universal. His death gives faith an occasion to universalize this concept. It then becomes faith in the universal presence of spirit. As Christian faith, spirit comes closer to its goal by imagining its empirical universality in the church.

The passage from immediate consciousness to imagination changes the shape of spirit to the "universality of actuality, the allness of selves" (407.29). In imagination, "spirit remains [the] immediate self of actuality, but as *the universal self-consciousness* of the community" (408.6–7) in which God dwells. As it was the logical subject of the earthly incarnation earlier, so now is divine "substance . . . [the] universal subject" (408.8) of the primitive Christian community that lives for God. And this universal presence of spirit is connected to the original revealer of spirit, the incarnate God who lives in the consciousness of his church: "not the individual [incarnate God] for himself [alone] but together with the consciousness of the community . . . is the complete whole of that same" (408.8–10) divine person. The church knows itself to be spirit because it believes in the universal presence of God incarnate.

Of course, this universality is deficient, insofar as imagination produces it. For believing consciousness, "the immediate mode [of God incarnate] is mediated or posited universally" (408.12) only because of its *"past* and *distance"* (408.11), namely its "disappearing" (408.4); were it still immediately present, it would not be universal. For faith, spirit's universal presence results from the disappearance of Jesus, who was its immediate and individual existence. God incarnate then "is only superficially dipped into the element of thinking . . . and is not posited as one with the nature of thinking itself" (408.13–14). In other words, God incarnate (spirit) is not yet understood as a universal concept that applies to every human existence (407.23–26). Instead, spirit "is only elevated into *imagining*, . . . the synthetic linking of sensory immediacy and its universality or thinking" (408.14–16). The sensory immediacy of God incarnate is multiplied into the "universality of actuality, the allness of selves" (407.29) who give him a universal existence on earth. Such universality is empirical; it finds its universality in real existence. But Hegel's concept is pure *a priori* thinking, necessary and universal, which *therefore* exists in multiple occurrences. For Hegel, the incarnate God *is* the concept of human existence. Because faith has not yet comprehended this, it gives to spirit an empirical universality in the church rather than a sheer and simple *a priori* universality valid for every human being.

Faith also gives divine being a transcendent existence when spirit "is only superficially dipped into the element of thinking [and] is preserved in it *as* [a] sensory mode" (408.12–14) of objectivity. Though universally present, God incarnate remains (for faith) a supernatural person qualitatively different from earthly existence. This God is close to humans but still not their concept. Therefore, the church can imagine itself as the earthly temple of a transcendent God. But "the spiritual essence is still afflicted with an unreconciled division into this [world] here and [a world] beyond" (408.21–22). When spirit is not comprehended as divine essence becoming human, in every human, it is imagined as a transcendent object present in the church.

Christian theology deals with such an object. Since it "is not yet self-consciousness [which has] progressed to its concept as concept" (408.18–19), it lacks the signs of true comprehension. For example, it cannot unify[27] its content: its "moments [are] posited in the element of imagining [and so] have the character of not being comprehended, but appear as completely independent sides which relate themselves to one another *externally*" (408.23–25). Another sign of incomprehension is theology's inability to discover the necessary reasons (410.34–37) for what it believes; the mysteries of faith remain mysteries, contingent happenings (412.31–35; 418.19–25), or God's "voluntary doing" (414.38), which faith cannot explain. Not only do various aspects of God remain unrelated (411.1–3), but the human recipient of revelation is externally related to the divine object revealed (411.3–6). When faith does not comprehend humanity as divine self-differentiation, it considers itself external to its transcendent God.

For consciousness to advance to the concept, a "higher formation" (408.26) is necessary: Christian consciousness must "*for itself* balance its consciousness with its self-consciousness" (408.28–29) or discover that its divine object of consciousness appears as every self-consciousness. Until then, spirit knows itself in the shapes developed by Christian theology, the "*form of imagining* . . . in which spirit is conscious of itself in this its community" (408.17–18). Despite this limitation, Christianity's "*content* is the true [one]" (408.22) since it portrays God as universally present among humans. From this truth, spirit unfolds a rich trinitarian theology that Hegel analyzes in much detail.

TRINITARIAN THEOLOGY (408.30–421.18)

Aware of spirit in its midst, believing consciousness now knows God in a threefold way: as eternal, as incarnate in Jesus, and as universally present. This threefold manner of knowing the same God calls for a synthesis, which trinitarian theology provides. Hegel examines "this content . . . as it is in its consciousness" (408.30), namely in imagination.

The content is "absolute spirit . . . in the shape of its *truth*" (408.31), which is "to become actual self, to reflect itself into itself and be subject . . . in its community" (408.34–36). Here, spirit is divine essence as the actual self of humans, who sacrifice themselves to their universal knowing, so that universal divine essence appears as the controlling subject.[28] But although universal knowing is indispensable to its appearance, absolute spirit is more than pious "inwardness" (408.33) and more than the "objectivity of imagining" (408.33–34) found in theology. Knowing leads to doing; therefore, spirit is fully itself only in "the life" (408.36) of the church. Its "rich life in the community" (408.38) shows "what this self-revealing spirit *in and for itself* is" (408.36–37).

As a result, theology has for its proper topic divine essence revealing itself in Christian living. Hegel criticizes the zealous modern interest in "the images of the first incomplete community or . . . what the actual human [God] said" (408.39–409.1). Such historical research does not yield the concept of spirit since it "confuses the *origin* as the *immediate existence* of the first appearance with the *simplicity of the concept*" (409.3–4). The true origin of Christianity is found in the concept of spirit that defines history, rather than in "the spiritless recollection of an individual . . . shape and its past" (409.8–9). Indeed, Jesus is the first empirical appearance of spirit. But this revelation ultimately depends not on historical fact, but on the concept of divine essence appearing as human subjectivity.[29] Jesus illustrates this concept as the first acknowledged instance of the principle that "divine nature is the same thing as human [nature]" (406.8–9). He is not however the ultimate origin of the concept, which derives from an *a priori* necessity of universal essence. Dogmatic theology comes closer to the truth when it explores the concept of spirit present in its imagination, which it does, for "spirit is [the] content of its consciousness" (409.10).

Morever, this content makes Christian theology trinitarian. As divine essence becoming human, spirit contains three moments or phases: pure essence, individual existence (for God incarnate), and universal existence (for the church). The phases are mutually related as universal essence, individual existence as opposed to universal essence, and individual existence reconciled with universal essence. In more concise language, they indicate identity, otherness, and reconciliation, respectively. In his introduction to the Trinity, Hegel describes them, respectively, as "*pure substance*" (409.10–11); "*other-being*" (409.15); and "the return out of . . . other-being" (409.14–15) in "self-consciousness" (409.15), "existence or individuality" (409.12). These "three moments make up spirit" (409.16).

In addition, each moment contains the other two. If essence becomes human, there must be something within essence itself calling for its incarnation.[30] Pure essence, therefore, contains its becoming other as well as the reconciliation of both; essence implies its own triplicity. This holds true for the other two moments as well: otherness implies the original identity, as well as the subsequent reconciliation; and reconciliation presupposes otherness and a prior unity. Therefore, each moment contains the same triplicity, but from a different starting point, which gives triplicity another milieu.

Since each moment implies the other two, each one contains the full triplicity of spirit. Therefore, spirit's "detailed movement is ... to spread its nature out in each of its moments as though in an element" (409.18–20). The three moments are circles or elements displaying the same triplicity in another form. When "each of these circles completes itself within itself, its reflection into itself is also the transition to the next" (409.19–21) circle. Hegel's analysis of trinitarian theology in *PhG* obviously foreshadows the conceptual system of his *Enzyklopädie*.

This triple development determines the rest of "Manifest Religion." Theology begins with "spirit ... in the form *of pure substance*" (409.10–11), the object of "pure consciousness" (409.11) or "*pure thinking*" (409.37). Spirit is the pretemporal Trinity of abstract thought (409.37–411.33). Spirit as essence then becomes the otherness of human existence and so becomes the world (412.1–4) and then human being, which because of its individuality falls into sin (412.15–35); here, spirit multiplies itself into many conflicting individuals. Theology thus enters the "*element of imagining*" (419.3), or "the consciousness of becoming other" (409.13–14). Reconciliation begins when divine essence assumes this form of otherness in a single person (414.8–415.10). Finally, spirit unifies the separate individuals, each knowing itself and its companions as divine presence. Then spirit becomes "the return out of ... [its] being other" (409.14–15), because universal essence appears as universal in the "*universal self-consciousness*" (417.6–7) of the "*community*" (417.7). Furthermore, spirit also becomes empirical "self-consciousness" (409.15; 415.16). Spirit is now "not only [the] *content* of self-consciousness and not only object *for it* but it is also *actual spirit*" (419.33–35); it exists as the Christian church (417–21). The universal church combines the universality of pure essence (the first moment) with individual existence (the second moment); this leads to the completion of spirit, as Hegel indicates earlier (408.36–38).

Three moments, therefore, constitute the movement of spirit: pure universal essence equal to itself (the pretemporal Trinity); worldly existence, other than universal (therefore sinful) yet (as God's otherness) capable of reconciliation with divine essence (thus the incarnation); and finally redemption, where universal divine essence incorporates its otherness (as the universal church) and so becomes equal to itself.[31]

The role of imagination in these three moments calls for comment. Imagination governs all of them, yet it corresponds most strongly to the second moment (409.21–25), where otherness separates individuals from each other (411.34–39). In this moment, abstract essence becomes real existence (creation) in separate individuals (sin and incarnation) and, thus, "the consciousness of becoming other or imagining as such" (409.13–14). Even God incarnate[32] is an individual distinct from other humans. But since imagining is also "spread out over all these elements and [is] their common determinacy" (409.24–25), it occurs in the first and third moments as well. How? The answer lies in the nature of imagination as a "synthetic linking" (409.13, 24) of pure essence with individual existence or self-consciousness (409.10–15, 21–22). Imagination links the moments of spirit synthetically rather than analytically, failing to comprehend their necessary connection. The same kind of thinking also pictures God as transcendent (408.20–22) by separating universal essence from human existence. In trinitarian theology, spirit fails to understand itself as a necessary development of divine essence. Christianity thus continues the imaginative thinking it acquired after the death of Jesus.

The Pretemporal Trinity (409.37–411.39)[33]

Hegel begins his analysis of the Trinity with "spirit . . . imagined as substance in the *element of pure thinking*" (409.37–410.1). Since "the simple eternal *essence* equal to itself . . . has the meaning of absolute spirit" (410.1–3), it must develop into human existence because it must become "actual" (410.4). This point is obvious from the preceding revelation, wherein "absolute spirit is . . . its rich life in the community" (408.31, 37–38).

But essence does not pass directly into existence. It first defines itself into an essential Trinity that underlies the earthly appearance of the incarnate Son and the indwelling Spirit. Prior to its appearance, divine otherness must be "in" God. Christianity formulates this otherness without grasping its logic: "because imagination apprehends and pronounces the . . . *necessity* of the concept as a *happening*, it is said that the eternal essence *begets* itself an other" (410.12–14)—a divine "Word" (410.23) or "Son" (410.36) eternally generated within God. The Son is a mystery for Christian theology, which (as imagination) separates essence and its otherness.

For Hegel, however, divine otherness is a logical requirement. Essence first develops within itself the logical exigency for its later development into human existence. Thus, essence differentiates itself according to the "*necessity* of the concept" (410.12–13) into something else: "the simple essence however, because it is abstraction, is in fact the *negative in itself* . . . the absolute *distinction* from itself, or its pure becoming other" (410.6–7, 8–9).

Hegel's argument here is not obvious: why must an abstraction become other? Elsewhere, such as in *PhG*'s Preface, he explains that a pure self-identical abstraction dissolves itself (39.29–32) because its identity is a quality differing from other qualities (39.22–24). The original abstraction implies these other qualities and therefore contains them logically. By positing them explicitly, it goes beyond its original identity. This argument makes pure essence other than itself.

Its otherness is not indefinite, but rather quite specific. "As *essence* it is only *in itself* . . . ; but just because this purity [of essence] is abstraction or negativity, it is *for itself*, or the *self*, the *concept*" (410.9–11). Pure essence differentiates itself into a subject that knows the essence, and for which the initial essence is "*objective*" (410.12), so that essence is a "self-knowing *in the other*" (410.20). An argument for divine selfhood is contained in an allusion to earlier developments: "spirit is this, . . . to be the actual" (410.3–4). God has appeared as actual human selfhood in Jesus and the church and, therefore, selfhood must be implied by divine essence.

But as a logical requirement within divine essence, it is not yet actual; when spirit in the Trinity becomes actual, it becomes the otherness (411.30–33) of creation (412.1–3). Within the pretemporal Trinity, selfhood occurs as a logical requirement rather than as a reality.

Thus, the pretemporal self of essence is not an actual (divine) consciousness, but only the idea for a subjectivity[34] that does not yet exist. When it does exist, it will be human.

And just as the incarnate otherness leads to unifying spirit in real existence, within essence itself this otherness (divine subjectivity) implies a third and unifying moment. Because otherness is a "difference *in itself*" (410.16) within eternal essence, it belongs to essence and is, therefore, "unity returned into itself" (410.17). Deity thus completes[35] its pretemporal essence by defining itself as a Trinity of essence, subjectivity, and the self-knowing of essence through subjectivity. Hegel describes it in these words: "thus there differentiate themselves the three moments of *essence*, of [subjective] *being for itself*, which is the being other of essence and for which the essence is, and of *being for itself* or self-knowing *in the other*" (410.18–20). The third moment differs from the second in a subtle way. Whereas the second moment is already a knowing of the first essence since it is that "for which the essence is" (410.19), the third moment explicitly states what the first two moments imply. Since essence posits the subjectivity as a knowing of essence, "the essence views only itself in its being for itself; it is in this renunciation only with itself, [because] the being for itself which excludes itself from essence is the *knowing* of *its own essence*" (410.20–23). Insofar as subjectivity is a knowing of essence, then essence knows itself in the subjectivity it posits. The subjectivity is "the Word which [when] pronounced leaves the pronouncer [as] renounced and emptied but [which] is nevertheless immediately heard [by the pronouncer as itself], and [so] the Word's existence is merely this hearing[36] [one]self" (410.23–25).

When essence knows and hears itself in its other, it returns to itself. Thus, the pretemporal Trinity portrays itself as a logical cycle of differentiation and unification: "the differences that are made are dissolved as soon as they are made, and made as soon as they are dissolved" (410.25–27). Self-identity implies otherness, and otherness implies identity. Here, the identity occurs more precisely through *knowing*, through the subjectivity in which divine essence knows itself. This kind of subjectivity is what Hegel means by "spirit"; therefore, "this movement within itself pronounces absolute essence as *spirit*" (410.29).

As pure essence, deity demonstrates that spirit is essential to its concept, even prior to its realization in fact as human being. Spirit is a logical requirement of eternal essence that knows itself through its own subjectivity. These moments of spirit are "the restless concepts that are only their opposite . . . and . . . rest in the whole" (410.32–33). But since "the *imagining* of the community is not . . . *conceptual* thinking . . . it has the content without its necessity, and [so] brings into the kingdom of pure consciousness the natural relations of Father and Son instead of the form of the concept" (410.34–37). In such an image, "the moments . . . come . . . apart, so that they do not relate themselves to one another through their own concept" (411.1–3) but appear as "isolated unbudgeable substances or subjects" (411.9–10).

Conceptual knowing, on the other hand, comprehends God as pure thought whose moments require one another. Consequently, it also knows God as the eternal essence that appears as human thinking because this is the meaning of spirit. But theological imagination "steps back from this its pure object [and] relates itself only externally to it; it is [then] revealed to it by an alien [incarnate God], and in this thought of spirit it does not know itself, not the nature of pure self-consciousness" (411.3–6). Thus, imagining knows God as a transcendent spirit that communicates with human being by special revelation, rather than as eternal reason appearing in human reason.

Hegel approves of modern theology's attempt to go beyond imagination in trinitarian doctrine (411.6–12), but he criticizes theologians who dismiss the pretemporal Trinity as a historically conditioned[37] heirloom (411.12–14). For such thinkers, "faith's . . . *inner* [meaning] has disappeared, because this would be the concept which knows itself as concept" (411.15–17). For Hegel the real substance of Christian faith is the rational Trinity as the concept of spirit, eternal reason that knows itself through human subjectivity.

This criticism again points to human thinking as the real existence of spirit. The pretemporal Trinity demonstrates the logical necessity of spirit, but not its actual existence. The abstract Trinity of "pure thinking" (411.34) must move away from itself into "the proper element of *imagining*" (411.35–36) in which otherness rules; "abstract spirit . . . thus *creates* a world" (412.1, 2–3). Of course, "this *creating* is the word of imagination" (412.3); the concept requires only an otherness, or a world, or real existence. Essence thus becomes existence, and a new phase of spirit begins.

There is an intrinsic necessity for this transition, according to Hegel, because what is abstract implies an other, something different from itself (411.22–23). But in the abstract pretemporal Trinity, otherness is not really posited:

> the relation of eternal essence to its being for itself is the immediate simple [relation] of pure thinking; in this *simple* viewing of self in the other, *other-being* is not posited as such; it is difference as it in pure thought is immediately *no difference*; an acknowledging of *love* wherein both are not *opposed* to one another according to their essence. (411.25–30)

In other words, abstract essence differentiates itself into subjectivity so as to know itself in this other. But insofar as the subjectivity remains within divine essence, it represents only abstract essence knowing itself. Therefore, abstraction has not yet produced something other than itself. It has demonstrated only the abstract idea of subjectivity. Spirit within essence thus "has the same lack . . . which *essence* as essence has" (411.21–22). Just as pure essence implies the otherness that leads to spirit, so too "*spirit* in the element of essence is the *form* of *simple unity* which . . . is essentially a becoming other" (411.23–24).[38] If pure essence leads to otherness, then it must lead to something other than essence. But spirit was to be the other of essence. Therefore, spirit must "be *actual* [spirit], for in its concept lies *other-being* itself, i.e., the surmounting of the pure concept [which is] only thought" (411.31–33). Consequently, abstract spirit requires an actual world.

And so a transition is made from essence to existence, or from logic to nature:

> . . . the element of pure thinking . . . consequently passes over into the proper element of *imagining*—the element where the moments of the pure concept not only get a *substantial* existence against one another but also are *subjects* which . . . reflected into themselves separate themselves from one another and oppose [one another]. (411.34–39)

Pure thinking posits essence, then subjectivity as individual, and finally subjectivity as essence's self-knowing. Imagination separates these moments into God, selfish subjectivity, and spiritual subjectivity. In real existence, the two forms of subjectivity become evil and good consciousness, or sin and God incarnate.

Evil and Reconciliation (412.1–417.5)[39]

Because it is divine essence as human, spirit requires the human world of time and space. For imagination, essence "thus *creates* a *world*" (412.2–3). But "for the *concept*" (412.3), it is a rational necessity: divine essence, "the simple [essence] pronounced as absolute . . . because it is the abstract, is rather the negative and herewith self-opposed or *other*" (412.4–6), for reasons that I indicated earlier in this chapter. More precisely, "that [which is] posited as *essence* is simple *immediacy* or *being*" (412.7–8), and even more precisely it is being which has no self (412.8–9), being which is "*passive* or *being for [an] other*" (412.8–9), or nature in general. And because any abstraction contains implications, nature in general develops further into "*a world*" (412.10) full of determinate "particularity" (412.13–14).

Since this world is divine spirit in external form, or "spirit in the determinacy of *being for [an] other*" (412.10–11), it also contains "*existing* spirit, which is the individual self which has consciousness" (412.17–18), namely human being. Obviously, Hegel sketches his position without explaining it in detail. The system itself provides a fuller justification for these logical transitions.

Existing spirit then falls into sin and later obtains redemption, according to Christian theology. For Hegel, this history becomes a logical necessity: essence posits first its otherness and then its reunion with otherness. Hegel's reinterpretation differs from Christian belief not only by its logical character, but also by deriving human sin from divine essence. Evil is a moment of divine otherness; essence's own unfolding requires its occurrence and subsequent reconciliation with essence. Evil, then, is actually a stage in the development of good.

Here, Hegel consistently follows his concept of spirit. The otherness of God is different from pure essence and therefore has a potential for evil. This evil is nothing other than the moment of subjectivity, posited abstractly as the second moment of the pretemporal Trinity and now given real existence in human being.[40] But such individual subjectivity can also surmount itself by sacrificing its egoism to its universal knowing. Human being then becomes the subjectivity in which essence knows itself. Through this higher type of human knowing, essence reconciles itself with its evil otherness and transforms it into good. This is the moment of spirit, in which human being duplicates the pretemporal Trinity's third moment and gives it real existence. The earthly example of spirit or human goodness is God incarnate, whose individual shape reproduces itself in the many individuals constituting the Christian church. Reconciliation, then, belongs to those who imitate the incarnate God by their universal knowing and who thereby become spirit themselves.[41]

These considerations anticipate religion's conclusion. Initially, however, human being simply exists. Insofar as it shares in the world's immediate existence, human being is innocent animal sensuality, "dispersed into the manifold of its consciousness" (412.24–25). In this initial stage, it is "not yet *spirit for itself*" (412.20), not yet human subjectivity; "thus it *is* [but] not *as* spirit" (412.20). Up to this point, "it can be called *innocent* but not indeed *good*" (412.20–21)—for goodness comes through universal knowing, which in turn requires individual thinking.

This individual subjectivity comes into being when "immediate existence turns into thought, or the merely sensory [innocent] consciousness into the consciousness of thought"[42] (412.26–27), which would be good if it were a pure knowing of universal essence. However, "because it is thought coming from immediacy or [thought which is] *conditioned* [by sensory individuality], it is not pure knowing, but thought which has in it the being other [of immediate sensory individuality]" (412.28–30).[43] It is therefore "the self-opposed thought of *good* and *evil*" (412.30–31), "the knowledge of [both] *good* and *evil*" (412.39)—good coming from its thought and evil from the sensual orientation of this thought. Since its knowing is not pure but rather makes innocent consciousness "*unequal* to itself, *evil* appears as the first existence of consciousness gone into itself" (412.37–38).[44] Nevertheless, the possibility for self-renunciation is also given when thought arises, so that "*good* consciousness" (413.2) is also "at hand" (413.3). Since the first good human consciousness is God incarnate, Hegel may be alluding here to the promise of a savior in Genesis 3:15.

Evil's relation to God calls for special treatment because evil appears in human being as the real existence of the (individual) subjectivity posited by the pretemporal Trinity. Just as the pure divine essence posits as its second moment the logical idea of subjectivity and as its third moment the self-knowing of essence in that same subjectivity, so, too, does human being pass from a state of natural innocence into individual subjectivity, which contains the further possibility for spirit as the self-knowing of essence in human subjectivity. In the pretemporal Trinity, divine essence posits as its second moment the logical idea of subjectivity and as its third moment the self-knowing of essence in that same subjectivity. Human being duplicates this movement by passing from its natural innocence into individual subjectivity (the second moment) before becoming the good consciousness of spirit, the self-knowing of essence in human existence (the third moment). These three phases of human existence reproduce the pretemporal Trinity, which is their essential pattern and which gives itself real existence in human being. Human evil, therefore, belongs to divine essence, and this unity grounds their ultimate reconciliation.

The second moment, however, does not receive its due in the pretemporal Trinity, where it quickly passes over into the third. But now "insofar as immediate [human] existence turns into *thought,* and [in this] *being within oneself* . . . the moment of essence's *becoming other* is thereby more closely determined" (413.3–5), human subjectivity captures the second moment of the Trinity, which one can then imagine as a pretemporal Son without the Spirit. Consequently, "becoming evil can be transferred . . . from the existing world . . . into the first kingdom of thought" (413.5–7). In religious imagination, this concept appears as the story of Lucifer, "the firstborn Son of Light [who] by going inward is the one who fell, but in whose place another was quickly begotten" (413.8–9). Hegel criticizes the story for bringing such images as "Son" and "Father" into the concept (413.9–12), but not for introducing evil into pretemporal essence; the latter contains individual ("evil") subjectivity as the necessary condition for spirit.

Hegel's position also implies that pretemporal essence need not correspond exactly to the Christian Trinity. The possibility of a subjectivity that does not become spirit means that the second moment can be subdivided into a good and a bad version, so that a quaternity is conceivable; the bad version would still belong to essence, from which there can be no "fall."[45] The bad subjectivity would not, however, be pure evil but rather the unfulfilled potential for good.

Hegel's entertainment of this possibility again reveals the true purpose of his pretemporal "Trinity." For him, the pretemporal essence defines the logical requirements of spirit and thus can include its incomplete moments, too. As the subjectivity that has not yet become spirit, Lucifer legitimately belongs to essence. Perhaps more accurately, the pretemporal Trinity and Lucifer are images produced by religion when it attempts to describe the logical foundations of human spirit. For Hegel however these foundations define God, who contains all the essential features of human existence. By including the possibility for evil, Hegel's God cannot correspond exactly to three divine persons.

Essence also has room for the concept of angels, who appear when pretemporal subjectivity is expanded into a multitude by "subordinating a whole manifold of other shapes to the simple thought of *other-being* in eternal essence, and transferring to them [the moment of] *going within oneself*" (413.13–15). These other shapes differ from "the Son, the simple [subjectivity] knowing itself as essence" (413.18–19); by their constant worship, they are subjective "being-for-self's renunciation, which lives only in praise of essence" (413.19–20). Thus, they represent another incomplete form of spirit, whose fullness requires a self-knowing subjectivity like the Son's; they apparently correspond to human being's innocence before the fall. Like Lucifer, they make pretemporal essence into a "quaternity" (413.23). And since "the going within oneself of evil" (413.21) can be put into this group as well, the angels divide into subjects who have "remained good and [those who have] become evil" (413.24), to give a "five-in-one" (413.25).

Hegel discourages the counting of moments for a number of reasons (413.25–36), the simplest of which is that "the mere difference of quantity and multitude is unconceptual and says nothing" (413.35–36) because it has no content other than a difference of number. This remark does not, however, detract from the trinitarian supplements that make "spirit more determinate in its moments" (413.22–23). Hegel approves of these further determinations insofar as they contain a conceptual content. Indeed, his objection to counting would also apply to the Trinity, which is merely a convenient way of referring to pure essence's most significant moments. His willingness to include angels in divine essence indicates once again his free interpretation of Christian doctrine.

More significant than the number of moments is their cohesive unity within divine essence. If evil subjectivity falls within essence, then its reconciliation[46] is already posited "in itself" or in principle; evil consciousness then must become good in fact and "for itself" by actually subordinating itself to essence. In this way, human being becomes the real existence of divine spirit, or essence's knowing itself in subjectivity. Christianity discovers this reconciliation when it universalizes the presence of spirit that first appeared in Jesus; this universality has already been examined in Hegel's treatment of the incarnation. In his analysis of trinitarian theology, he returns again to these themes for they contain the concept of spirit on which reconciliation depends. But in his portrayal of trinitarian theology, reconciliation has not yet occurred; evil has been posited, but not its reunion with essence.

As abstract opposites, good and evil can "be imagined as essences of thought, each of which is independent for itself" (414.1–2) in the shapes of the Spirit and Satan, respectively. On earth, "human being is then the self without essence and the synthetic terrain of their existence and struggle" (414.2–3). But in fact, "the self is their actuality" (414.4–5). Evil exists as human being[47] and is "nothing other than spirit's natural existence going within itself" (414.6); and eventually, "good steps into actuality and appears as an existing self-consciousness" (414.7–8). This appearance of good in the world is of course the incarnation, whereby "divine essence assumes human nature" (415.18–19).[48] For Christian faith or "imagining" (414. 9–10), the incarnation is "the self-abasement of divine essence which renounces its abstraction and unactuality" (414.10–11). But for the concept, this incarnation is in fact "divine essence's becoming *other*" (414.8) than the pretemporal Trinity in which spirit is posited within pure essence.

With the incarnation, "the alienation of divine essence is thus posited in its doubled mode" (414.16)—first as evil consciousness, for which "*being for itself* . . . counts . . . as the essential [thing] and the simple divine [essence] as the unessential" (414.23–25), and second as the good consciousness for which "*divine essence* counts as the essential [thing], but natural existence and the self as the unessential and [something] to be surmounted" (414.22–23).[49] Good and evil are, therefore, opposed as the incarnate God on the one hand and sinful human being on the other.

Since their reconciliation is already guaranteed by the concept of spirit within pure essence, religion correctly attributes the reconciliation to a divine initiative by the good consciousness,[50] which is the incarnation of divine "being in itself" (414.37). This initiative—the death (415.3) of Christ—is "imagined as a voluntary doing" (414.38) by religion, but for Hegel "the necessity of its renunciation lies in the concept that the [good or divine] being in itself, which is so determined only in opposition [to evil], has just for that reason no true subsistence" (414.38–415.2). In other words, there is no lasting truth for the figure of God incarnate as a singular good person separated from evil persons, because God can have no opposite: "the absolute essence would only have this empty name [of absolute essence] if in truth there were an *other* for it, if [there were] a *fall* from it" (415.23–24).[51] Consequently, the individual human existence of God passes away (when Jesus dies) and is replaced by a more universal existence in the church, the multitude of persons who by themselves are evil but who are now elevated into goodness by the presence of God. I have already described how this occurs.[52] Reconciliation occurs when the church knows itself as divine presence. The death of Jesus removes him from view as the sole expression of spirit, and so enables the church to see itself as universal spirit.[53] Hegel's concept thus requires no special theory of atonement for sin.

When spirit becomes universal, "it reconciles absolute essence with itself" (415.3–4) because essence itself is universal. In the church, essence "portrays itself as *spirit*" (415.4) by overcoming the limitation imposed on it by a single incarnation. For the "abstract [divine] essence is alienated from itself, [inasmuch as] it has natural existence and personal[54] actuality" (415.5–6) in Jesus alone (the good consciousness), but not in anyone else. The individual incarnation means that essence has only a single human actuality rather than a universal one. It becomes universal when its incarnate "being other or its sensory presence is taken back . . . and posited as surmounted, as *universal*" (415.6–8), or present in all members of the church. And such a universalizing is what "reconciles absolute essence with itself" (415.3–4) because as universally present, "essence has become itself in it[s sensory presence]; the immediate existence of actuality has ceased to be an [existence] alien or external to it, by being surmounted, universal" (415.8–10). Jesus's "death is consequently its rising as spirit" (413.10) in the church. Essence recovers its universality when the universal presence of spirit replaces the singular presence of God in Jesus.[55] Thus, divine essence is reconciled with itself when it is reconciled with existing subjectivity, which by itself is evil but when reconciled to God is good. The reconciliation of good and evil is also the reconciliation of divine essence with itself because evil is a moment of that same essence.

Even though Christianity may consider Jesus as now living in heaven at the right hand of God, Hegel's interpretation requires only the risen existence of Jesus on earth as the spirit of the church, which is "universal divine human [being], the community" (421.4). The main point of Hegel's interpretation is this movement from the individual earthly presence of God to a more universal earthly existence in the church.[56] When God's presence thus incorporates many human beings, their "evil" is perforce eliminated.

In his earlier description of the incarnation, Hegel alludes to this expansion. In contrast to "*this individual* self-consciousness" (407.19) of God incarnate in Jesus, the full content of revealed religion (as well as of speculative knowing) is to know God (407.1) or spirit as "*this* [individual] and [also] universal self" (407.6). The universal self of God is, of course, the Christian community. When God incarnate (in one individual) dies in order to be viewed as present in the whole church, "the surmounted immediate presence of self-conscious essence is . . . universal self-consciousness; consequently, this concept of the surmounted individual self, which is absolute essence, immediately expresses the constitution of a community" (415.11–14). In other words, God's incarnation is universally actual in the church.

Christianity cannot easily explain this transition from the individual holiness of Jesus to the holiness of the whole church. For Christianity, divine grace is an object of *faith* because God's gracious disposition cannot be taken for granted. Hegel, however, explains it simply: God is not a willful individual but a universal essence including all reality; its universal extension is necessary and so appears in religion, but only as the image of Christ's universal presence. According to Hegel's concept, though, the universality of God's presence is based on the self-identity of essence as universal.

Hegel concludes his analysis of reconciliation with a long discussion (415.16–417.1) of its logical implications. They merit more than a passing mention here. For Christian "imagining . . . divine essence assumes human nature" (415.17–19). For Hegel, this image has already "*pronounced* that *in themselves* both are not separated" (415.19–20); divine and human nature belong together. One should understand their unity as potentially universal since essence itself is the universal form of many human beings. Though evil and unredeemed, human being still belongs to the self-differentiation of deity: "divine essence renounces itself *from the beginning*; its existence goes within itself and becomes evil" (415.20–21). Therefore, "*in itself* this evil existence is not an alien to it; absolute essence would only have this empty name [of absolute essence] if in truth there were an *other* for it, if [there were] a *fall* from it" (415.22–24). Even as evil human being belongs to God because "the moment of *being within oneself* . . . constitutes the essential moment of the *self* of spirit" (415.24–26). By itself this moment is "evil," and religion views it as a setback or fall from grace. But for Hegel, it is absolutely necessary for the existence of spirit, where divine essence knows itself through human subjectivity. Without such individual subjectivity, spirit could not exist at all. Thus, "*being within oneself* and [along] with it . . . *actuality* [as human being] belongs to essence itself . . . [and] is for us [the] *concept*" (415.26–27). God contains human being "*from the beginning*" (415.20), so that even humanity's incomplete existence as "evil" falls within the concept of God.

Religion, however, knows divine-human unity as beginning "later, in the renunciation of divine essence that becomes flesh" (415.32–33). Religion knows this not as a concept, of course, but "as an unconceptual *happening*; the [essence] *in itself* assumes the form of *indifferent being*" (415.28–29) because for Christianity, human nature does not belong intrinsically to God. But the conceptual significance of the incarnation is just the opposite, namely that "absolute essence and the self [that] is for itself are not separated" (415.30–31). A single incarnation, however, fails to convey the concept's universality. Christianity remedies this defect by its doctrine of reconciliation, which expresses more fully the meaning of the risen Christ as ecclesial spirit.[57]

Hegel's criticism of the individual incarnation has already been discussed. There, faith is "the imagination which . . . still is *immediate* and consequently not spiritual, or [which] first knows the human shape of essence only as a particular [individual shape] not yet universal" (415.33–35). This faith becomes "spiritual in the movement of [humanly] shaped essence's offering back its immediate existence and returning to essence; the essence is spirit only as *reflected into itself*" (415.35–38) in ecclesial universality. As a result, the resurrection means "the *reconciliation* of divine essence with [its] *other* in general and specifically with *evil*, the *thought* of [otherness]" (415.38–39). But conceptually, this reconciliation is already contained in the universal fact of human being as the existing subjectivity of divine essence.

This divine-human unity does not exactly mean that "*in itself evil is the same* as *good*" (416.2–3). Technically, evil and good are different moments: "in that evil is *the same* as good, is evil precisely not evil nor good good, but both are instead surmounted" (416.6–8) in the concept of their unity. Indeed, when evil is defined as the subjective "being for itself that is within itself and good [as] the selfless simple [knowing of essence],[58] . . . their unity is immediately clear" (419.8–10) because pure subjective knowing is also the simple knowing of objective essence.[59] Thus, "the being for itself that is within itself is the simple knowing [of essence as its object]; and the selfless simple [knowing of essence] is precisely so the pure being for itself that is within itself" (416.10–12). When it looks away from itself to its rational objectivity, evil subjectivity becomes good by its knowing of universal divine essence.[60] The two types of knowing differ only by their different orientation. And since they mutually imply one another, they also illustrate Hegel's logical method in which any incomplete content implies another one as part of its wider self-identity (416.12–417.1).

A similar pattern applies to the relation between essence and nature, the respective objects of good and evil consciousness. As the universal essence, "divine essence is *the same* as nature in its whole extent" (416.3–4), so that nature "is divine in its essence" (416.28). Divine essence exists as the natural universe and thus includes evil human subjectivity within its compass.

But there is also a difference in the "*sameness* of divine essence and nature in general and human [nature] in particular; the former is nature insofar as it is not essence" (416.26–28), namely insofar as it posits itself as existence rather than as essence. And this existence as distinguished from essence has an insubstantial yet firm foothold in the chain of logical development: "nature is *nothing outside* its essence; but this nothing itself nevertheless *is*" (416.31–32) because it has the form of pure being that implies other determinations. Later (at the beginning of his *Logik*), Hegel identifies being with nothing to constitute becoming, which ultimately defines itself as pure personality.

This is also true of *PhG*, in which empty being "is the absolute abstraction, thus [eventually] pure thinking or being within oneself, and with the moment of its opposition to spiritual unity it is *evil*" (416.33–34). Without going into much detail, Hegel refers to the argument that later appears in the *Logik*. Here, he applies it to the development of evil as divine otherness: pure being becomes pure thinking, and as individual it turns away from essence to affirm itself as a subjective thinking that knows no objective essence. Thus, it is evil. But thinking does in fact have a content since its pure objectivity is also the divine essence that differentiates itself into a world and then into thinking itself. Evil, therefore, can maintain itself only by abstracting from the dialectical development of its objective thought, thus remaining in the "moment of its opposition to spiritual unity" (416.34). In their unity, "the moments both *are* and *are not*" (416.36–417.1) because they negate themselves by their mutual implication. As a result, good and evil, or essence and nature, belong to a "unity where the differences are only as moments or as surmounted" (417.1–2).

Christian faith obviously has no grasp of such a logic. But it "possesses the true content" (415.32) of this logic by imagining God as human—first as the individual incarnation and later as divine presence in the church, where human evil meets trinitarian goodness. Thus, the unity contained in Hegel's concept has "come to be for imagining consciousness in that reconciliation" (417.3) of God with sin. And since the reconciliation is potentially in every human or in "the universality of self-consciousness, the latter ceases to be [the] imagining" (417.4–5) of God as a being separate from itself. Instead, God is known to be present in every self-consciousness that renounces itself and turns to its Lord. The community then "turns back into itself as into the self; and spirit then passes out of the second element of its determinacy, imagining, into the *third*, self-consciousness as such" (415.14–16), in which spirit belongs to every self.

Ecclesial Spirit (417.6–421.18)[61]

Spirit now becomes the Christian church, "the allness of selves" (407.29) referred to earlier. Here, "spirit is . . . posited in the third element, in *universal self-consciousness*; it is its *community*" (417.6–7). Hegel's phrase "universal self-consciousness" may refer to an intersubjective community spirit, but primarily it means the many individuals who constitute the community. Elsewhere, the term refers to all individuals in contrast to the single self of Jesus alone, who is "*this individual* self-consciousness opposed to *universal* self-consciousness" (407.19–20; see also 407.6 and 418.27–28) or to "every self" (407.23–24). Its meaning of individuality (as a universal occurrence) is confirmed by an earlier description of the third element as "the element of self-consciousness itself" (409.15), with no reference to universality.

In this third element, reconciliation is actually appropriated by individual subjectivity; in the second element, it is offered in principle to the world at large. In the third element, essence appears in (hitherto evil) subjectivity to reconcile itself with such subjectivity; the movement is personal for each individual self-consciousness. But since the pattern occurs in a multitude of individuals, it is also universal. Divine essence, then, overcomes the difference between itself and its otherness.[62] In religious history, this occurs when the early church experiences the universal presence of spirit.

This third element reproduces the movement of spirit found in earlier elements. In the first element, the pretemporal Trinity determines the logical pattern of human existence as essence's knowing itself through subjectivity. Thus, in the third element human subjectivity has to become such a knowing. In this respect, it imitates the second element's good consciousness and does so in two related ways. First, as the knowing in which essence knows itself, human being imitates the earthly incarnation of God. Second, as the passage from individual (evil) knowing to universal (good) knowing, it also imitates the incarnate God's movement from individual (earthly) existence to universal (ecclesial) existence—Christ's death and resurrection. Within individual knowing, this imitation of Christ is obviously subjective and refers to universal thinking.[63] Its larger significance is, however, objective: through universal thinking, universal divine essence appears as individual consciousness and so reconciles itself with its (hitherto evil) otherness.

Hegel describes this development of ecclesial spirit in the following way. As the pattern of pretemporal spirit come into human existence, "the deceased divine human, or human God, is *in itself* universal self-consciousness" (417.9–10); God incarnate illustrates a universal truth. But for the truth to pass from possibility to actuality in a given individual, the incarnate God's universal exemplarity "has to become this *for this* [individual] *self-consciousness*" (417.10–11), which for itself must "*produce* what has come to be *in itself*" (417.8–9) within essence's universal resurrection. Human "evil, for which natural existence and individual being-for-self counts as essence . . . has . . . to raise itself to spirit, or portray in its [own existence] the movement of [spirit]" (417.12–16). In other words, human individuality must unite itself with universal divine essence by rejecting its naturally existing evil self. It then appropriates the reconciliation it has come to know through Christ.

Human individuality's initial attempt, however, is unsuccessful and illustrates evil's enduring power. Hegel's analysis of this point reflects the Christian (especially Pauline) view of sin as intrinsic to human being. Since evil then turns to the risen Lord for help, Hegel's analysis also alludes to the Christian idea of sinful humanity's helplessness before it receives God's grace.

The evil self "*is natural spirit*; the self has to withdraw itself out of this naturalness and go into itself, which would mean becoming *evil*" (417.17–18) all over again. But since its naturalness "is already *in itself* evil" (417.18–19), its further "going within itself consequently consists in *convincing itself* that [its] natural existence is evil" (417.19–20) by "*knowing evil* as . . . [intrinsically] *in itself* in existence" (418.1–2). Acknowledging evil as essential is an appropriate first attempt at reconciliation since evil needs to join itself to essence. This goal requires evil to surmount the sensory factual images of evil and reconciliation through a pure knowing (417.20–25) that unifies those opposing images (417.25–35).

Consciousness thus attempts to escape sin by "the *thought* of evil . . . [which] is consequently acknowledged as the first moment of reconciliation" (418.3–4). Recognizing evil as essential takes the self beyond the sensory character of sin, "for as a going back into oneself out of the immediacy of nature which is determined as evil it is an abandoning of that [nature] and a dying to sin" (418.4–6). But this explains evil only by the universality of evil, which occurs "because nature has already [objectively] in itself gone into itself; because of evil humans must go into themselves, but *evil* is itself the [same] going into oneself" (418.10–12). As such, it is merely the "*simple concept*" (418.13) of sin rather than "becoming other" (418.14) than sin. And so the reconciliation of divine essence with evil subjectivity has not yet been appropriated by the latter. Humanity merely recognizes its innate sinfulness.

Consequently, "besides this immediacy [of evil] . . . the *mediation* of imagination is necessary" (418.16–17). Evil consciousness then turns to the risen Christ (418.23–34) who is present in the church; through this image, evil is reconciled with God. Hegel interprets the image in a rational way: reconciliation occurs when universal thought affirms itself as the truth of human individuality because the self then knows itself as essence rather than as evil. According to the concept of spirit "*in itself* the *knowing* is of nature as the untrue existence of spirit, and this inwardly developed [insich gewordne] universality of the self [is] the reconciliation of spirit with itself" (418.17–19). The text applies to individual (evil) subjectivity the movement of the pretemporal Trinity: as universal essence in the form of human subjectivity, spirit completes itself when subjectivity knows itself as universal essence. This universal knowing is pure *a priori* thinking, present in human knowing from its beginning but now freed from its (evil) dependence on nature. This knowing now recognizes universal essence as the real truth of natural existence and so is the reconciliation of universal essence with individual (evil) existence. Nature as individual and sensory is essence's otherness, but universal thinking "knows surmounted naturalness as universal [and] thus as reconciled with itself" (418.21–22). In such a pure universal thinking, spirit completes its development; it is now universal essence knowing itself through human subjectivity. Essence thus appears as human being and so is reconciled with its (evil) otherness.[64]

But in Christianity this concept becomes known through "the *mediation* of imagination" (418.16). Here, the concept of spirit "*in itself* gets for the uncomprehending [believing] consciousness the form of a *being*

... [that is] *imagined*" (418.19–20).[65] In particular, faith here is "a grasping of that *image* [affirming] that through the *happening* of divine essence's own renunciation, through its incarnation [which] happened and its death, divine essence is reconciled with its existence" (418.22–25). Reconciliation "now expresses more precisely what previously ... was called the spiritual resurrection, or [essence's] individual self-consciousness [in the shape of Jesus] becoming universal or the community" (418.26–28). The universal presence of God incarnate is recognized as the reconciliation of essence with its (evil) otherness.

Reconciliation thus requires the universal presence of God; this in turn requires only the universal thinking of each individual consciousness, rather than a genuine resurrection from the dead. Hegel describes the latter with his usual reserve about life beyond the grave: "the *death* of the divine human ... loses this natural meaning ... of the non-being of *this individual* [and is] transfigured into the *universality* of the spirit which lives in its community" (418.28–34). As ecclesial spirit, Christ acquires a universal meaning that overcomes his transitory individual existence. For Hegel, the resurrection of Jesus means that spirit is a universal concept rather than a single incarnation; a personal conscious immortality has no role in his analysis.

In the second element, Christ portrays spirit (418.35–37) through his death, which transforms his individual existence into universal (ecclesial) existence. Thus, he is present in every individual Christian. But this individual presence actually refers to an individual's universal thinking, the true presence of God in human being. As a result, in the third element, this "nature of spirit ... is ... transferred into self-consciousness itself, into the knowing that preserves itself in its [objective][66] *being other*" (418.37–38). Since in this element spirit appears as universal knowing, individual self-consciousness "does not therefore actually *die* as the *particular* [incarnate God] is *imagined*[67] to have *actually* died, but its particularity dies away in its universality, that is, in its *knowing*" (418.38–419.2). Hegel's reference to universal knowing indicates that for him this presence is reason itself, individual subjectivity as universal thought. Christianity is not so conceptual but nevertheless has this universal knowing by imagining within itself the presence of universal essence: "it is no longer I who live, but Christ who lives in me."[68]

This universal knowing is reconciliation, "essence reconciling itself with itself" (419.2). In the mass of evil human beings, essence does not appear in its rational purity. Their sensory knowing is a human existence of essence, but in a form different from essence itself. But when human subjectivity now surmounts its natural sensory intellect for pure universal knowing, it becomes a genuine presence of universal essence. Thus, essence is reconciled with its otherness.

Furthermore, such a reconciliation is not a return to the transcendent God or pretemporal Trinity of pure thinking, the first element of spirit. The second element gives essence a real human self as the incarnate God. The third element, then, is not simply pure abstract thinking but *self*-consciousness, which knows *itself* to be divine presence: divine spirit is present within the soul of every Christian. The "preceding [second] *element of imagining* is thus posited here as [a] surmounted [element], or it has returned into the self . . . ; the [incarnate God,] mere being in that [prior element], has become subject" (419.2–5) as every Christian self. In the second element God incarnate is a sensory being for believing consciousness (418.19–20); in the third element, God incarnate is believing consciousness itself. Since the church interprets the death of Jesus as his resurrection or universal presence, "the mediator's death [as] grasped by the self is the surmounting of his *objectivity* or his *particular being for himself*; this *particular* being for self has become universal self-consciousness" (419.8–11) as the individual members of the church.

Now that spirit becomes real subjectivity in the multitude of (hitherto evil) human beings, it also surmounts its first (pretemporal) element: "the *first element* [or] *pure thinking* and its eternal spirit is no longer beyond imagining consciousness nor [beyond] the self" (419.5–7). Pretemporal essence or "the *universal* [essence] is thereby self-consciousness, and the pure or unactual spirit of mere thinking [has] become *actual*" (419.11–13) as every human being. This pretemporal essence remains a factor in religion for as long as the earthly incarnation continues because the incarnate Son recognizes a transcendent Father. The Son enters an evil world as the good consciousness who "knows as *essence* the simple [universal God] of thought in contrast to actuality; this extreme of the [actual evil] self does not yet have equal worth [compared] with essence; this [worth] the self first has in spirit" (419.17–19) after "the death of the mediator" (419.13). During the Son's earthly existence, other human beings remain evil, separated from God and from the individual incarnation. Only after his death do they recognize that spirit includes them, too. Consequently, God is not beyond them and so is no longer the transcendent Father of the earthly Son. Thus, the latter's death is also "the death of the *abstraction* of *divine essence* which is not posited as [every] self" (419.20–21). When this abstract essence is posited as the human self (in the shape of ecclesial spirit), it loses its abstract identity and therefore seems to die.

Thus, consciousness echoes its pre-Christian state as "the painful feeling of the unhappy consciousness that *God himself* is *dead*" (419.21–22).[69] These are the birth pangs of spirit[70] in the moment of reconciliation. Henceforth, divine essence is known only in "the most inner simple knowing [of] self, the return of consciousness into the depth of the night of the I=I, which [depth] knows and distinguishes nothing more outside itself" (419.23–24).

Knowing itself as divine presence, believing consciousness must now give up its transcendent God because "this feeling [of pain] is in fact the loss of *substance* and its being opposite to consciousness" (419.25–26). But this loss on the other hand creates "the pure *subjectivity* of substance or pure certainty of self, which were missing in [substance] as the object [of consciousness] or the immediate [incarnate God] or the pure [pretemporal] essence" (419.26–28).[71] This painful "knowing thus is the *spiriting* by which substance has become subject . . . *actual* and simple and universal self-consciousness" (419.28–30). When divine substance is known as human self-consciousness, "its abstraction and lifelessness [are] dead" (419.29); God is no longer the transcendent Father, but the spirit within.

Spirit (essence as human) then knows itself in a shape identical to itself; "spirit thus is spirit knowing *itself*; it knows *itself*" (419.31) in the shape of the Holy Spirit who dwells within its people. The human subjectivity that knows itself as divine presence is here the knowing subject and also the object known. As a result, spirit knows itself as real: it is "not only [the mental] *content* of self-consciousness and not only [a mental] object *for it* but it is also *actual spirit*" (419.33–35); "that which is object for it is" (419.31–32) real since the object is God as ecclesial spirit.[72]

Hegel also points out that spirit in the church continues the concept of spirit that appears in "Evil and Its Pardon" (419.38–420.5). The idea is the same: just as the beautiful soul pardons evil consciousness and gives up its immutability (420.1–3), so too in the church essence reconciles itself with evil and gives up its abstract transcendence. The "religious consciousness to which absolute essence is manifest *views* this concept" (420.5–6) through the image of God present in (hitherto evil) human being. And since that human being is religious consciousness itself, the latter "surmounts the *distinction* of its [own] *self* from its *viewed* [object and] is [therefore] the [human] subject[73] as well as the [divine] substance, and *is* itself spirit precisely because and insofar as it is this movement" (420.5–8) of reconciliation.

To the extent that the goal of religion is to surmount the difference between spirit as an incarnate divine object and spirit as human self-consciousness (369.23–26), the goal has now been reached for deity has also absorbed human self-consciousness; the object of religious consciousness now equals the human subject that knows it. Such a result is not only the completion of religion, but also the beginning of absolute knowing, where absolute essence comprehends itself through human consciousness.

Yet Christianity is not yet this conceptual comprehension. According to Hegel, "this community is however not yet completed in this its self-consciousness" (420.9–10) because imagination affects all three elements of spirit (409.21–25) in trinitarian theology. Thus, the community's "content is in general for it in the form of *imagining*" (420.10), which gives its object a separate otherness. And so the third element, "the *actual spirituality* of that [community] also has this division" (420.10–11) from having an object (here, the reconciling spirit) distinct from oneself. Instead of knowing spirit as its own concept, it imagines divine presence as an essence other than itself. Consequently, the community "does not have the consciousness of what it is; it is the spiritual consciousness which [for] itself is not this [holy] object, or [which] does not open itself to consciousness of itself" (420.13–15).

In the church's consciousness of God's interior presence, human "self-consciousness . . . becomes *inward* and reaches a *knowing* of [this] *being within oneself*" (420.16–18). The church recognizes God as the spirit within and so "gains the pure negativity" (420.19) of intellectual knowing. But it does not know that reconciliation occurs through its own thinking, which fulfills the concept of spirit and so is essence knowing itself as human. That its "negativity or pure *inward-*

ness of *knowing* is also the [self-identical] *essence equal to itself*, or that substance herein becomes absolute self-consciousness—this is an *other* for devout consciousness" (420.20–22), which knows absolute spirit not as its own thinking but as a holiness different from itself. Christianity correctly knows its interior spirit as God but wrongly explains it as a Spirit present only through Jesus's merit: "that the pure becoming inward of knowing is *in itself* absolute simplicity or [divine] substance it grasps . . . as the image of something that is not so according to the *concept* but as the action of an *alien* satisfaction" (420.23–26) accomplished by a Savior, who died for people's sins. Christianity thus attributes its universal knowing to the work of Christ instead of to its own concept as the real existence of divine essence.

Christianity also does not realize that because of this concept, its own thinking effects the presence of God within itself. Thus this truth "is not for it, [namely] that this depth of the pure self is the might by which *abstract essence* is pulled down from its abstraction and elevated to the self through the force of its [own] pure devotion" (420.26–28).[74] Christianity fails to realize its own role in reconciliation because it does not comprehend the concept of divine essence as human existence. The concept of deity's becoming human or "substance's self-renunciation . . . is for that [Christian consciousness] an [object] *in itself* which it does not . . . find in its *own* doing as such" (420.29–31), and so essence's development into human being remains an object separate from Christian thinking. The separation is, of course, the work of imagination: "since this unity of essence and self [has] come about [by divine objectivity] *in itself*, consciousness . . . has this *image* of its reconciliation, but as image" (420.31–34). Hegel's description corresponds well to the church's belief in Jesus risen from the dead, and present in the hearts of Christians as the Spirit pledging their own future resurrection.

Thus reconciliation remains in God alone, who (for Christian imagination) is other than the self. Christian piety "reaches contentment by *externally* adding to its pure [subjective] negativity the positive significance of its unity with essence" (420.34–36). It knows that divine essence contains reconciliation but does not know this essence as itself. Consequently, its empirical existence remains unreconciled. Its reconciliation is present only in the otherness of essence. As a result, "its contentment itself remains afflicted with the opposite of a beyond"

(420.36–37), namely the reconciling essence of God who is other than human.

Actual reconciliation then becomes the object of Christian eschatological hope, "whose own reconciliation consequently steps into its consciousness as a *distant* [thing], a distant [thing] of the *future*" (420.37–421.1), existing only in God but not yet in the actual world. Since individual reconciliation requires a person's universal knowing, "the universal divine human, the community[75] has . . . its *own doing* and *knowing* for its father" (421.4–5). But since ecclesial spirit does not identify its universal knowing with divine essence (420.19–28), it has "for its mother[76] . . . *eternal love* which it only *feels* but does not view in its consciousness as an actual immediate *object*" (421.5–7). The forthcoming birth or appearance of its reconciliation lies in God, who contains the future. Thus, "the world . . . still has to wait for its transfiguration" (421.11–12). Knowing God by its universal thinking, the community's "reconciliation is consequently in its heart" (421.7). But since divine essence is not identified with human universal knowing, it constitutes another world, leaving the church "with its consciousness still divided and its actuality still broken" (421.7–8).

Since the self's universal knowing is also an essential *a priori* knowing of the world,[77] the Christian separation of God and self also separates God from the actual world. Even ecclesial spirit keeps them apart. It is conscious of "the reconciliation lying beyond; but what [it knows] as *present*, as . . . *immediacy* and *existence*, is the world which still has to wait for its transfiguration" (421.10–12) in a future kingdom of God. Thus, for Christianity the world is "to be sure *in itself* reconciled with essence; and essence . . . to be sure no longer knows[78] the object as alienated from it but as equal to it in its [divine] love" (421.12–14). Such doctrines refer to a divine essence whose loving plans have not yet been fulfilled. The world, then, waits for its redemption; "for [Christian] self-consciousness this immediate present does not yet have [the] shape of spirit" (421.14–15). Through its eschatological hope, "the spirit of the community is thus in its immediate [empirical] consciousness separated from its religious [consciousness]" (421.15–16).[79] Faith affirms that both sides of its consciousness "are not separate *in themselves*, but [this is] an [object] *in itself* that [has] not been realized or that [has] not yet also become absolute being for itself" (421.17–18) in a human subjectivity that knows its identity with divine essence. Such a subjectivity would know its reconciliation with God as a necessary and universal truth, valid for all times. It would thus view its present existence as the fulfillment of reconciliation.

But bringing together empirical existence and religious consciousness (364.33–365.5) was to be "the completion of religion" (365.1–2). On the one hand, Christianity completes[80] the sequence of world religions by giving a human shape to God; on the other hand, Christianity is not yet complete because it continues to separate God from the actual world and empirical human being. As *religion*, however, it is complete since it imagines God as present in real human being. Its deficiency is remedied not by another religion but by absolute philosophical knowing.

But Christianity gives God an *actual* human shape when it believes in Jesus as God incarnate (404.33–405.13). While this incarnate God is the "*highest* essence" (406.7) God can attain, a single incarnation of God is an individual sensory being separated from the rest of the human race (407.18–23). After his death, a multitude of other selves do make up "the universal divine human, the community" (421.4), yet the church's empirical existence is not considered to be the incarnation of God. In the church, religious consciousness and empirical consciousness are, therefore, dissociated.

In this respect the church returns to the end of "Evil and Its Pardon," in which God appears as the identification of universal and individual subjectivity—a "pure knowing" (362.29) without material actuality. What, then, is gained by the chapter on "Religion"? At least two things: a full incarnation of God in human being in the single case of Jesus; and the universalizing of this incarnation in the church, which as universal surpasses the single incarnation of Jesus. But since the universal version is not as intensive as the incarnation of God in Jesus (but rather reverts to the pure interiority of the appearing God in *PhG* VI–C), there is room for further development. Spirit will then become "Absolute Knowing" when it comprehends the whole world (material and spiritual) as the universal existence of divine essence.

Hegel's concept thus offers a bold reinterpretation of Christianity: divine essence differentiates itself into human being and so is the concept of every individual human person. This concept is present in the church's image of ecclesial spirit but because imagination separates the divine and human realms, it attributes the world's transfiguration to a divine plan to be realized in the future. For Hegel, however, the world is already transfigured by thought insofar as human reason knows itself to be the real existence of divine essence. The kingdom of God is already present.

Is there also a future kingdom as well? Hegel's position makes this possibility very unlikely since his criticism aims precisely at the Christian hope for a world qualitatively different from the present one. Such a refusal of eschatology is consistent with his interpretation of Jesus's resurrection as the church, which universalizes the incarnation by its awareness of an interior divine presence and so becomes "the universal divine human" (421.4). The possibility of an afterlife (whether for Jesus or his followers) has no place in Hegel's analysis of Christian theology. In his concept of God as the essence of this present world, there is no room for a different world. The fullness of God produces only this one.

Christianity, of course, believes otherwise because religion (by definition) thinks by imagination. Its object, then, is something other than present reality: for example, a transcendent God or an eschatological future. Reason, on the contrary, produces only itself and therefore deals with present reality in its essential (or divine) form. It knows reality as thought, and thus empirical reality as the material otherness of divine essence, which returns to its essential form in human thinking. Spirit is just such thinking: reason that knows itself as the present existence of divine essence.

Christianity knows this concept as ecclesial spirit, which is an image of divine presence in a nonrational form and which displaces rational transparency into a future kingdom. Thus, if in Christianity spirit "attains its true *shape*, then *shape* itself and [its originating] *imagination* is still the unconquered side from which it [namely spirit] must go over into the *concept*" (368.32–34). In the concept, spirit will "completely dissolve . . . the form of objectivity" (368.34–35) because reason will know divine essence as itself. The world's objectivity offers no obstacle to this project because the world is divine essence in space and time, and thus has the same essence as thinking itself.

One can already see this direction of Hegel's thought in his analysis of the church. When he writes that the church fails to grasp the "*concept*" (420.25) according to which its "pure *inwardness* of *knowing* is also the *self-same essence*" (420.20–21), he means that human subjectivity is the existence of divine essence as "absolute self-consciousness" (420.21–22). But the Christian church does not think in this logical way. It is not aware that its own universal thinking belongs to essence and indeed brings essence to selfhood (420.26–28). Furthermore, the church does not see itself as divine because its imagination separates divine essence from actual existence. The unity of God and the world, therefore, is not a present reality for Christianity but only a distant goal, kept transcendent by theological imagining that views God as a substance separated from the world. Thus, the Christian church of the New Testament eventually becomes the unhappy consciousness of Roman Christianity (*PhG* 122–31). Its image of spirit contains a transcendent God who is *externally* related to the world and to human being.

NOTES

1. For commentary, see Kojève, pp. 255–64; Hyppolite, pp. 537–49; Lauer, pp. 244–55; Kainz, 2: 154–71; Solomon, pp. 614–16, 625–30. Kojève is sketchy for this division of *PhG* VII, but his discussion contains a detailed outline of Hegel's text. Brito covers important parts of Hegel's text in his pp. 120–34, and his pp. 172–222 examine very carefully *PhG* 413.37–417.5.
2. It is "Die offenbare Religion" (400.2), "the manifest religion" in which "divine essence [is] *revealed [geoffenbart]*" (405.23) or "manifest [offenbar]" (407.16). Consequently, it is also "the absolute religion" (405.15–16). The German connection between "offenbaren" ("to reveal") and "offenbar" ("manifest") is hard to render in English.
3. An allusion to I John 1:1.
4. In Campe's dictionary (1: 916), "sich entäußern" is explained as meaning "Sich einer Sache . . . begeben, sie von sich geben," i.e., "to give up something, to renounce it." Luther uses "sich entäußern" for Christ's *kenôsis* in Phil. 2:7 to indicate a "self-emptying" or self-renunciation. Hegel echoes this usage when he refers to divine essence as "renounced and emptied" (410.24) by pronouncing its eternal Word. Making an inner aim "external" or "äußere" may also be suggested by some contexts, but this meaning is not the primary one of "entäußern." Thus, "in the Phenomenology *Entäusserung* and *entäussern* are never used in the same context as *Erinnerung*, except on the last page," according to Joseph Gauvin, "Entfremdung et Entäußerung dans la Phénoménologie de l'es-

prit de Hegel," *Archives de Philosophie* 25 (1962): 563. In fact, the verb sometimes refers to internalization, such as when Christian consciousness "becomes *inward* . . . [by] renouncing its natural existence" (420.17–18), or when "*being* . . . renounces itself and becomes an ego for consciousness" (404.20–22). The latter passage also indicates another feature of Hegel's usage: the subject of "entäußern" is not necessarily a conscious one.

5. Even in St. Paul, spirit can often be interpreted as human thought. See C. E. B. Cranfield, *The Epistle to the Romans*, 2 vols., ICC (Edinburgh: T. & T. Clark, 1975; 1979), 1: 371; Edward Gordon Selwyn, *The First Epistle of St. Peter*, second ed. (London: Macmillan and Co., 1947), reprint ed. (Grand Rapids: Baker Book House, 1981), pp. 282–83. This parallel to Hegel is only superficial, however. Paul does not consider human thinking itself to be the manifestation of God, even though it testifies to the existence of the Creator (Rom. 1:19–21).

6. Here, the "unhappy consciousness" must be pre-Christian Rome. In *PhG* III (see my chapter II), it is Roman Christianity. Apparently Hegel saw Roman Catholicism as a Christian continuation of Rome's unhappy consciousness, the "actual spirit" (405.7) preceding Christianity. In both phases, the unhappy consciousness is separated from God.

7. The unhappy consciousness also loses its "knowing of self" (401.34). Deprived of its people, the self loses both its political "immediate personality" and the people's personification in "*thought*" (402.1–2) as a national god.

8. According to Kojève, Roman consciousness is unhappy because the human spirit has lost the freedom it enjoyed in Greek political life; it "weeps for the loss of the real world (= [the free] State) and imagines [or] constructs in and through its thought a transcendent world beyond" (p. 256), which becomes the God of Roman Christianity. Kojève's interpretation is correct but incomplete. It fails to acknowledge divine substance as the essence of reality, and so does not properly appreciate its human appearance.

9. Here, "subject" refers to the subject of a proposition. However, Hegel also uses the term for conscious human subjectivity, as when "through the religion of art spirit stepped out of the form of *substance* into the [form] of *subject*" (400.3–4). That both meanings occur on the same page illustrates one of the major difficulties of *PhG*: its imprecise terminology.

10. The phrase "universal self" recalls two passages describing the death of Antigone's brother Polynices. In the first, his unburied corpse regains the "*universal individuality*" (245.7) of the "earth" (245.14). In the second passage, after its burial the same corpse becomes a shade or "universal

self" (363.29). The latter meaning would fit the death of Jesus. But Hegel's discussion of "Culture" (*PhG* VI–B) suggests a noetic meaning: the individual self renounces itself to become "the *universal self*, the consciousness grasping the *concept*" (266.4–5).

11. He does, of course, "renounce himself [when] he goes to his death" (415.30); so, too, does the Christian community "renounce its natural existence" (420.18) by its universal knowing (420.19–21; 419.1–2).

12. "*Schwärmerei*," which Kojève (p. 257) links to Neoplatonism. See TWA 19: 440–45 for Hegel's discussion of Neoplatonism and its reputation for "Schwärmerei."

13. "Einbildung" (404.4; 404.12). For verbal consistency, I translate "Einbildung" as "fancy" instead of "imagination," which has been used for "Vorstellung."

14. Not as directly as in *Logik* and *Enzyklopädie*, however, because the topic of *PhG* is knowledge rather than being (404.14–17). But since immediate knowing has for its object immediate being (404.15–16), the latter is the object that unfolds into knowing (404.17–22). Even though thinking and being are different (404.22–24), they are unified by the concept of immediate being that becomes knowing (404.24–28).

15. An indication that for Hegel, God has no consciousness apart from human being.

16. Another indication that for Hegel, a transcendent God is not a self-conscious being, but only an abstraction. God *is* a self-consciousness only as human.

17. Conversely, the empirical self recognizes in the incarnate God its absolute worth. Oriental religions do not value the empirical self so highly (370.12–14). The Greek religion of the underworld honored only the departed self, and Roman law acknowledged only the abstract self of thought.

18. The logical or metaphysical subject, divine substance, is present in its human appearance or "accidentality" (405.20) because a substance appears through its properties or accidents. The term "self" (405.22) must refer to this human accidentality, as in the rest of the paragraph (most clearly in 405.29–30 and 406.4–5). Human subjectivity thus becomes a divine predicate. The combination of divine logical subject and its human self appears again in 406.1–3. I interpret "subject" in 405.22 as referring to God, in order to give it the same meaning as in 406.1–3: "essence, the *subject* itself, . . . *this pure universal*." However, if one understands "subject" in 405.22 as the human subject or self in which God appears, the sentence (405.19–22) quoted in the text is clearer. But "subject" then loses the meaning it has in 406.1–3.

19. The *Logik* (*GW* 12) culminates in "*pure personality*, which . . . *comprises everything within itself*" (251.11–12). This is the "divine *concept*" (253.5) that has differentiated itself into human personality.

20. Earlier in *PhG*, Hegel describes the passive intelligibility of being (313.19–20) as "the concept of Cartesian metaphysics, that *in itself being* and *thinking* is the same . . . *pure abstraction* . . . ; *thinking* is *thinghood*, or *thinghood* is *thinking*" (313.25–31). The passage occurs in a longer discussion (311–13) in which Hegel identifies pure matter with transcendent divine essence: both are the same abstraction of pure being.

21. "*Exists*" is the common rendering; "*being there*" emphasizes the empirical objectivity of God's appearance.

22. A reference to the Hegelian system rather than to *PhG*, which is not "speculative philosophy" (168.18–23).

23. Jesus alone, as in 407.19–20, 23

24. Here, "every self" (407.23–24). Christianity regards Jesus as everyone's access to God; but for Hegel, Jesus illustrates a universal truth.

25. *GW* 8: 280.21–26.

26. Hegel compares this universal presence to "the thing of *perception*" (407.31–32), for the thing is universally present in its many properties. Higher still is "the *universal* of understanding" (407.32), in which a thing embodies the universal law of force common to all things. At this level, Jesus would represent the universal concept of spirit common to all humans.

27. Lauer's rendering of "begriffen" as "comprehended in unity" (p. 249) is very good.

28. When the sacrifice is voluntary, human knowing remains a subject but also becomes the predicate for a higher metaphysical subject, namely God.

29. "That this meaning . . . not be mere fancy, it must . . . spring forth for consciousness out of the *concept* and emerge in its necessity" (404.12–14).

30. See above, n. 29.

31. Kainz uses a similar outline in his treatment of "revealed religion" (2: 161, 162, 164). He observes correctly that for Hegel, divine-human unity is not past but present (2: 161).

32. Known earlier by sensory consciousness but now (after Jesus's death) only by imagination.

33. For brief commentary, see Kainz, 2: 161–62.

34. In the *Logik*, it becomes "the absolute idea" of personality (*GW* 12: 235.29–38; 251.10–13).

35. Does Hegel preserve the equality of the three divine persons? The ques-

tion is inappropriate, since for him the pretemporal Trinity does not refer to three divine persons, but rather to the logical requirements for deity's *human* existence.

36. Since "Vernehmen" means both "hearing" and "understanding" (Campe, 5: 338), it preserves both meanings of *Logos*. Hegel's reference to "pronouncing" makes "hearing" preferable as a translation, but the other meaning is implied; "understanding" is always present when one hears a *word*.

37. Hegel offers a similar criticism of purely historical research into Christian origins (408.36–409.9).

38. At the end of the *Logik*, pure subjectivity is the knowing of pure being: "So then has logic also returned in the absolute idea to this simple unity which is its beginning, the pure immediacy of being" (*GW* 12: 252.25–26). Pure subjective thinking leads to nature. But Hegel makes no clear allusion to such an argument in *PhG*'s analysis of the Trinity. Similar arguments do, however, occur elsewhere in *PhG*; e.g., spirit as the pure knowing of conscience leads to spirit as immediate being in the religion of light.

39. For brief commentary, see Kainz, 2: 162–64.

40. As individual subjectivity isolated from essence, human being corresponds to Lucifer, the pre-existent Son who does not become spirit (413.7–12).

41. Thus, "absolute spirit is . . . its rich life in the community" (408.31, 36–37).

42. Since human thought is conscious of logical ideas or universal thoughts, the word "thought" can refer either to this objective content "in itself" or to a subjective (actively psychological) thinking "for itself." And because objective universality is the content of pure individual thinking, the latter is more than itself; its thoughtful character makes it spirit, or the appearance of universal (divine) essence.

43. Hegel's version of the fall corresponds to the modern idea of a human evolution from animal nature rather than to the older theological idea of human perfection in paradise.

44. Kainz interprets this thinking as alienation from nature (2: 163). But Brito's understanding of evil as the natural self (p. 174) is better since "evil . . . [is that consciousness] for which natural existence . . . counts as essence" (417.12–13). See also 417.19–29 and 414.22–23.

45. According to Hegel, "absolute essence would have only this empty name [of absolute essence] if in truth there were an *other* [than] it, if [there were] a *fall* from it" (415.23–24).

46. For a detailed commentary on Hegel's analysis of this reconciliation

(*PhG* 413.37–417.5), see Brito's discussion, which emphasizes the logical and structural aspects of Hegel's text (pp. 172–222).

47. Because imagination separates good and evil, it cannot attribute evil to a good God. Thus, "imagining takes evil as a happening alien to divine essence" (414.12)—as a fall due to the free will of a creature.

48. As an individual incarnation, Jesus corresponds to individual subjectivity, the second moment of the pretemporal Trinity; as good consciousness, he corresponds to spirit, its third moment. Which divine person then is incarnate in Jesus? The question is inappropriate for Hegel's interpretation, in which the pretemporal moments of deity are not actually persons at all.

49. Brito interprets this passage to mean that for Christ humanity is less essential than divinity (p. 184); thus, the revelation of God in a human being must lead to the latter's death and resurrection (p. 187). While this interpretation provides a good speculative foundation for the death of Christ, it also makes the earthly incarnation of God something like an unstable compound. Such instability suits the appearance of essence, according to Brito, because the being in which essence appears is nonessential in comparison with essence itself (pp. 181–82), and so must disappear. The essence itself can appear (i.e., be truly incarnate) only by making the flesh disappear (pp. 203, 523). But this interpretation does not seem compelling for a number of reasons. It envisages *PhG*'s discussion of trinitarian theology only after the death of Christ (where, of course, there is no longer an earthly incarnation) and leaves out of consideration Hegel's earlier analysis of the incarnation as an *immediate* experience (404.33–407.13) of an "*immediately* present God" (407.35) who *then* disappears in death and rises in spirit (407.35–408.1). Thus before his death, Christ is a true and stable incarnation of God; Brito's reading of Hegel excludes this possibility. The appearance of God in human being precedes death, when (for Hegel) it ceases. It also refers to more people than Jesus. When any self sacrifices its individuality to its universal thought, it "is preserved in its renunciation" (400.27–28) and does not die literally. This knowing actualizes "the unification and penetration of both natures [divine and human], in which [unification and penetration] both [natures] are with equal worth just as *essential* as [they] are also only *moments*" (400.34–401.2) of their unity. A similar equilibrium occurs in "the appearing God" of "Evil and Its Pardon" at the end of *PhG* VI–C (363.28–29), as well as in Hegel's portrayal of "the universal divine human, the [Christian] community" (421.4) as universal knowing (419.1–2). Finally, it also allows God to appear as philosophical thinking (407.1–4). Consequently, the incarnation in Jesus must refer to his earthly

existence. When Hegel claims that Christianity brings "this joy . . . of seeing oneself in absolute essence" (407.9–10), he refers to the appearance of God in earthly human life rather than to a higher life beyond this one.

50. Brito's discussion of this point is quite good (p. 196). For St. Paul, sinners cannot save themselves but need a Savior from God; for Hegel, divine essence itself implies the conquest of sinful existence, and so the reconciliation is accomplished in history by God incarnate rather than by sinful human being.

51. According to Kojève (pp. 261–62), statements like this one are aimed at Böhme and Schelling.

52. In my section entitled "After Jesus."

53. Cf. Saint Augustine, *Confessions*, trans. R. S. Pine-Coffin (New York: Penguin Books, 1961), p. 82: "He departed from our sight, so that we should turn to our hearts and find him there."

54. Hyppolite's translation, 2: 281, of "selbstische."

55. Brito's interpretation of this passage emphasizes very well the logical meaning, namely that by submitting to universal divine substance (pp. 207–8), the death of Jesus implies his own resurrection and also reveals God as the subject (pp. 208–9) in control of the situation. Brito then links the risen Christ to the Christian community (p. 213), as Hegel himself does. But is one to take these developments in the traditional Christian sense or to give them a demythologizing interpretation? For me, Hegel's text demythologizes the traditional understanding: by his death and resurrection, Jesus passes over into a "universal self-consciousness" (415.12), which is the early Christian "community" (415.13–14). Hegel makes no explicit mention of a distinct personal survival of the Son by returning to the Father; the resurrection of Christ *is* the church. In Brito's description of the text, this meaning does not appear clearly, if at all.

56. I agree with Kojève's identification of the risen Jesus with the Christian church (p. 259), but not with his claim that the church foreshadows the Napoleonic empire (p. 262), which realizes the Christian goal of universality (p. 264). Kojève's proposal that Jesus anticipates the combination of Napoleon and Hegel (p. 258) is not proven by any clear evidence from Hegel's text. Hegel's argument for the universal "incarnation" of God in human spirit does, however, call for a universally minded spirit, without limiting it to a particular government.

57. Hegel identifies the risen Jesus with spirit in the church; see, for example, 418.26–28.

58. Good consciousness in real existence was God incarnate, who in the pretemporal Trinity is "the Son, the simple [subjectivity] knowing itself

as essence" (415.18–19); this passage helps illuminate the meaning of "the selfless simple" (419.9).

59. The same unity emerges as "the appearing God" in "Evil and Its Pardon" at the end of *PhG* VI–C.

60. Such a conversion produces Christian faith; see my section entitled "Self-Renunciation" earlier in this chapter.

61. For commentary, see Kainz, 2: 164–71.

62. See Hyppolite, *Structure*, pp. 545–46.

63. "Universal" has different applications in *PhG*, referring to the self-identical divine essence as well as to essence's occurrence in "all" individuals of a given type. These objective applications have subjective counterparts in an individual's universal thinking, which is the individual appearance of divine essence as well as the basis for intersubjectivity. As divine essence, universal human thinking is absolute spirit.

64. Reconciliation depends on the self-renunciation described at the beginning of "Manifest Religion": when *"self-consciousness* renounces itself and makes [itself] into thinghood or the universal self" (403.19–20), it becomes objective reason, the subjective knowing of universal thinghood; universal essence then appears as human subjectivity. This renunciation turns pagan despair into Christian faith and enables it to recognize divine essence as human, first in Jesus and then in itself. Self-renunciation identifies consciousness with objective essence and thus makes possible all the doctrines of trinitarian theology.

65. The same pattern is observed by the incarnation (407.14–32): its immediate presence is followed by the universal presence of God incarnate as an *image* (ecclesial spirit) rather than as a universal concept. Here in trinitarian theology, the very same image reconciles God with evil.

66. Its *"being other"* is its objectivity (422.18–22).

67. Imagination gives his factual death a universal meaning: his resurrection as ecclesial spirit.

68. Gal. 2:20. For Christianity, this presence of Christ occurs by way of the Holy Spirit who dwells in the individual self. Lauer thus claims that Hegel has in mind two related spirits, a divine and a human one (p. 254), with the former elevating the latter to its highest freedom in absolute knowing (p. 255). But this interpretation still considers God to be an imagined self distinct from the actual self, even if both of them are connected. Hegel, however, criticizes the church for not recognizing that human thinking is the true means by which divine essence descends to earth (420.26–28). Thus for Hegel, divine presence is not an actual Holy Spirit but human reason, in which the logical idea of pretemporal spirit has its actual existence.

69. This mention of unhappy Roman consciousness indicates that the Christian church envisioned here is the primitive community. At the beginning of "Manifest Religion," one meets "the pain which pronounces itself as the hard saying *that God is dead*" (401.34–35); this pain is the unhappy consciousness that follows Greek comedy (401.28–35).

70. Cf. the similar description of the Greek artist who recreates from the self the lost substance of his culture (377.31–378.9).

71. Another indication that for Hegel, deity becomes conscious only through human being.

72. Solomon rightly emphasizes the individual incarnation of God in Jesus (p. 615) and the universal incarnation of God in all humanity (pp. 627–29). But Solomon collapses the distinction between divine and human, thereby making Hegel an atheist (pp. 627, 629). Having little appreciation for the logical God of Hegel, Solomon sees only its human existence. As a moment of spirit or divine-human unity, divine essence exists only as nature and human being; as essence however it has its own importance, which is to be the underlying substance of all that exists. Everything derives from such a substance, which gives the universe its objective rationality prior to any human thinking.

73. Here, the conscious human subject; however, in 419.37–38, the term "subject" refers to the metaphysical concept of spirit.

74. Another clear indication that for Hegel, divine selfhood is human selfhood.

75. Hegel's wording makes the community as objectively divine as Jesus, who is "the *individual* divine human" (421.2–3). The church universalizes the individual incarnate God.

76. Who brings forth its reconciliation only within divine essence (Gal. 4:26). Jesus, on the contrary, has a human mother (421.2–4) since his divinity came into the world.

77. Pure thought is identified with pure being, essence, or thinghood (e.g., *PhG* 313.25–31). The self-sacrifice by which consciousness makes itself into universal thinghood (403.19–20) leads to Christian belief in the incarnation. When consciousness identifies itself with essence, it can recognize God as human.

78. Christian faith imagines God as having a divine mind.

79. In Kainz's interpretation (2: 164–68, 170–71), the community Hegel envisions here is the contemporary Protestant church, which can cooperate with civil government in order to bring about a final integration of divine and human being in "Absolute Knowing." But this view is unlikely for a number of reasons. The church Hegel has in mind is the one that has just emerged from the unhappy consciousness of pagan Rome

(see above, n. 69). Furthermore, the primitive Christian community offers a much better chronological successor to Jesus than the Protestant church of modern times. Finally, "Absolute Knowing" is philosophical thinking rather than institutional cooperation. The church contributes the objective content to "Absolute Knowing" (*PhG* 425.23–26); the beautiful soul (425.37) provides the subjective thinking (425.29, 33). Kainz's contention holds true for Hegel's later works, but not for the church in *PhG* VII.

80. Christianity is called the "completed religion" in Hegel's later lectures on religion. See Lasson's editorial remarks on the text in Hegel's *VPR*, ed. Georg Lasson, *Die absolute Religion*, Philosophische Bibliothek 63, pp. 234–38. The remarks are still pertinent, even though Lasson's edition has been superseded by Jaeschke's. In his editorial introduction to the English translation of Jaeschke's new German edition, Peter C. Hodgson offers a clear discussion of the title "vollendete Religion." See Hegel's *LPR*, ed. Hodgson, 3: 1–5.

CHAPTER VI

CONCLUSION: HEGEL AND CHRISTIANITY

HAVING EXAMINED ALL the principal texts on religion in Hegel's *PhG*, I now attempt a synthetic overview of their underlying meaning. Hegel's argument leads to a speculative reinterpretation of Christianity,[1] the religion that comes closest to his concept of God. Since other types of religion are significant only insofar as they prepare the way for Christianity, I have left them out of this concluding survey. Thus, my overview compares Hegel's concept of spirit with various Christian theological topics, using the interpretation developed by the long analyses of texts in my four preceding chapters. If I have properly interpreted Hegel's book, his religious thought may now be summarized as follows.

HEGEL'S INTERPRETATION OF CHRISTIANITY

A review of Hegel's interpretation of Christianity should begin by describing the concept of spirit by which he measures all religions. The term and its meaning of a communication from God to human being already occur in the Bible, but the precise concept used by Hegel emerges within German idealism as described in "Evil and Its Pardon" at the end of *PhG* VI. Hegel then uses it for his analysis of incarnational religions in *PhG* VII. Although these religions predate his concept, its application to them is not anachronistic. If spirit is essence revealing

238

itself as human thinking, it is a perennial feature of human consciousness and thus can reveal itself in the centuries before Hegel. Indeed, its gradual discovery by earlier ages furnishes the method for *PhG* VII: knowing the concept that should be discovered, Hegel can trace its emergence through a number of religions that flourished long before his time.

These religions are evidence for the human awareness of "absolute essence" (363.5, 7), the object of consciousness developed by *PhG*. Its nonempirical religious character appears in the very first chapter when empirical individuality shows itself as universal (65.15–17, 29–30; 68.20–21; 69.14–17; 70.26–27). Gradually this universal object forms itself into absolute spirit, universal essence appearing as the existing individuality (361.23–25) of human thinking. Incorporating human subjectivity within itself, the phenomenological object is now "absolute essence *in and for itself* . . . the self-consciousness of spirit" (363.7–8).

In this formula, one finds the specific topic (incarnational religion) for *PhG* VII, as well as the general goal of the whole work. Before *PhG* VII, absolute essence was known as an objective universal essence; deity was an object for human consciousness, and different from it. This divine object is now known more accurately as an objective essence that becomes human consciousness. Christianity imagines its becoming human as a gracious descent of God into the world, but for Hegel this divine humanization is a metaphysical necessity. His analysis of trinitarian theology indicates that the hidden absolute essence logically differentiates itself into human being; the essence is intrinsically incarnational. It does this in order to perfect itself: in human knowing, the absolute essence becomes conscious of itself, reaching its ultimate lucidity in speculative philosophy. Hence for Hegel, philosophy *is* God (407.1–3), absolute knowing or the consciousness in which absolute essence knows itself truly.[2]

Because the essence or idea[3] of thinking subjectivity is the highest determinacy of divine essence as essence, the pure *idea* of human being is ultimately the same thing as divine essence. In Hegel's analysis of trinitarian theology, this point appears as the pretemporal Trinity, in which simple essence differentiates itself into spirit prior to actual existence.

But Hegel's thought goes further than essence in order to bring forth from the concept real human existence as well. In Christianity, normal human existence appears "evil" and so does not fulfill its concept of being divine appearance. This concept first appears as God's incarnation in Jesus, but its limitation to a single person is a deficiency that Hegel criticizes. Ecclesial spirit improves on the single incarnation by universalizing divine presence, but still fails to make individual Christians as divine as Jesus was. As a result, it too leaves other human beings outside the universal essence. This conclusion to Hegel's analysis of Christianity in *PhG* implies that his own concept of God will include every instance of individual human existence. Such universality corresponds to a concept's universal coverage; as the concept of spirit, divine essence includes every instance of spiritual human subjectivity.

But how can universal essence appear as individual subjectivity? The answer is found in the nature of thinking, in which universal essence appears as universal; it appears precisely as the universal thinking of the individual self, whose thinking reproduces the universal essence of nature. Though all existing beings manifest God, in them divine essence has the form of otherness. Only in human thinking does essence appear in its true form. And though all human knowing provides essence with consciousness, only in the *universal* knowing of individual human thinking does universal essence appear as itself and also as individual subjectivity.

Essence, then, becomes the subject of human subjectivity. When human being submits to its universal knowing, it submits itself to universal essence, the content of this knowing; divine essence thus appears as a higher subject in human intellectual subjectivity. As the controlling agent of individual thinking, deity then fulfills Hegel's definition of something "reflected into itself, a subject" (21.5–6). The two subjects then belong to each other: divine essence is the logical or metaphysical subject, whose conscious predicate is human subjectivity. But since its universal thinking *is* its own rational subjectivity, human reason retains its own subjective autonomy. In the images of Christianity, "both natures . . . are with equal worth *essential* and also only *moments*" (401.1–2). Insofar as human being sacrifices its individuality to its universal thinking, it preserves itself while manifesting universal divine substance, and so is the incarnation (or appearance) of divine essence.

Therefore, in both Hegel's philosophy and in Christianity (407.1–7), "divine nature is the same [thing] as human [nature]" (406.8–9). Spirit is divine "essence that is essentially [human] *self-consciousness*" (405.25), or divine "*essence* . . . that *essentially* assumes human shape" (387.26–27). In these definitions, one should not overlook the adverb "essentially," which emphasizes the subjective activity of essence. As the metaphysical subject, divine essence directs the development; its own essential requirements differentiate it into human being.

Hegel's position identifies God and human being, but also makes a clear distinction between them. For even if divine essence differentiates itself into rational human being so that the two are ultimately one, the obvious difference between an eternal originating idea and its resulting temporal existence establishes a firm distinction between eternal divine essence and its actual existence as nature and human being. In *PhG*, however, this distinction is not explained in any great detail. It may be clarified by a brief look at Hegel's later works; for example, the shorter version of the *Logik* which constitutes the first part of his *Enzyklopädie*. Parts of this work help one to understand *PhG*'s bold claim that in Christianity, "divine nature is the same [thing] as human [nature]" (406.8–9). As Hegel says elsewhere in *PhG*, such a proposition "must necessarily awaken misunderstandings" (416.6) that should be cleared away if possible.

When divine essence differentiates itself into the pure idea of a thinking being, it remains an essence whose thinking existence is necessary only *in general*. Definite individual instances of this idea have no necessary existence because, like all existing things, they come into being as the products of other things and then pass away into something else. They fulfill the definition of contingent existence first of all as one that "has the ground of its being not within itself but in another"[4] and then as one that is "a *possibility* and has the determinacy of being surmounted—of being the possibility of an other—[or] the *condition*"[5] of something else. These texts refer, respectively, to the temporal beginning and end of all natural beings. When one applies them to human being, one easily sees that individual persons must also be contingent. On the other hand, from the point of view of its concept human being is necessary because it is a necessary development of divine essence itself. As the pure idea that calls forth a thinking existence in general, God's differentiation into human being is necessary; however, specific instances of human being—namely particular nations and individual persons—are contingent and temporal.

In *PhG*, Hegel does not formally use these categories for the distinction between God and humans. Nevertheless, his terminology in that work indicates another difference between them: deity is essence, whereas humans belong to nature (416.3–5, 26–28, 32). Correlative to this difference is the one between good and evil (416.2–3, 6–8, 13), which is the difference between universal essence and individual (or natural) existence. The point of these passages in *PhG* is that good and evil (or essence and nature) are different, yet they are also unified by the concept of God as a dialectical movement; God is an essence that posits its own existence as human being. The Christian image of an incarnate God already indicates this unity in an unconceptual way.

Each term of the dialectic then *implies* the other, or logically entails it, so that each term is more than itself. Thus, Hegel writes: "inasmuch as [human] evil is *the same* as [divine] good, precisely [for this reason] is evil not evil nor good good, but both are rather surmounted" (416.6–8) by their conceptual unity. Since each implies the other, they are ultimately the same, but since their sameness is only by implication, they must also be different. And so Hegel affirms: "as much as [it] must be said that according to this their concept good and evil are *the same*, i.e., insofar as they are not good and evil [because each implies the other], so must [it] just as much be said that they are *not* the same, but simply *different*" (416.12–15). Without using the term, Hegel is describing the procedure of his later dialectic, according to which an initial idea has logical implications that develop into something quite different, so that the latter may be called a differentiation of the former.

Thus, divine essence posits itself as something different: first as the world, and ultimately as individual human existence. This difference, however, is not the final word since the concept's unity requires essence to overcome its otherness. Hegel uses this unity to show that God's reconciliation with evil is a conceptual necessity, even though Christianity sees it as a work of grace. The unity emerges, in fact, whenever an individual consciousness surrenders its individuality to its universal knowing. It then becomes the subjectivity through which essence knows itself, or spirit.

In the later system, the same concept of divine-human unity is developed into the absolute idea of the *Logik* and the absolute spirit of the *Enzyklopädie*. A number of reasons can be given for this resemblance. Hegel intended *PhG* as an introduction to the system,[6] and so one expects points of convergence. *PhG* even points out (407.1–7) that its concept of spirit occurs in both Christianity and in "pure speculative knowing" (407.2), which must be Hegel's own system as then conceived.[7] *PhG* and the system both begin with being: *PhG* with an empirical consciousness of being, and the system with pure being in itself prior to human consciousness. And when *PhG* portrays the movement of absolute spirit by its analysis of the Trinity, it begins with pure essence itself, as the *Logik* and *Enzyklopädie* do more fully later on. Obviously, *PhG* is not the system; Hegel distinguishes phenomenology from the "speculative philosophy" (168.20–21) of purely logical reasoning. But their concepts of spirit are similar, as the reasons mentioned prove. *PhG*'s concept of spirit as divine-human unity thus anticipates the later system.

Hegel finds that many specific themes in Christianity agree with his concept. Since God is universal essence differentiating itself into human being, many Christian doctrines prove to be correct: creation, human evil, the incarnation, and the reconciliation of evil with God. But Hegel reinterprets these doctrines in light of his own concept, which universally identifies God with human being. Thus, God's incarnation in Jesus is true. But so is a similar identification of God with every human being, which Christianity expresses in its doctrines of ecclesial spirit and reconciliation. Hegel's conceptual outlook is especially good at reproducing the Biblical idea of divine sovereignty; thus universal knowing in the church is "essence reconciling itself with itself" (419.2) by overcoming the otherness of human subjectivity. In this way, God is the first and the last: first as the simple idea of being, and last as the perfection of being in its highest kind of thinking. Hegel's theory of spirit, then, enables him to interpret several major Christian doctrines as a single conceptual necessity. His theory even explains why religion precedes philosophy: the concept first appears in religion because human being initially formulates its thoughts through sensory images.

Hegel's concept of spirit also diverges from Christianity in some important respects. His God is not infinite in the traditional sense of "immeasurable perfection," which is not comprehensible by human reason. On the contrary, Hegel's concept is accessible to people's minds because it is the pure idea of the finite world they already know. Therefore, Hegel's God is indeed a pure essence, but not one that possesses good qualities to an infinite degree, since an unlimited degree of anything divine would place it beyond human reason. However, Hegel's God *is* infinite in another sense. Precisely by positing the world of nature and spirit, divine essence proves itself to be not finite or not bounded by its own abstract essence, according to the definition of "*infinity*" as "difference *in itself*" (99.7–8).[8]

One important example of such infinity is God's knowing, which exists as human thinking. Does Hegel really mean that divine consciousness does not exist prior to human being? His pretemporal Trinity does contain a subjectivity in which essence knows itself, but this knowing seems to be no more than the logical pattern for its actual emergence as *human* thinking. Moreover, since Hegel considers that divine essence "reaches its *highest* essence" (406.17) in human being, he cannot view God as an eternal and superior consciousness. In such a case, human being would add nothing higher to divine essence. If so, God is not conscious prior to human being, even though God is, of course, the eternal reason or essence that provides itself with rational existence as human being.

Although many passages in *PhG* suggest such an interpretation, two in particular are cited here. The first (from Hegel's introduction to natural religion) claims that in some religions, "God is *imagined* as *self-consciousness*" (369.28), but this "*imagined* [divine] self is not the *actual* [self]" (369.29) of real human being. According to this distinction, God has no self-consciousness apart from human being, which is the only real self that exists. Of course, God can be imagined as a self-consciousness having its own existence (and, in fact, God is usually imagined in this way); however, in that case one has to do with an image without actuality. In Hegel's view, such a transcendent mind is rather an image for essence's real existence as human thinking.

The second passage points in the same direction. In his analysis of Christianity's belief in a divine incarnation, Hegel writes: "the renunciation of substance, its becoming self-consciousness expresses . . . the unconscious transition of *necessity*" (403.22–24) since it is a necessary development within divine essence. In Hegel's view, God becomes human by an "unconscious . . . *necessity*." This necessity may be interpreted in various ways, but the text itself seems to exclude at least one interpretation, namely that God's incarnation is due to a conscious decision. On the contrary, writes Hegel, it is not due to anything conscious at all. It follows that God is first conscious in human self-consciousness, and so is not a conscious thinking prior to human being. As the essence that becomes human, God must be self-determining and therefore free; the essence follows only its own intrinsic necessity. But such freedom does not require an initial consciousness. This consciousness comes only later, when universal essence becomes human.

A definitive answer to this question of divine consciousness in Hegel requires a careful study of his later writings and lectures, and such a task is obviously beyond the scope of my study.[9] My conclusion for *PhG*, however, is that Hegel's God does not think prior to human being.[10] Likewise, in the *Logik* Hegel's concept of God includes thinking, but only as human being. In both works, divine essence differentiates itself into human being for the same reason: to manifest itself in thinking, which is the appearance of essence.[11]

As God incarnate, Jesus expresses the same truth for Christian faith. He signifies the first appearance in time of Hegel's concept of spirit, according to which "divine nature is the same [thing] as human [nature]" (406.8–9) and is therefore welcomed with joy by the world (407.9–10). But Hegel's analysis attributes the incarnation to believing consciousness rather than to anything unique in Jesus himself: when Roman unhappy consciousness renounces itself, it becomes capable of recognizing God incarnate in any suitable person. This capacity in turn demands a universal divine-human presence, which emerges as ecclesial spirit. And though Christianity does not acknowledge this presence as equal to the personal divinity of Jesus, Hegel's criticism of Christian eschatology aims precisely at its timidity on this point: the church should recognize itself as the incarnate presence of God because the incarnation is a general fact accessible to any self-renouncing universal thinking.

Thus, this universal divine presence corresponds to the factual occurrence of (universal) thinking in every human being. But behind this factual universality lies the concept itself: because divine essence differentiates itself into human thinking, it must include every instance of such thinking. The concept as a self-identical unity is the idea of human existence, and so replicates itself wherever human being is found. The factual universality of divine-human unity properly depends on the concept itself: God is human wherever human being occurs because the concept of God ultimately thinks itself through human subjectivity.

Christianity grasps this concept by its image of ecclesial spirit, "the universal divine human" (421.4), but the image does not provide the simple clarity of the concept. As a result, the church defers its complete unity with God to an eschatological future. But the divine-human unity revealed in Christianity properly refers to an actually present unity, as in the earthly life of God incarnate. The church's eschatological hope indicates a failure to grasp God as present in its own thinking. And so the Christian church declines in the course of time into the unhappy consciousness described earlier in *PhG* IV–B.

Thus religion must be surpassed by a better knowing of the divine concept, which itself calls for such a development because philosophy (and not religion) is the ultimate differentiation of divine essence thinking itself. Since religion does not yet know itself as essence's own thinking, the concept of God must be completed by philosophy rather than by religion: "God is only attainable in pure speculative knowing, and is only in it and is only itself" (407.1–3).

In absolute knowing, human reason will know itself as divine essence's internal differentiation into thinking. Absolute essence then becomes human reason itself, as the real existence and life of God. At the beginning of this concept lies the pure simplicity of divine essence, or "being in general" (403.39); at its completion, the concept is fully enriched by the whole content of the world, whose perfection is the thinking existence of rational being. Therefore, God is not only the object of human thought, but also the human subjectivity of thinking. God's existence *as* human subjectivity is what Hegel means by "spirit." Since Christianity preserves divine transcendence, it is not yet aware that its interior spiritual knowing is essence thinking itself. Though Christianity advances the "self-consciousness of spirit" (363.8) in comparison to previous religions, it has not reached full self-consciousness. Only a thinking that knows itself as pure objectivity, and thus as divine essence, can complete the movement of spirit.

ASSESSING HEGEL'S INTERPRETATION

In Hegel's own system, reason[12] understands *itself* as the worldly existence of divine essence. But what proof does he offer for this concept of God? In his discussion of manifest religion, he explains that the incarnation can be necessary only if "being in general or substance . . . *in itself* . . . renounced itself and became self-consciousness" (403.39–404.1). By its own internal necessity, being's universal essence must become human thought, and then God appears as human self-consciousness.

Hegel then points out that this very development occurs as a conceptual necessity (404.12–14) in earlier chapters of *PhG*, in which two parallel movements are traced. In one of them, sensory consciousness becomes spirit knowing itself (404.14–17); this movement corresponds to Hegel's chapter headings. It begins, however, with subjective knowing rather than with objective being; therefore it does not provide the objectivity needed for the argument, which intends to place the incarnation in the conceptual development of being itself. Hegel thus appeals to the other movement, whereby objective being is turned into subjective knowing (404.17–22).[13] By combining the two movements, one obtains the concept of being as a necessary development into spirit, the thinking that knows itself as objective being (404.22–28). By itself, this development seems to have nothing to do with religion and means only "that actual world-spirit has reached this knowing of itself" (404.29–30), as earlier chapters describe (404.31–32).

For such a spirit to be religious, it must also know itself as the appearance of objective *divine* essence and not simply as objective being. But Hegel understands God as the essence or substance of objective being, which turns into human thinking. Belief in God's incarnation thus occurs in a thinking that identifies itself with universal essence, and more particularly in the self-renunciation through which unhappy Roman consciousness becomes Christian faith: when "*self-consciousness* renounces itself and makes [itself] into [objective] thinghood or the universal self" (403.19–20), it knows itself as universal objectivity. It then becomes a "*simple* positive self" (405.6–7), accepting its *a priori* simple reason as positive existing objectivity, or as universal essence. In this intellectual conversion, God appears as human thinking, as in "Evil and Its Pardon" or in the good consciousness of the pretemporal Trinity.

But if being objectively proves itself to be thinking, and if thinking is the appearance of deity, then this divine appearance is contained in being itself. Universal being turns into thinking, which then opens itself up to universal essence. Therefore God objectively appears as real human being (404.34), and so the incarnation of God (404.34–37) is "not fancy but is *actually in*" (404.37–405.1) real existence.

The argument requires that divine essence be the universal essence of being, which transforms itself into human thinking. Hegel's God is indeed this "being in general or substance" (403.39), the universal essence that develops itself into human thinking. When this thinking discovers essence within itself, it knows human reason to be the presence of God and so is able to recognize God in human being. Such a consciousness can then propose the incarnation as an objective fact.

Hegel's position is not simply that the universe is rational, but also that its rationality appears as human thinking. He shares the former view (that the universe is objectively rational) with Greek philosophy and its followers. The latter view (that such rationality transforms itself into subjective thinking), on the other hand, is his own contribution to the tradition of Greek philosophy. Thus, Hegel unifies the ancient view that reason is objective with modernity's insistence on subjectivity.[14] This synthesis provides him with an argument for belief in the incarnation of God: since objective essence (or God) turns into subjective reason (or human being), God is incarnate in human being. Hegel's argument presupposes that God is already present in being as its essence. The argument then seeks to establish that objective being is also subjective thinking, by necessity. If being is thinking, then being's essence must also be human thinking. Therefore, God appears as human being.

Hegel's position obviously differs from traditional Christian theism, in which divine being has a personality all its own, and thinks and wills the natural world into existence. But Hegel interprets this traditional view as attributing an imaginary personality to God, who is "imagined as [a] self-consciousness. The imagined [divine] self [however] is not the actual [self of human being]" (369.28–29). For Hegel, God is an essence existing as the natural world and having personality only in human being, the final result of divine self-differentiation.

Which view is correct? This difficult question does not find its final answer in these pages. The following observations are offered only as an approach toward understanding the problem Hegel's philosophy raises for traditional theism. My approach confronts Hegel's argument with a representative statement of the traditional view, and points out what seem to be the strengths and weaknesses of each position. To illustrate the traditional view, I select Bernard J. F. Lonergan's *Insight*. In this work, Lonergan argues that "the real is completely intelligible"[15] only as "unrestricted understanding,"[16] which by definition is God. This God is not simply thought or the world's intrinsic intelligibility, but also a thinking that is prior to human thinking and that understands far more than one can hope to understand in this life. If such an understanding has produced the universe, it must be a mind whose thoughts one does not possess perfectly. Thus, it is a beyond of the sort Hegel rejects. The difference between Hegel and Lonergan can, therefore, be stated as follows: if the universe is completely comprehensible by human reason, is it comprehensible by its own intrinsic essence which comes to know itself in human thinking, as Hegel maintains? Or is it comprehensible because of a complete understanding that has produced it, as Lonergan argues? In simpler terms, does universal intelligibility imply only a divine substance and human thinking, or does it also require a divine thinking?

My study of Hegel's *PhG* cannot answer such a question. But there is no doubt that Hegel offers a tempting alternative to the traditional theism that Lonergan expounds. There must be a divine understanding, argues Lonergan, because "intelligibility either is material or spiritual or abstract."[17] But abstract intelligibility refers to concepts produced by thinking; "material intelligibility necessarily is incomplete, for it is contingent in its existence and in its occurrences"; and human spiritual intelligibility is incomplete because of its many questions. Therefore, "the only possibility of complete intelligibility lies in a spiritual intelligibility that cannot inquire because it understands everything about everything. And such unrestricted understanding is the idea of being" or God.

Of course, it would be anachronistic to make Hegel respond to this argument. But because he offers an alternative explanation for the world's intelligibility, one should consider his system here as a possible solution. Hegel might say in particular that Lonergan's three types of intelligibility—material, abstract, and spiritual—do not set forth all the possibilities. Because Hegel explains the real world as the material existence of an abstract essence, the world is neither simply material nor simply abstract but both of them simultaneously since the pure thought of being refers to both essence and existence. From this pure thought of being, the whole system is developed logically, so that the absolute idea is not simply an abstract intelligibility but also a material one. Therefore, the so-called abstract idea is not abstract at all because it exists with a material body. And if one follows Hegel beyond the material existence of the universe into the appearance of actual thinking, then the absolute idea contains thinking as well—the spiritual intelligibility of Lonergan's typology.

Taken by itself, of course, a material body could be considered contingent, and since "the contingent is not self-explanatory,"[18] a material existence could not provide complete intelligibility. However, as the real existence of the idea, it is no longer contingent but necessary and, therefore, quite intelligible. Similarly, an abstract concept by itself is incomplete because it is derived from something else through an act of understanding. But since the Hegelian concept exists by necessity, it is not an abstract idea. Rather, the idea or concept or whatever else it may be called has both an outer and an inner side, and is simultaneously material and abstract because it is the logical idea of being; it is both being and thought at the same time. And since thought does not remain passive being for Hegel but passes over into real thinking, the Hegelian concept is also a spiritual one. Thus, it explains the intelligibility of being in a dialectically unified way not envisaged by Lonergan's trichotomy of material, abstract, and spiritual intelligibility.

For Lonergan, only the spiritual intelligence of an unrestricted understanding can account for the universe's complete intelligibility, which is indicated by our infinite desire to know: "the real is the objective of an unrestricted desire to understand correctly; to be such an objective, the real has to be completely intelligible. . . ."[19] Hegel would agree that the universe is completely intelligible; his own logical system intends to prove it. But for Hegel, complete intelligibility is accounted for by the logical idea, which gives the world an intrinsic intelligibility not produced by a prior divine understanding. Of course for Hegel, too, there is complete understanding, but it occurs in human being and is clearly derivative, depending on the logical idea (or God) for its existence. And everything that human understanding or reason can discover is already contained in that logical idea, whose determinate parts make up a coherent unity. What human reason finally uncovers as the intelligibility of the universe is not a divine thinking or personality, but rather a divine thought or logic or idea that thinks itself only near the end of its logical dialectical development. That idea stands alone as the basis for complete intelligibility because it unifies essence and existence and spirit in the idea of what *must* be. This unity contains a completeness not found in the separate possibilities considered by Lonergan. When confronted by the Hegelian system, Lonergan's argument for the existence of a prior divine thinking no longer seems to be a cogent one. It concludes with an unrestricted divine understanding by showing the insufficiency of either purely material or purely abstract intelligibility; however, it overlooks the possibility proposed by Hegel's logical idea, which combines these two kinds of intelligibility (along with spirit) in a single concept.

According to Hegel, therefore, the world is necessary as the existence of the idea. But when existence and idea are separated (as they are in views like Lonergan's), the material world appears contingent, and its existence is explained by appealing to "an unconditioned intelligent and rational consciousness that freely grounds the universe in much the same fashion as the conditioned intelligent and rational consciousness of man freely grounds his own actions and products."[20] Since the universe does not follow by necessity from this rational consciousness of God but is rather a "reasonable choice"[21] made by divine consciousness, there can be no question of a concept linking divine essence to human existence through an internal necessity. The world has its full rationality only in a divine thinking that understands the reason for its existence.

But for Hegel, the universe is rational in itself because it is the existence of a logical idea that is God. Ultimate rationality is found in conceptual necessity rather than in a rational divine personality, which would be an imagined self. Thus, Hegel's view of divine personality is that it falls within the conceptual necessity of the logical idea, and is itself an idea whose real existence is the actual self-consciousness of human being. Ultimately, being is intelligible not because it derives from a higher consciousness that freely grounds the universe but because it is intrinsically intelligible and rational as the outward expression of a logical idea that is God. And since this idea is intrinsically thinkable, it is accessible to human reason at the present time.

Whether Hegel ultimately succeeds or not is a question beyond the scope of my examination of *PhG*. But it should at least be clear that he explains the universe in a way that has not been considered seriously enough by the traditional theism developed by Lonergan. And if Hegel's system is true, then *PhG*'s interpretation of Christianity has a good chance of being correct, for it understands Christian faith in light of the system itself. However, the Hegelian system is not unassailable. In particular, its claim that the world exists by intrinsic necessity (rather than by a divine decision) may not be fully proven.

In *PhG*, God is the universal substance or essence of immediate being.[22] But *why* does this being exist in the first place? Empirical being carries no explanation for its existence, nor does the pure universal essence of such being provide a convincing explanation for its existence. Such an essence is the God one finds in *PhG*, but its concept lacks the absolute necessity one expects from divine essence. Indeed, Christian thinking argues toward the existence of God precisely because the being people experience is full of mystery; its existence in particular seems unexplained. In Lonergan's argument material objects are contingent, and their existence is explainable only by the hypothesis of an unrestricted (or divine) mind that understands everything. This mind answers the fundamental question of existence, as well as all further questions about the character of the universe and the types of beings it contains.

The rich analyses of human experience found in Hegel's *PhG* explain much about the character of the universe, but they do not answer the question of its existence. Hegel's discussion of trinitarian theology, however, offers a brief discussion of the passage from pure essence to material existence, in this respect anticipating the outline of his *Enzyklopädie*. His argument in *PhG* is that pure essence is abstract and therefore implies its completion by an actual world. The argument, then, presupposes material existence, from which essence is abstracted, because God is the universal essence of being, and apart from real being such a God is necessarily abstract. But this abstract universal essence is hardly an explanation for material existence, which remains as mysterious as ever. Yet for Hegel, existence needs no explanation. His main question is rather the difference between objective existence and subjective thinking, and his goal is to show that subjective reason should understand itself as objective being. Thus, Hegel's God functions as the universal objectivity of being, the thought present in thinking. God grounds the whole shape of existence and *is* pure existence itself. But how can pure being, which Hegel in his *Logik* identifies with nothing,[23] be the sufficient ground of real existence? Is pure empty being an adequate foundation for material existence?

Perhaps a deeper study of the *Logik* would solve this difficulty. But since it remains a question, it prevents me from agreeing with Hegel's reinterpretation of traditional Christianity. The question suggests that the full truth of being lies beyond the Hegelian system and perhaps beyond all human reason. If some fundamental truths elude human thinking, then some aspects of God must remain hidden. And if so, Hegel's claim to know God[24] would have to be judged as another case of philosophical hubris.

CHRISTIAN FAITH AFTER HEGEL

If these tentative reflections are correct, then traditional Christianity remains possible after Hegel. The full intelligibility of being still escapes humans, and its elusiveness has often been invoked as a proof for the existence of God. Lonergan himself (the modern thinker selected here to represent Christian tradition) places this intelligibility in an unrestricted understanding, which he calls God. Insofar as he puts it beyond contemporary human understanding, he seems to approach the truth better than Hegel does. Lonergan's identification of this beyond as an infinite mind may be hasty, however, since he pays too little attention to the Hegelian alternative of an intrinsic intelligibility for the existing universe. But at least he glimpses ultimate explanations in a principle higher than people's own understanding. And if such a principle surpasses their native powers, it is currently a mystery to them, and can serve as a basis for faith. For according to Hegel, a beyond calls for belief (287.33–34).

However, belief in a beyond cannot be reconciled with Hegel's approach, in which a completely comprehensible concept supersedes Christian faith. Once belief in a beyond is admitted into Christianity, Hegel's interpretation tumbles down like a house of cards. For if God is a mystery beyond one's knowing, then a complete comprehension of divine essence is impossible. The Hegelian system would then provide a profound metaphysical grasp of the universe, but it would not give us divine essence itself. One could not agree with Hegel's claim that "divine nature is the same thing as human [nature]" (406.8–9), because the system would not reveal divine essence at all and could say nothing about human being's place in that essence. Nor could one accept Hegel's completely realized eschatology, in which all hope of meeting God in the future fades away, because the true vision of God is to be found in philosophy on earth. If philosophy does not provide this vision, then a better knowledge of God could become a worthy object of hope, and the basis for a futuristic eschatology.

Such an eschatology could also include a hope for life eternal, which has no place in *PhG*. In the Greek religion of the underworld, departed spirits have actuality only in their earthly families (261.2; 287.34–35). This is similar to Hegel's analysis of the resurrection of Jesus, whose "rising as Spirit" (415.10) is only "the constituting of a community" (415.13–14), and not also his elevation to divine power nor a conscious life with God. In this restriction of life to earthly forms, Hegel develops his concept of God: since divine essence exists as nature and as human being, there is no possibility of any life hidden from current view; it illustrates a beyond of the sort Hegel always rejects.[25] Private remarks attributed to Hegel confirm this interpretation of *PhG*. In them, he reveals a firm disbelief in a possible afterlife.[26] These remarks are clear evidence for the view that Hegel was not a traditional Christian, however much he may have used Christian themes in his philosophy.[27]

Finally, the system itself recognizes only the being of one's experience—a being shaped into transient things and mortal animals. The highest form of life in the system is the absolute idea, which is the idea of a thinking life or rational animal. Since what it thinks is the logical idea of the universe, this absolute idea is "the idea thinking itself, here namely *as* thinking, as *logical* idea."[28] Insofar as this idea remains only an idea, it is eternal and necessary, but it has real existence only in the shape of individual human beings who are perishable and contingent. Thus, there is a disparity between the idea as an essence and the idea's real existence. Such a disparity characterizes finitude in general: "the *finiteness* of things consists . . . in this, . . . that their existence and their universal nature (their body and their soul) are of course united, [for] otherwise the things would be nothing, but that these their moments are already different and altogether separable."[29] This difference applies to every existing thing, and thus to human life as well. The absolute idea is, therefore, that of a finite and mortal existence in which eternal divine essence thinks itself.

Now if the Hegelian system were a true portrayal of divine essence, then all the individual beings that derive from it would necessarily be transient. No kind of eternal existence would be possible, except for the universe in general; individual beings, however, would come into existence and then perish. But if (as I wondered earlier) *PhG*'s concept of God as "being in general" (403.39) assumes the being of one's experience without giving a fundamental explanation of why it exists and why it has the character it does, then it lacks absolute necessity and should not be considered a divine kind of essence. In that case, the being of experience remains unexplained, and its ultimate reason is a mystery. People then have some basis for believing in a God whose essence eludes them. Furthermore, they can entertain the possibility of another kind of being for humans—another life depending (like this one) on the mystery of God. An eschatology that aims for a better knowledge of God can include in its aim a knowing proportionate to the object known. Eschatological knowing would then be proportionate to its divine object and could hope for some share in its divine being. And since one's questioning of Hegel deals with his apparent failure to provide absolute necessity, the mysterious basis of being (namely divine essence) would have to be an absolutely necessary being. One's knowing of this object, however, could not be absolutely necessary because it would have a beginning; but it could fittingly hope for a neverending duration, since a permanent knowing would come closer to an absolutely necessary object than a transient knowing would. And so the eschatological knowledge of God would also be a life eternal, or something like it.

So far, my sketch of Christian faith has included belief in God and in a future knowing, which would have some share in God's immortality. This last point needed some development since Hegel excludes it from his philosophical reconstruction of Christianity. For him Jesus is not the eschatological Savior but God incarnate, or more precisely, an example of spirit as divine essence in human subjectivity. But if Hegel's argument is not accepted, the incarnation could have grounds other than the Hegelian system. In particular, one could cite the need for helping humans reach their eschatological goal of knowing God. The incarnation, then, would accomplish an aim opposite to that which Hegel envisions. Instead of making deity comprehensible by revealing it as finally human, the incarnation instead would turn human thinking toward a mystery beyond itself. Since the Word incarnate does not remain visible but rejoins the hidden God, it does not make deity fully accessible to human reason; instead, it points reason toward another goal unobtainable in this life.

Such doctrines must be based on faith since they all pertain to God as a mystery that can be known adequately only through some future discovery. Their appeal to faith in something beyond human reason is a special victim of Hegel's ambition to replace them by a thoroughly rational system. He claims that the system offers the same content; however, this claim seems dubious when one discovers that it has no eschatology, and rather than eternal happiness offers earthly minds a comprehension of the intelligible universe.

In addition, the system does not impose itself as absolutely necessary. Its divine essence universalizes the type of being that is given to one's consciousness in experience. Thus, essence has a necessity relative to the being of experience, but this necessity does not seem absolute. Why does the being of experience exist at all? And why does it have the character it has, namely that of a being that (according to Hegel) has no determinate content and so equals nothingness? If such questions are legitimate, they indicate that the Hegelian system does not necessarily impose itself on human reason. Leaving such fundamental questions unanswered, the system does not dislodge Christian faith, which believes in the solutions but finds them still beyond its present comprehension. And so faith remains possible, despite Hegel. His version of Christianity does not impose itself even on rational grounds.

Nevertheless, the Hegelian system is a major achievement of speculative thought. As a preparation for the system, Hegel's *PhG* offers a stimulating survey of Western consciousness on its way toward his own philosophy. In that preparatory work, he analyzes religion in great detail, only to replace it with philosophy's absolute knowing. Thus, one should not consider him a modern Aquinas who reinterprets traditional faith in a rational and systematic way. Whereas Aquinas respects faith as beyond reason and places its object beyond philosophy (so that theology becomes another science, one dealing with revealed truth rather than with reason alone),[30] Hegel reduces faith to reason and theology to philosophy, whose object is the intrinsic intelligibility of the material universe. Theology, then, seems to lose its proper depth since it has no more mysteries to probe. A better comparison likens Hegel to Aristotle, a philosopher whom he admired greatly and who (like Hegel) accepted no revelation beyond reason. But Aquinas found ways of using Aristotle to comprehend parts of Christian faith even while respecting its revealed character. In his own view, Hegel would probably regard himself as a modern Aristotle bringing thinkers like Aquinas (and the whole Christian tradition) to a purely rational conclusion. But to Christian faith, Hegel seems to be an Aristotle waiting for his Aquinas.

NOTES

1. Hegel's religious thought is best understood as a purely rational speculative theology, or philosophy of religion. When Christian theology begins with faith, it can rightly distinguish itself from the rational philosophy of religion. But for Hegel, faith disappears in the concept, where God is completely comprehensible to human reason. Since faith and reason provide the same content (in Hegel's view), faith is then superfluous. Moreover, the concept gives a *truer* account of God, who is reason itself or the logic of the universe. Thus, Hegel claims that "true theology is . . . also philosophy of religion." See *Enzyklopädie* § 36, *Zusatz*; *Werke*, TWA, 8: 104. Hegel's *Enzyklopädie* is referred to hereafter as *Enz.*

2. Deity also knows itself in pre-philosophical religious thinking, but in an inferior way.

3. I use terms like "essence," "idea," and "concept" as more or less equivalent. In his *Logik*, Hegel distinguishes them in a way that need not concern one here. In the first part of his *Enz.*, which parallels the *Logik*, he observes the sequence of "being, essence, substance, concept, and idea," with each of these terms being a higher differentiation or refinement of the previous one. He remarks that "the different steps of the logical idea can be considered as a series of definitions of the absolute"; see *Enz.* § 160, *Zusatz*; *Werke*, TWA, 8: 308. Therefore they can also be used as synonyms for God, as they are in *PhG*, where for example "essence and substance" (406.7) along with "*pure universal*" (406.3) refer to "the divine nature" (406.8–9). Hegel uses other names for God in *PhG* as well.

4. *Enz.* § 145, *Zusatz*; *Werke*, TWA, 8: 284–85.

5. *Enz.* § 146; *Werke*, TWA, 8: 287.

6. On this point, *PhG*'s own title page (*GW* 9, pp. V, 1, 3) agrees with Hegel's 1812 preface to the first part of his *Logik* (*GW* 11: 8.21–26).

7. By the time he wrote *PhG*, Hegel had already worked out the plan of his later system, at least as far as the concept of divine-human unity is concerned. That concept appears in the "Vorlesungsmanuskript zur Real-philosophie (1805/06)" (*GW* 8: 282.15–283.16; *GW* 8: 286.9–15), written before *PhG*.

8. Although this definition refers to the supersensible world of *PhG* III rather than to the Trinity of *PhG* VII, it seems applicable to the latter as well.

9. In his lectures on the history of philosophy, Hegel agrees with Spinoza's claim that divine substance has in human individuals the attribute of thinking, and in the world of nature the attribute of extension (*Werke*, TWA, 20: 163), from which it seems to follow that God is not a thinking consciousness prior to human existence. But it also follows that human thinking is derived from divine substance. According to Hegel, Spinoza fails to demonstrate the necessity of these connections (ibid., pp. 173, 175). Hegel's dialectic, therefore, tries to prove the logic, or strict conceptual necessity, of divine substance's differentiation into natural existence and spiritual human thought. Apart from its lack of logical necessity, Spinoza's one substance with its two attributes of extension and thought resembles in rough outline Hegel's trinitarian concept of logic, nature, and spirit.

10. Hegel does designate God as "*thinking*" (407.4) prior to the world's existence, but such "*Denken*" is a synonym for "pure essence" (407.4)

and refers to thought rather than to the act of thinking. Such a purely logical object is *prior* to its being thought by any thinker; it is true "in itself," much as (to use a simple example) "2+3=5" is true prior to its being thought by any human thinker.

11. Hegel's position obviously diverges from such church doctrines as the formula of Chalcedon, which ascribes to the incarnate Son of God two different natures. The doctrine implies two intellects, a human and a divine one; the latter transcends the former. Hegel's concept has no place for a divine transcendence beyond human reason.

12. I use "reason" to designate subjective "thinking" as well as objective "thought." In *PhG* III, Hegel uses the term "Vernunft" (usually translated as "reason" in English) for a limited kind of empirical thinking that wrongly seeks itself in material bodies; phrenology is an extreme example. In *PhG* VII, Hegel remarks that such a reason has no religion because it "knows and seeks *itself* in the *immediate* present" (363.20) of sensory certainty rather than in a present mediated by thought. The limited sense that "Vernunft" has in *PhG* III is not intended by my use of the term "reason."

13. In *PhG* III (see "*The Supersensible Inner*" in my chapter II), the transition from object to subject occurs when objective "appearance or the play of forces . . . steps forth as *explaining* . . . [and] thus consciousness [of the object] is *self-consciousness*" (100.32–35) through "understanding's *explaining*" (100.35–36). Human thought is now the object that hitherto has been understood as an objective play of forces; to explain an object is to enter one's interior thought. The object is now not only contained in thought, but also *is* thought itself. Thus, objective being posits itself as thinking subjectivity. And though the play of forces belongs to the eighteenth century, the resulting subjectivity also occurs in classical culture (*PhG* IV begins with Stoicism), where it helps produce Christian faith.

14. Hegel's disagreement with Kant on this point is obvious. Whereas Kant's critical philosophy leaves human reason helpless before the object it cannot know "in itself," Hegel's revision of Kant identifies human thinking and real objectivity.

15. Bernard J. F. Lonergan, *Insight: A Study of Human Understanding* (revised ed. 1958; reprint ed., San Francisco: Harper & Row, 1978), p. 672.

16. Ibid., p. 674.

17. Ibid., p. 674. The other quotations in this paragraph are from the same page in Lonergan's *Insight*.

18. Ibid., p. 659. In Lonergan's argument, contingent being is intelligible as a value chosen by God's rational consciousness. See also pp. 656–57.

19. Ibid., p. 676.
20. Ibid., p. 657.
21. Ibid.
22. Traditional Christianity would not agree with Hegel's identification of God with universal being. For example, Aquinas conceived God as the pure self-subsistent being that causes all other beings and that does not share their limitations because it is prior to all of them. For Hegel, however, the character of the material universe reveals the content of its underlying divine essence. Therefore Hegel's God has a limited form that corresponds to the existing universe as a totality. Within this totality, God is unlimited or infinite since divine essence crosses over every fixed moment.
23. *GW* 11: 44.5–6, 15–17.
24. In the "Einleitung" to his *Logik*, Hegel claims: "this content is the portrayal of God as He is in His eternal essence before the creation of nature and a finite spirit" (*GW* 11: 21.19–21).
25. Still another example is furnished by Egyptian religion in Hegel's *Philosophy of History*. Here, Hegel interprets immortality to mean something other than survival after death: "this proposition that the soul is immortal, is intended to mean that it is something other than Nature—that Spirit is inherently independent. . . . The idea that Spirit is immortal, involves this—that the human individual inherently possesses infinite value" (trans. J. Sibree, pp. 215–16).
26. See Kaufmann, pp. 358–59, which quotes from Heine's *Geständnisse* of 1854. When Heine asked Hegel about a reward after death, Hegel "said cuttingly: 'So you want to get a tip for having nursed your sick mother and for not having poisoned your dear brother?' " Heine (born in 1797) claims the incident occurred when he was twenty-two.
27. Solomon (p. 583) refers to Hegel's conversation with Heine (as found in Kaufmann) to support his interpretation of Hegel as an anti-Christian atheist. My own view is that Hegel is a philosophical theist who rejects Christian otherworldliness: God is the essence of this world, beyond which nothing can exist.
28. Hegel, *Enz.* § 236; *Werke*, TWA, 8: 388.
29. Ibid., § 168; *Werke*, TWA, 8: 319.
30. According to the very first article of Aquinas's *Summa theologiae*, theology differs from philosophy only because God has revealed an end beyond this life. (See any edition, I. q. 1 a. 1.) Without such a supernatural goal theology becomes philosophy, as Hegel's example illustrates.

APPENDIX

Page and line numbers for each paragraph in *GW* 9 are on the left; the corresponding § numbers from Miller's translation are on the right. Lines for titles and subtitles (in *GW* 9) are omitted, because Miller does not number them.

9.2–10.2	§ 1	21.16–22.2	§ 24	34.28–35.13	§ 47
10.3–24	§ 2	22.3–20	§ 25	35.14–36.10	§ 48
10.25–11.12	§ 3	22.21–23.28	§ 26	36.11–16	§ 49
11.13–23	§ 4	24.1–12	§ 27	36.17–37.3	§ 50
11.24–12.2	§ 5	24.13–25.13	§ 28	37.4–38.14	§ 51
12.3–16	§ 6	25.14–26.7	§ 29	38.15–21	§ 52
12.17–13.8	§ 7	26.8–20	§ 30	38.22–39.18	§ 53
13.9–28	§ 8	26.21–27.9	§ 31	39.19–40.7	§ 54
13.29–14.2	§ 9	27.10–28.4	§ 32	40.8–31	§ 55
14.3–22	§ 10	28.5–32	§ 33	40.32–41.6	§ 56
14.23–15.5	§ 11	28.33–29.6	§ 34	41.7–23	§ 57
15.6–21	§ 12	29.7–13	§ 35	41.24–42.6	§ 58
15.22–16.5	§ 13	29.14–28	§ 36	42.7–23	§ 59
16.6–21	§ 14	29.29–30.12	§ 37	42.24–43.29	§ 60
16.22–17.11	§ 15	30.13–24	§ 38	43.30–44.5	§ 61
17.12–18.2	§ 16	30.25–31.16	§ 39	44.6–24	§ 62
18.3–17	§ 17	31.17–24	§ 40	44.25–37	§ 63
18.18–28	§ 18	31.25–34	§ 41	45.1–6	§ 64
18.29–19.11	§ 19	31.35–32.25	§ 42	45.7–24	§ 65
19.12–27	§ 20	32.26–36	§ 43	45.25–46.14	§ 66
19.28–20.10	§ 21	32.37–33.11	§ 44	46.15–36	§ 67
20.11–25	§ 22	33.12–34.4	§ 45	46.37–47.15	§ 68
20.26–21.15	§ 23	34.5–27	§ 46	47.16–48.4	§ 69

48.5–24	§ 70	71.4–25	§ 111	93.7–94.4	§ 152
48.25–49.22	§ 71	71.26–33	§ 112	94.5–25	§ 153
49.23–30	§ 72	72.1–36	§ 113	94.26–95.17	§ 154
53.1–54.6	§ 73	72.37–73.17	§ 114	95.18–39	§ 155
54.7–19	§ 74	73.18–34	§ 115	96.1–26	§ 156
54.20–29	§ 75	73.35–74.11	§ 116	96.27–97.4	§ 157
54.30–55.31	§ 76	74.12–75.6	§ 117	97.5–26	§ 158
55.32–39	§ 77	75.7–28	§ 118	97.27–98.26	§ 159
56.1–35	§ 78	75.29–76.3	§ 119	98.27–99.8	§ 160
56.36–57.17	§ 79	76.4–23	§ 120	99.9–29	§ 161
57.18–58.9	§ 80	76.24–39	§ 121	99.30–100.28	§ 162
58.10–22	§ 81	77.1–12	§ 122	100.29–101.16	§ 163
58.23–35	§ 82	77.13–32	§ 123	101.17–102.7	§ 164
58.36–59.3	§ 83	77.33–78.13	§ 124	102.8–30	§ 165
59.4–25	§ 84	78.14–23	§ 125	103.4–27	§ 166
59.26–60.14	§ 85	78.24–30	§ 126	130.28–104.31	§ 167
60.15–32	§ 86	78.31–79.2	§ 127	104.32–105.10	§ 168
60.33–61.27	§ 87	79.3–10	§ 128	105.11–30	§ 169
61.28–30	§ 88	79.11–23	§ 129	105.31–106.2	§ 170
61.31–62.5	§ 89	79.24–80.4	§ 130	106.3–107.9	§ 171
63.4–8	§ 90	80.5–81.14	§ 131	107.10–19	§ 172
63.9–33	§ 91	82.4–24	§ 132	107.20–24	§ 173
64.1–11	§ 92	82.25–83.3	§ 133	107.25–32	§ 174
64.12–22	§ 93	83.4–19	§ 134	107.33–108.14	§ 175
64.23–28	§ 94	83.20–30	§ 135	108.15–28	§ 176
64.29–37	§ 95	83.31–85.8	§ 136	108.29–109.3	§ 177
65.1–14	§ 96	85.9–30	§ 137	109.8–18	§ 178
65.15–23	§ 97	85.31–86.11	§ 138	109.19–23	§ 179
65.24–30	§ 98	86.12–28	§ 139	109.24–28	§ 180
65.31–37	§ 99	86.29–87.8	§ 140	109.29–34	§ 181
66.1–11	§ 100	87.9–37	§ 141	110.1–13	§ 182
66.12–21	§ 101	88.1–9	§ 142	110.14–16	§ 183
66.22–36	§ 102	88.10–89.3	§ 143	110.17–29	§ 184
66.37–67.8	§ 103	89.4–10	§ 144	110.30–34	§ 185
67.9–22	§ 104	89.11–15	§ 145	110.35–111.17	§ 186
67.23–32	§ 105	89.16–90.7	§ 146	111.18–112.2	§ 187
67.33–39	§ 106	90.8–21	§ 147	112.3–20	§ 188
68.1–21	§ 107	90.22–91.16	§ 148	112.21–33	§ 189
68.22–33	§ 108	91.17–30	§ 149	112.34–113.24	§ 190
68.34–69.31	§ 109	91.31–92.26	§ 150	113.25–39	§ 191
69.32–70.29	§ 110	92.27–93.6	§ 151	114.1–7	§ 192

174.33–175.26	§ 316	196.23–36	§ 356	215.3–13	§ 395
175.27–37	§ 317	197.1–30	§ 357	215.14–29	§ 396
176.1–30	§ 318	197.31–34	§ 358	216.4–9	§ 397
176.31–177.16	§ 319	197.35–198.16	§ 359	216.10–30	§ 398
177.17–178.3	§ 320	198.19–35	§ 360	216.31–217.8	§ 399
178.4–16	§ 321	199.1–4	§ 360	217.9–24	§ 400
178.17–179.22	§ 322	199.5–11	§ 361	217.25–219.9	§ 401
179.23–180.3	§ 323	199.12–32	§ 362	219.10–19	§ 402
180.4–7	§ 324	199.33–200.35	§ 363	219.20–220.2	§ 403
180.8–28	§ 325	200.36–201.10	§ 364	220.3–18	§ 404
180.29–36	§ 326	201.11–29	§ 365	220.19–221.22	§ 405
180.37–181.16	§ 327	201.30–36	§ 366	221.23–39	§ 406
181.17–182.11	§ 328	202.4–10	§ 367	222.1–14	§ 407
182.12–183.2	§ 329	202.11–14	§ 368	222.15–31	§ 408
183.3–31	§ 330	202.15–31	§ 369	222.32–223.18	§ 409
183.32–184.5	§ 331	202.32–203.12	§ 370	223.19–34	§ 410
184.6–11	§ 332	203.13–27	§ 371	223.35–224.16	§ 411
184.12–29	§ 333	203.28–204.11	§ 372	224.17–25	§ 412
184.30–185.13	§ 334	204.12–30	§ 373	224.26–225.5	§ 413
185.14–186.13	§ 335	204.31–205.10	§ 374	225.6–19	§ 414
186.14–33	§ 336	205.11–23	§ 375	225.20–34	§ 415
186.34–187.27	§ 337	205.24–206.4	§ 376	225.35–226.19	§ 416
187.28–35	§ 338	206.5–32	§ 377	226.20–227.19	§ 417
187.36–188.21	§ 339	206.33–207.11	§ 378	227.20–228.17	§ 418
188.22–189.10	§ 340	207.12–27	§ 379	228.20–30	§ 419
189.11–30	§ 341	207.28–39	§ 380	228.31–229.14	§ 420
189.31–190.7	§ 342	208.3–28	§ 381	229.15–21	§ 421
190.8–30	§ 343	208.29–209.14	§ 382	229.22–26	§ 422
190.31–191.24	§ 344	209.15–31	§ 383	229.27–35	§ 423
191.25–39	§ 345	209.32–210.7	§ 384	229.36–230.36	§ 424
192.1–29	§ 346	210.8–18	§ 385	230.37–231.26	§ 425
193.5–17	§ 347	210.19–211.19	§ 386	231.27–37	§ 426
193.18–34	§ 348	211.20–31	§ 387	231.38–232.3	§ 427
194.1–16	§ 349	211.32–212.3	§ 388	232.4–7	§ 428
194.17–29	§ 350	212.4–22	§ 389	232.10—233.2	§ 429
194.30–195.23	§ 351	212.23–213.11	§ 390	233.3–33	§ 430
195.24–30	§ 352	213.12–22	§ 391	233.34–234.16	§ 431
195.31–34	§ 353	213.23–39	§ 392	234.17—27	§ 432
195.35–196.7	§ 354	214.1–5	§ 393	234.28–33	§ 433
196.8–22	§ 355	214.9–215.2	§ 394	234.34–235.7	§ 434

235.8–18	§ 435	258.19–260.6	§ 475	280.1–11	§ 515
235.19–37	§ 436	260.7–23	§ 476	280.12–19	§ 516
235.38–237.7	§ 437	260.26–261.11	§ 477	280.20–37	§ 517
238.3–27	§ 438	261.12–15	§ 478	280.38–281.7	§ 518
238.28–239.14	§ 439	261.16–33	§ 479	281.8–37	§ 519
239.15–39	§ 440	261.34–262.27	§ 480	282.1–30	§ 520
240.1–7	§ 441	262.28–263.12	§ 481	282.31–283.32	§ 521
240.8–21	§ 442	263.13–29	§ 482	283.33–284.14	§ 522
240.22–26	§ 443	263.30–264.6	§ 483	284.15–35	§ 523
240.30–241.5	§ 444	264.10–265.4	§ 484	284.36–285.18	§ 524
241.6–20	§ 445	265.5–15	§ 485	285.19–30	§ 525
241.25–242.2	§ 446	265.16–266.23	§ 486	285.31–286.24	§ 526
242.3–17	§ 447	266.26–267.5	§ 487	286.27–287.26	§ 527
242.18–25	§ 448	267.9–25	§ 488	287.27–288.1	§ 528
242.26–31	§ 449	267.26–268.17	§ 489	288.2–289.20	§ 529
242.32–243.5	§ 450	268.18–35	§ 490	289.21–26	§ 530
243.6–244.13	§ 451	268.36–269.11	§ 491	289.27–37	§ 531
244.14–245.17	§ 452	269.12–34	§ 492	289.38–290.7	§ 532
245.18–30	§ 453	269.35–270.9	§ 493	290.8–15	§ 533
245.31–37	§ 454	270.10–35	§ 494	290.16–37	§ 534
245.38–246.26	§ 455	270.36–271.22	§ 495	290.38–291.4	§ 535
246.27–247.10	§ 456	271.23–272.3	§ 496	291.5–11	§ 536
247.11–248.10	§ 457	272.4–15	§ 497	291.12–292.10	§ 537
248.11–16	§ 458	272.16–31	§ 498	292.13–18	§ 538
248.17–32	§ 459	272.32–273.10	§ 499	292.19–34	§ 539
248.33–249.5	§ 460	273.11–20	§ 500	293.1–17	§ 540
249.6–28	§ 461	273.21–30	§ 501	293.18–20	§ 540
249.29–250.19	§ 462	273.31–274.11	§ 502	293.24–294.3	§ 541
250.20–251.4	§ 463	274.12–20	§ 503	294.4–21	§ 542
251.9–23	§ 464	274.21–32	§ 504	294.22–37	§ 543
251.24–252.14	§ 465	274.33–275.11	§ 505	294.38–295.7	§ 544
252.15–34	§ 466	275.12–26	§ 506	295.8–296.7	§ 545
252.35–253.30	§ 467	275.27–276.4	§ 507	296.8–15	§ 546
253.31–254.37	§ 468	276.5–30	§ 508	296.16–22	§ 547
255.1–24	§ 469	276.31–277.13	§ 509	296.23–297.19	§ 548
255.25–256.1	§ 470	277.14–34	§ 510	297.20–298.24	§ 549
256.2–14	§ 471	277.35–278.25	§ 511	298.25–299.15	§ 550
256.15–34	§ 472	278.26–279.16	§ 512	299.16–23	§ 551
256.35–257.31	§ 473	279.17–29	§ 513	299.24–300.7	§ 552
257.32–258.18	§ 474	279.30–39	§ 514	300.8–18	§ 553

300.19–301.21	§ 554	321.25–323.10	§ 594	342.4–13	§ 634
301.22–34	§ 555	323.11–21	§ 595	342.14–343.13	§ 635
301.35–302.28	§ 556	323.25–324.4	§ 596	343.14–18	§ 636
302.29–303.15	§ 557	324.5–20	§ 597	343.19–39	§ 637
303.16–37	§ 558	324.21–27	§ 598	344.1–12	§ 638
304.1–22	§ 559	324.30–325.15	§ 599	344.13–29	§ 639
304.23–305.16	§ 560	325.16–24	§ 600	344.30–345.21	§ 640
305.17–23	§ 561	325.25–37	§ 601	345.22–36	§ 641
305.24–35	§ 562	326.1–34	§ 602	346.1–23	§ 642
305.36–306.12	§ 563	326.35–328.15	§ 603	346.24–347.15	§ 643
306.13–27	§ 564	328.16–26	§ 604	347.16–348.10	§ 644
306.28–307.19	§ 565	328.27–329.3	§ 605	348.11–349.9	§ 645
307.20–308.6	§ 566	329.4–29	§ 606	349.10–30	§ 646
308.7–24	§ 567	329.30–36	§ 607	349.31–37	§ 647
308.25–36	§ 568	329.37–330.7	§ 608	350.1–23	§ 648
308.37–309.11	§ 569	330.8–15	§ 609	350.24–31	§ 649
309.12–29	§ 570	330.16–26	§ 610	350.32–351.2	§ 650
309.30–37	§ 571	330.27–331.10	§ 611	351.3–10	§ 651
310.1–21	§ 572	331.11–26	§ 612	351.11–18	§ 652
310.22–311.6	§ 573	331.27–34	§ 613	351.19–352.7	§ 653
311.9–312.2	§ 574	331.35–37	§ 614	352.8–34	§ 654
312.3–12	§ 575	331.38–332.11	§ 615	352.35–353.2	§ 655
312.13–22	§ 576	332.14–24	§ 616	353.3–35	§ 656
312.23–33	§ 577	332.25–333.7	§ 617	353.36–354.12	§ 657
312.34–313.31	§ 578	333.8–35	§ 618	354.13–355.6	§ 658
313.32–314.7	§ 579	333.36–334.23	§ 619	355.7–33	§ 659
314.8–315.11	§ 580	334.24–36	§ 620	355.34–356.10	§ 660
315.12–316.8	§ 581	334.37–335.8	§ 621	356.11–25	§ 661
316.12–22	§ 582	335.9–336.17	§ 622	356.26–357.7	§ 662
316.23–317.13	§ 583	336.18–29	§ 623	357.8–16	§ 663
317.14–26	§ 584	336.30–337.2	§ 624	357.17–37	§ 664
317.27–318.6	§ 585	337.3–21	§ 625	358.1–359.2	§ 665
318.7–16	§ 586	337.22–338.8	§ 626	359.3–23	§ 666
318.17–26	§ 587	338.9–19	§ 627	359.24–360.16	§ 667
318.27–319.17	§ 588	338.20–35	§ 628	360.17–30	§ 668
319.18–28	§ 589	338.36–339.2	§ 629	360.31–361.10	§ 669
319.29–320.13	§ 590	339.3–27	§ 630	361.11–25	§ 670
320.14–33	§ 591	339.28–340.25	§ 631	361.26–362.29	§ 671
320.34–321.12	§ 592	340.30–341.16	§ 632	363.3–8	§ 672
321.13–24	§ 593	341.17–342.3	§ 633	363.9–20	§ 673

363.21–33	§ 674	382.28–35	§ 714	402.34–403.16	§ 754
364.1–9	§ 675	382.36–383.12	§ 715	403.17–35	§ 755
364.10–16	§ 676	383.13–21	§ 716	403.36–404.11	§ 756
364.17–32	§ 677	383.22–35	§ 717	404.12–32	§ 757
364.33–365.17	§ 678	383.36–384.30	§ 718	404.33–405.13	§ 758
365.18–366.8	§ 679	384.31–385.15	§ 719	405.14–406.10	§ 759
366.9–34	§ 680	385.18–386.3	§ 720	406.11–27	§ 760
366.35–367.26	§ 681	386.4–23	§ 721	406.28–407.13	§ 761
367.27–368.18	§ 682	386.24–37	§ 722	407.14–32	§ 762
368.19–37	§ 683	387.1–11	§ 723	407.33–408.10	§ 763
369.3–370.21	§ 684	387.12–19	§ 724	408.11–16	§ 764
370.24–371.3	§ 685	387.20–388.2	§ 725	408.17–29	§ 765
371.4–24	§ 686	388.3–27	§ 726	408.30–409.9	§ 766
371.25–32	§ 687	388.30–389.17	§ 727	409.10–25	§ 767
371.33–372.3	§ 688	389.18–27	§ 728	409.26–36	§ 768
372.6–25	§ 689	389.28–390.8	§ 729	409.37–410.17	§ 769
372.26–373.9	§ 690	390.9–391.6	§ 730	410.18–28	§ 770
373.12–14	§ 691	391.7–32	§ 731	410.29–411.17	§ 771
373.15–26	§ 692	391.33–392.12	§ 732	411.18–33	§ 772
373.27–374.10	§ 693	392.13–34	§ 733	411.34–39	§ 773
374.11–23	§ 694	392.35–393.21	§ 734	412.1–14	§ 774
374.24–375.5	§ 695	393.22–32	§ 735	412.15–35	§ 775
375.6–11	§ 696	393.33–394.12	§ 736	412.36–413.36	§ 776
375.12–24	§ 697	394.13–395.2	§ 737	413.37–414.15	§ 777
375.25–36	§ 698	395.3–13	§ 738	414.16–26	§ 778
376.3–7	§ 699	395.14–34	§ 739	414.27–415.10	§ 779
376.8–20	§ 700	395.35–396.24	§ 740	415.11–417.5	§ 780
376.21–377.21	§ 701	396.25–397.5	§ 741	417.6–16	§ 781
377.22–30	§ 702	397.6–23	§ 742	417.17–35	§ 782
377.31–39	§ 703	397.24–27	§ 743	417.36–418.15	§ 783
378.1–9	§ 704	397.28–398.6	§ 744	418.16–34	§ 784
378.12–16	§ 705	398.7–30	§ 745	418.35–419.30	§ 785
378.17–32	§ 706	398.31–399.14	§ 746	419.31–420.8	§ 786
378.33–379.22	§ 707	399.15–35	§ 747	420.9–421.18	§ 787
379.23–380.11	§ 708	400.3–17	§ 748	422.3–23	§ 788
380.12–23	§ 709	400.18–401.4	§ 749	422.24–423.16	§ 789
380.24–381.4	§ 710	401.5–15	§ 750	423.17–32	§ 790
381.5–21	§ 711	401.16–23	§ 751	423.33–424.9	§ 791
381.22–382.19	§ 712	401.24–35	§ 752	424.10–22	§ 792
382.20–27	§ 713	401.36–402.33	§ 753	424.23–425.9	§ 793

BIBLIOGRAPHY

WORKS BY G. W. F. HEGEL.

Works published by Hegel (arranged chronologically)

Glauben und Wissen (1802). In *Gesammelte Werke*, herausgegeben im Auftrag der Deutschen Forschungsgemeinschaft, vol. 4: *Jenaer Kritische Schriften*, pp. 315–414. Edited by Hartmut Buchner and Otto Pöggeler. Hamburg: Felix Meiner, 1968.

Phänomenologie des Geistes (1807). *Gesammelte Werke*, in Verbindung mit der Deutschen Forschungsgemeinschaft [und] herausgegeben von der Rheinisch-Westfälischen Akademie der Wissenschaften, vol. 9. Edited by Wolfgang Bonsiepen and Reinhard Heede. Hamburg: Felix Meiner, 1980. (The principal source for my study of Hegel.)

———. Edited by Johannes Hoffmeister. Der philosophischen Bibliothek Band 114. Hamburg: Felix Meiner, 1952.

———. *Werke*, Theorie Werkausgabe, vol. 3. Edited by Eva Moldenhauer and Karl Markus Michel. Frankfurt am Main: Suhrkamp Verlag, 1970.

———. *La phénoménologie de l'esprit*. Translated by Jean Hyppolite. 2 vols. Paris: Aubier, Editions Montaigne, 1941.

———. *The Phenomenology of Mind*. Translated by J. B. Baillie. second ed. London: Macmillan, 1931; reprint ed. (Harper Torchbook), New York: Harper & Row, 1967.

———. *The Phenomenology of Mind*. Electronic edition of Baillie's translation. Washington, DC: The Center for Text & Technology, Academic Computer Center, Georgetown University, 1990.

———. *The Phenomenology of Spirit*. Translated by A. V. Miller. Oxford University Press, 1977.

Wissenschaft der Logik (1812–1816). *Gesammelte Werke*, in Verbindung mit der Deutschen Forschungsgemeinschaft [und] herausgegeben von der

Rheinisch-Westfälischen Akademie der Wissenschaften, vols. 11–12. Edited by Friedrich Hogemann and Walter Jaeschke. Hamburg: Felix Meiner, 1978–1981.

"Ueber Friedrich Heinrich Jacobi's Werke" (1817). In *Sämtliche Werke*, Jubiläumsausgabe, vol. 6: *Enzyklopädie der philosophischen Wissenschaften im Grundrisse [1817] und andere Schriften aus der Heidelberger Zeit*, pp. 313–47. Edited by Hermann Glockner. Stuttgart: Fr. Frommans Verlag/ Günther Holzboog, 1956.

Enzyklopädie der philosophischen Wissenschaften im Grundrisse (1830). Edited by Friedhelm Nicolin and Otto Pöggeler. Philosophische Bibliothek Band 33. Hamburg: Felix Meiner, 1959.

Enzyklopädie der philosophischen Wissenschaften im Grundrisse (1830), Erster Teil, Die Wissenschaft der Logik, mit den mündlichen Zusätzen. Werke, Theorie Werkausgabe, vol. 8. Edited by Eva Moldenhauer and Karl Markus Michel. Frankfurt am Main: Suhrkamp Verlag, 1970.

Works published posthumously

Aesthetics. Translated by T. M. Knox. 2 vols. Oxford University Press, 1975.

The Christian Religion. Edited and translated by Peter C. Hodgson. American Academy of Religion Texts and Translations, no. 2. Missoula, MT: Scholars Press, 1979. (Part III of Hegel's *Lectures on the Philosophy of Religion*, in a preliminary translation by Hodgson prior to the full three-volume edition published by University of California Press.)

Hegel: The Letters. Translated by Clark Butler and Christiane Seiler, with commentary by Clark Butler. Bloomington, IN: Indiana University Press, 1984.

Jenaer Systementwürfe III. Vorlesungsmanuskript zur Realphilosophie (1805/06): Naturphilosophie und Philosophie des Geistes. Gesammelte Werke, in Verbindung mit der Deutschen Forschungsgemeinschaft [und] herausgegeben von der Rheinisch-Westfälischen Akademie der Wissenschaften, vol. 8. Edited by Rolf-Peter Horstmann with assistance from Johann Heinrich Trede. Hamburg: Felix Meiner, 1976.

Lectures on the Philosophy of Religion. Translated by Rev. E. B. Speirs and J. Burdon Sanderson. 3 vols. 1895; reprint ed., New York: The Humanities Press, 1962.

———. Edited by Peter C. Hodgson. Translated by R. F. Brown, P. C. Hodgson, and J. M. Stewart. Assisted by J. P. Fitzer (vol. 1 only) and H. S. Harris (vols. 1–3). 3 vols. Berkeley, Los Angeles, London: University of California Press, 1984–1987.

———. Electronic version of Hodgson's edition. Washington, DC: The Center for Text & Technology, Academic Computer Center, Georgetown University, 1990.

Philosophy of History. Translated by J. Sibree. 1899; reprint ed., New York: Dover Publications, 1956.

Vorlesungen über die Geschichte der Philosophie. Werke, Theorie Werkausgabe, vols. 18–20. Edited by Eva Moldenhauer and Karl Markus Michel. Frankfurt am Main: Suhrkamp Verlag, 1971.

Vorlesungen über die Philosophie der Religion. Edited by Georg Lasson. 4 vols. in 2. Philosophische Bibliothek 59–60, 61, 63. 1925; reprint ed., Hamburg: Felix Meiner, 1966.

Vorlesungen über die Philosophie der Religion (Vorlesungen, Bände 3–5). Edited by Walter Jaeschke. 3 vols. Hamburg: Felix Meiner, 1983–1985.

WORKS BY OTHER AUTHORS

Augustine, Saint. *On the Free Choice of the Will.* Translated by Anna S. Benjamin and L. H. Hackstaff. Indianapolis, IN: Bobbs-Merrill, 1964.

———. *Confessions.* Translated by R. S. Pine-Coffin. New York: Penguin Books, 1961.

Behler, Ernst. "Friedrich Schlegel und Hegel." *Hegel-Studien* 2 (1963): 203–50.

Brito, Emilio, S. J. *La christologie de Hegel.* Traduit par B. Pottier, S. J. Bibliothèque des Archives de Philosophie, Nouvelle Série, 40. Paris: Beauchesne, 1983.

Campe, Joachim Heinrich. *Wörterbuch der Deutschen Sprache.* 5 vols. Braunschweig: in der Schulbuchhandlung, 1807–1811.

Copleston, Frederick, S. J. *A History of Philosophy.* Vol. 4: *Descartes to Leibniz.* Paramus, NJ: The Newman Press, 1958.

———. *A History of Philosophy.* Vol. 7: *Fichte to Nietzsche.* Westminster, MD: The Newman Press, 1963.

Cranfield, C. E. B. *The Epistle to the Romans.* 2 vols. International Critical Commentary. Edinburgh: T. & T. Clark, 1975–1979.

Fackenheim, Emil L. *The Religious Dimension in Hegel's Thought.* Bloomington, IN: Indiana University Press, 1967.

———. S.v. "Hegel," *Encyclopaedia Judaica.* New York: Macmillan, 1971.

Gadamer, Hans-Georg. "Die verkehrte Welt" (1964). In *Gesammelte Werke,* vol. 3: *Neuere Philosophie* I, pp. 29–46. Tübingen: J. C. B. Mohr (Paul Siebeck), 1987.

Gauvin, Joseph. "Entfremdung et Entäusserung dans la Phénoménologie de l'esprit de Hegel." *Archives de Philosophie* 25 (1962): 555–71.

Goethe, J. W. von. *Wilhelm Meister's Apprenticeship*. Translated by Thomas Carlyle. 1824; reprint ed., Harvard Classics, New York: P. F. Collier & Son, 1917.

Hirsch, Emanuel. "Die Beisetzung der Romantiker in Hegels Phänomenologie." *Deutsche Vierteljahrsschrift für Literaturwissenschaft und Geistesgeschichte*, 2 (1924): 510–32.

Hyppolite, Jean. *Genèse et Structure de la Phénoménologie de l'Esprit de Hegel*. 1946; reprint ed., Paris: Aubier, Editions Montaigne, 1974.

Jaeschke, Walter. *Reason in Religion: The Foundations of Hegel's Philosophy of Religion*. Translated by J. Michael Stewart and Peter C. Hodgson. Berkeley and Los Angeles: University of California Press, 1990.

Jamros, Daniel P., S. J. " 'The Appearing God' in Hegel's *Phenomenology of Spirit*." *CLIO* 19 (1990): 353–65.

Kainz, Howard P. *Hegel's Phenomenology, Part I: Analysis and Commentary*. Studies in the Humanities 12. Tuscaloosa, AL: University of Alabama Press, 1976. *Hegel's Phenomenology, Part II: The Evolution of Ethical and Religious Consciousness to the Dialectical Standpoint*. Athens, OH: Ohio University Press, 1983.

Kant, Immanuel. *Kant's Werke*, vol. 4: *Grundlegung zur Metaphysik der Sitten*. Berlin: Georg Reimer, 1911.

———. *Kant's Werke*, vol. 5: *Kritik der praktischen Vernunft*. Berlin: Georg Reimer, 1913.

———. *Critique of Practical Reason and Other Writings in Moral Philosophy*. Translated by Lewis White Beck. Chicago: University of Chicago Press, 1949.

Kaufmann, Walter. *Hegel: Reinterpretation, Texts, and Commentary*. Garden City, NY: Doubleday, 1965.

Kimmerle, Heinz. "Dokumente zu Hegels Jenaer Dozententätigkeit (1801–1807)." *Hegel-Studien*, no. 4. Bonn: H. Bouvier, 1967.

Kojève, Alexandre. *Introduction à la lecture de Hegel*. Leçons sur la *Phénoménologie de l'Esprit* professées de 1933 à 1939 à l'Ecole des Hautes Etudes. Edited by Raymond Queneau. 1947; reprint ed., Paris: Editions Gallimard, 1979.

Lauer, Quentin, S. J. *A Reading of Hegel's Phenomenology of Spirit*. New York: Fordham University Press, 1976, 1982.

Lonergan, Bernard J. F. *Insight: A Study of Human Understanding*. Revised ed., 1958; reprint ed., San Francisco: Harper & Row, 1978.

Schlegel, Friedrich. *Friedrich Schlegel's Lucinde and the Fragments*. Translated with an introduction by Peter Firchow. Minneapolis: University of Minnesota Press, 1971.

Schulz, Franz, Prof. Dr. *Klassik und Romantik der Deutschen*, II. Teil, *Wesen und Form der Klassisch-Romantischen Literatur.* Stuttgart: J. B. Metzlersche Verlagsbuchhandlung, 1959 [1952, 1940].

Selwyn, Edward Gordon. *The First Epistle of St. Peter.* 2d. ed. London: Macmillan and Co., 1947; reprint ed., Grand Rapids, MI: Baker Book House, 1981.

Solomon, Robert C. *In the Spirit of Hegel: A Study of G. W. F. Hegel's Phenomenology of Spirit.* New York: Oxford University Press, 1983.

INDEX